Photo: Bill Marsden

About the Author

Bill Marsden, a native Albertan, has been called the "founding father of the Alberta film industry" by *Playback Magazine*. Originally a still photographer, Marsden went on to learn all aspects of the movie industry. He has made films throughout North America and Europe and has more than one hundred production credits to his name. Although he specialized in documentaries and industrial films, he was also behind the camera on Alberta's earliest feature films—*Wings of Chance* and *Naked Flame*.

In 1981, Marsden joined the Alberta government as director of film industry development (later re-classified as Film Commissioner). During his tenure, he helped develop the industry infrastructure and attracted film business opportunities worth millions of dollars from all over the world, including the Japanese epic *Heaven and Earth* and the Clint Eastwood box-office hit *Unforgiven*. Eastwood even gave Marsden a special thank you in the *Unforgiven* credits.

The recipient of numerous awards of excellence, both national and international, Marsden was honoured with a Governor General's Commemorative medal in 1992. He retired in 1993, but remains devoted to the motion picture industry. He has a passion for antique airplanes and is presently absorbed in writing another book.

To Danny Johns with
best wishes —
Bill Marsden

Big Screen Country

MAKING MOVIES IN ALBERTA

A Memoir by Bill Marsden

**FIFTH
HOUSE**

Cover and interior design by Kathy Aldous-Schleindl
Front and back cover photographs by Chris Large
Edited by Alex Frazer-Harrison
Copyedited by Geri Rowlatt
Proofread by Meaghan Craven
Scans by St. Solo Computer Graphics

The publisher gratefully acknowledges the support of The Canada Council for the Arts and the Department of Canadian Heritage.

THE CANADA COUNCIL | LE CONSEIL DES ARTS
FOR THE ARTS | DU CANADA
SINCE 1957 | DEPUIS 1957

We acknowledge the financial support of the Government of Canada through the Book Publishing Industry Development Program (BPIDP) for our publishing activities.

Printed in Canada by Friesens
04 05 06 07 08 / 5 4 3 2 1

Library and Archives Canada Cataloguing in Publication

Marsden, Bill, 1928-
    Big screen country : making movies in Alberta / Bill Marsden.
    Includes index.
    ISBN 1-894856-47-3
    1. Marsden, Bill, 1928- 2. Motion picture industry--Alberta--History. 3. Motion pictures--Alberta--History. 4. Motion pictures--Alberta--Biography. I. Title.

PN1993.5.C32A4 2004   791.43'097123   C2004-902926-6

First published in the United States in 2005 by
Fitzhenry & Whiteside
121 Harvard Avenue, Suite 2
Allston, MA 02134

Fifth House Ltd.
A Fitzhenry & Whiteside Company
1511, 1800 − 4 St. SW
Calgary, Alberta T2S 2S5
1−800−387−9776
www.fitzhenry.ca

Table of Contents

This book is dedicated to my wife, Sally; to our children, Cathy Faulknor and her husband Steve, Mark Marsden, and Tracy Marsden; to our grandchildren, Melanie Faulknor, Michael Faulknor, Amberley Marsden, Spencer Marsden, and Hillary Marsden; and to their great grandmother, a remarkable ninety-seven-year-old—my mother, Mabel V. Maguire.

It is also intended as a tribute to Alberta film greats who have passed on: Bruno Engler, Ken Hutchinson, Les Kimber, Larry Matanski, Bill Round, Gerry Wilson, and Nick Zubko.

Foreword

Bill Marsden started his career as a still photographer in the 1950s, then graduated to films, moved into directing and producing, and finally became Alberta's film commissioner. In the latter position, he was rightly described as the "founding father" of Alberta's film industry.

I first met Bill in 1951 when he was a photographer and I was a publicity writer for the Alberta government. We travelled the province together and I soon learned to appreciate his creative genius behind the camera. Whether taking views of official ceremonies, visiting dignitaries, family farms, or Hutterite colonies, the final results were always technically correct, expertly positioned, and a marvel to behold.

Bill and I both left the government but were together again a few years later at the newly formed Glenbow Foundation. Although Bill undertook many creative tasks, probably the most impressive was the recording of the 1961 Blackfoot Sun Dance. We had been asked by the tribe to film the event for posterity and Marsden had the task of directing and producing a one-hour documentary, as well as doing some of the photography himself. He was masterful in the task. He got along with everyone, made the old ladies giggle, and jollied and bribed the young men into moving their cars so they would not show up in the film. He directed the crew as they moved among the ceremonies, present but never intrusive. The end result was described by the Smithsonian Institution as one of the most important films ever made of a Plains Indian ceremony.

After the shooting was finished, the Blackfoot recognized Glenbow founder Eric Harvie, a Calgary millionaire, by giving him the honorary name of Old Sun, a great chief of the tribe. After the ceremony, Bill and I went to the officers' mess in Calgary (Bill was a lieutenant in the reserves) and the first person we met was one of Harvie's old law partners. Bill told him about the ceremony and that Harvie had been named Old Sun. "Old son of a what?" responded the disgruntled ex-partner.

After Glenbow, Bill formed William Marsden & Associates and became an independent producer at a time when practically no feature films and only a limited number of commercial productions were being made in Alberta. Films for Shell Oil, the Calgary Stampede, and the Red Cross helped to keep the wolf from the door, and in lean times he photographed children and even a few weddings. However, as business improved, he was able to concentrate entirely on motion pictures.

One of Bill's first active involvements in feature film production occurred in 1959 when he was a cameraman during the filming of *Wings of Chance*. The production included Hollywood actors Dennis O'Keefe and Kasey Rogers and told the story of a downed bush pilot. In 1963, Bill was a cameraman in another production, *Naked Flame*, a story about a Doukhobor sect that included nude scenes, arson, and murder. Later re-released as *Deadline for Murder*, it was described by *Variety* as a melodrama with "a hokey climax." However, it gave Bill an additional taste of Hollywood that never left him. As a result, when he was commissioned by the Alberta government to produce a film on pioneer life, he went Hollywood all the way. He engaged actor-singer Burl Ives as the star and had so many professionals involved that even his local Canadian players were obliged to join the actors' union, ACTRA.

I saw Bill frequently during those years and could not help but notice his unflagging optimism and enthusiasm. Simultaneously, he was shooting movies, renovating his old house in Calgary's Elbow Park, and building an aeroplane in his garage. Then Bill moved to Edmonton and I saw less of him, but we still kept in touch.

In 1973, Marsden and four other producers formed the Alberta Motion Picture Industries Association (AMPIA) to push for changes at the government's ACCESS television network, complaining that all the work was being done in-house. When they succeeded, they sought other reforms that would give them a chance to build a film industry in Alberta.

In 1976, Bill became president of AMPIA and a year later he was appointed to an Alberta government committee to study the film industry. Their investigations took them to Hollywood and then to Australia, which had a thriving film industry. With the information gathered, Bill and other members of the task force submitted a report to the Alberta government, recommending provincial involvement in the promotion of an Alberta film industry. The government accepted the report but it was not implemented until 1981, when Marsden was appointed Director of Film Industry Development for the Alberta government.

That signalled the end of Bill's career in film production and introduced him to the complex world of budgets and incentive loan guarantees. With $3 million provided by the government, he formed the Alberta Motion Picture Development Corporation (AMPDC) to provide seed money for Alberta's budding film industry. It was the first such program in Canada. By the time the program was up and running, another $7 million had been added to the funds.

As stated by writer Pat Barford, "Slowly, surely, under Marsden's direction, the Alberta film commission developed filmmakers committed to an indigenous film industry. It was with Marsden as a mentor that Anne Wheeler, Doug MacLeod, Arvi Liimatainen and Tom Dent-Cox became the rising stars of Alberta's budding film industry."

Besides developing a local film industry, Marsden was active in enticing Hollywood to come to Alberta. The province's wonderful scenery, its trained professionals, and a cooperative government made the area attractive to a number of major films and television programs. Over the years he was a major player in bringing in productions from France, Germany, Britain, Japan, and the United States. He was directly involved with such films as *Superman III* starring Christopher Reeve, *Running Brave* with Robby Benson, and *Draw!* with Kirk Douglas.

One of Bill's favourites was the $60 million Japanese epic *Heaven and Earth*, filmed in 1989. Another favourite was *Unforgiven*. Bill was responsible for bringing this Academy-Award-winning film to the province because he had done a favour for the Clint Eastwood group a few years before, prompting them to call him when they had a "western" that could be filmed in Alberta. Scouting for the film was done with a government helicopter, and knowing that Eastwood was a licensed helicopter pilot, Bill had an extra set of controls installed in the helicopter. Clint did most of the flying and found the site for his town of Big Whiskey.

By the time Marsden retired in 1993, he had made an impression in Hollywood, in the international film community, and in the Alberta film industry. On his retirement, he was praised for his role "in building our Alberta industry," for his "unmatched enthusiasm and dedication," and for his "support and hard work in developing the Alberta film industry." As one of my best friends, I know he enjoyed every minute of it, a fact that is clearly reflected in this book.

Hugh A. Dempsey
Author and Chief Curator Emeritus, Glenbow Museum

Acknowledgements

I gratefully acknowledge the assistance provided by the Honourable Mark Norris, minister of Economic Development, and Mr. Drew Hutton, MLA for Edmonton-Glenora. I also thank: Hugh Dempsey, Fil Fraser, the Glenbow Archives, Doug Hutton, Ken Jubenvill, Linda Kupecek, Chris Large, Arvi Liimatainen, Doug MacLeod, Mel Merrells, Tony Mokry, Murray Ord, the Provincial Archives, Paul Rayman, Chuck Ross, John Scott, Brock Silversides, Doug Steeden, Jaron Summers, Andy Thomson, Geordie Tocher, and Bob Willis.

Introduction

This book is both a memoir and a history. It focuses on key events, individuals, and some important years. I had the pleasure of working with, and learning from, the pioneers of moviemaking in Alberta, some of whom have not been publicly recognized until now. I use the word "film" frequently, which dates me, but of course I mean video and television as well.

The Governments of Canada and Alberta were both leaders in the use of motion pictures. The Canadian government led the way, engaging British film genius John Grierson to establish the National Film Board (NFB) of Canada in 1939. He is credited with developing the documentary film genre, which he defined as "a creative interpretation of reality."

By 1945, the NFB had become one of the world's largest movie studios, with a staff of 787. It produced more than five hundred films over a five-year period, movies that were acclaimed internationally. NFB distribution offices from coast to coast showed sixteen-millimetre movies in schools, community halls, and even campgrounds during the summer months.

The Film Board's mission was (and still is) to show Canada to Canadians and others. The NFB encouraged many Canadians to get involved in film production. It provided contract work to individuals such as Ottawa's Budge Crawley, Vancouver's Lew Parry, and Edmonton's Larry Matanski. All became prominent regional filmmakers, along with Regina's Evelyn Cherry, who was employed in Montreal as an assistant to John Grierson before returning to Saskatchewan to found Cherry Films, Ltd.

In the 1940s, Canadians who wanted to make movies had two choices: leave the country or work for the NFB.

The sixteen-millimetre documentary film was the television of its day. It took us to distant places to reveal wonderful sights. As a child in small-town Alberta, the first such film I ever saw was produced by the John Deere Company and showed the manufacture and use of its agricultural implements, in black and white. An audience of farmers filled the town hall, with wide-eyed interest and the occasional sharp intake of breath. They dreamed of owning such miracle machines, but we were in the middle of the Depression.

The first colour movie I remember seeing was at Keifer's once-a-week cinema in the village of Irma, Alberta. I was twelve years old and the show was *The Wizard of Oz*. It begins in black and white and then bursts into glorious Technicolor when Dorothy and Toto arrive in Oz. It was awesome—unforgettable!

I often dreamed of making my own movies. Even back then, I felt my place was behind the camera.

The availability of Commercial Kodachrome colour film in sixteen-millimetre, along with related production equipment, encouraged provincial governments to become involved with filmmaking in order to inform and influence. Alberta was among the first to take advantage of this opportunity. Over the next fifty years (from 1948 onward), there was considerable motion picture activity in Alberta, and I was fortunate to be involved in much of it.

As in *The Wizard of Oz,* there were undreamt-of pleasant surprises and events ahead.

WARNER BROS.

Warner Bros. Inc.
4000 Warner Boulevard
Burbank, California 91522
818 954-6000
Cable Address Warbros

13 September 1994

Mr. Bill Marsden
10th Floor, Sterling Place
9940 - 106 Street,
Edmonton, AB T5K 2P6
CANADA

Dear Bill:

I understand that you are being honored with a special dinner that acknowledges the invaluable contributions you've made in bringing filmmakers to the beautiful province of Alberta. True, Alberta is a producer's dream come true when one thinks of the spectacular scenery, the friendly people, the skilled crews. But it was you who convinced both Clint and me that it was the place to film "UNFORGIVEN" and for this we'll always be grateful.

"UNFORGIVEN" will go down in the cinema history books as a classic that garnered four Oscars. At the time of scouting locations back in the summer of '91, who would have thought we were going to be so blessed? I'm happy to hear that many other productions have followed in our wake, and that the world is finally discovering the beauty that all you Albertans have known since birth.

But the grandeur, the spectacular Rockies, the hospitable people aside, it is your conscientiousness, your 24 hour a day availability, your friendliness, your passion for the cinema that brings filmmakers to Alberta. I wish I could be present at your celebration to join in the toast that acknowledges you as the unique talent you are.

I look forward to doing it again with you soon.

Best wishes always,

David Valdes
DCV/lt

This letter was read aloud on the occasion of my receiving the Billington award from the Alberta Motion Picture Industries Association in 1994, an honour I treasure. It helped me recall the marvels that enabled a small-town Alberta boy to work with David Valdes and Clint Eastwood on a motion picture that won four Academy Awards.

Wings over Wetaskiwin

There was no runway that day in 1936, just a large grassy field that we were soon roaring down, faster and faster, clatter and bang, bump, bump, until one last big bump launched us airborne!

The noise of the engine lessened as we levelled off, and I loved listening to the humming sound of the wing wires.

We were visiting my grandmother in Wetaskiwin when my father took me for my first airplane ride. I was eight years old. The field used as an airport was northwest of town, alongside the highway, with a wooden hangar near the water tower. The aircraft was an American Eagle biplane, with open cockpits, yellow with black trim, and a big black radial engine. The pilot, Bert Wallis, occupied the rear cockpit. Father and I, wearing helmets and goggles, sat side by side in the wider front cockpit.

We were well above Wetaskiwin when I looked over the side in wonder. I'll never forget the sights, sounds, or smell of that adventure.

The cost of the ride in that depression year was an extravagance, but it was worth it. It launched my lifelong passion for flying; I knew then that I would someday take flight in my very own plane.

I arrived in this world in Wetaskiwin, Alberta, on 7 May 1928, and was christened William Deane McKinney Marsden.

In 1904, at the age of eight, my father, Thomas, had come to Canada with his family from Wigan, in Lancashire, England. My mother, Mabel, was from Strome, about eighty kilometres from Wetaskiwin. Her parents, Bernard and Kate McKinney, had come to Alberta from Iowa in 1903. My parents were married in 1927. I am proud that my grandparents on both sides arrived in Alberta before it became a province in 1905.

I was an only child until my fourth birthday in 1932 when my brother, Thomas, Jr., was born. My sixth birthday and his second were commemorated in a very fine studio picture by master photographer Carl Walin. Thomas and I wore black velvet short pants with white pearl buttons, matching jackets, and white silk blouses with frilly collars. The suits had been sent from England by two great-aunts and were known as "Little Lord Fauntleroy" suits.

I endured many humiliations in this outfit. My Grandfather McKinney's reaction to the suit terrified me. "Come out behind the barn with me and I'll piss in your ear so you'll at least smell like a man," he had said.

That same year, we moved to the village of Irma, 145 kilometres east of Wetaskiwin. It was a farming community where my father managed the local Imperial Lumber. I began school and was sent there wearing the infamous Fauntleroy suit. Nothing like it had ever been seen by my peers. I fought jeering classmates all the way home, arriving battered and bloody.

The suit fared even worse—I made sure it would never be worn again!

In 1938, I spent all my spare time building airplane models, and finally I built one big enough for me to sit in and, I hoped, maybe even fly!

The fuselage was a long, tapered wooden crate, in which bunches of bananas had been shipped, acquired from McFarland's General Store. From the local lumberyard, managed by my father, I had obtained materials for wings, ailerons, elevators, and a rudder. All were operable, with leather hinges and control cables made of binder twine. The wheels were borrowed from my wagon.

The test flight takeoff was down a steep hill, where I had built a summer version of a ski jump. My airplane went into the air off the jump and took wing like an elephant. It stalled, crashed, and splattered. I was badly bruised and disappointed, but vowed that one day I would build an airplane I could actually fly.

And I did.

My brother Thomas and I on our joint birthday, 7 May 1934. Thomas was two years old—I was six. He was born on my fourth birthday, and I've always told him that what I really wanted for that birthday was a puppy dog (not really!). We are dressed in our much disliked "little Lord Fauntleroy suits," sent to us by two great-aunts in England. Photo: Carl Walin (Wetaskiwin)

My parents separated and then finally divorced in 1940. Father moved to Edmonton to work at Clark Lumber. My brother and I went to visit him in 1942, catching a car ride with a neighbour.

Our first sight of Edmonton from gravelled Highway 14 was exciting. Dominating the skyline were the MacDonald Hotel and the Marshall Wells Building, the latter eight storeys high with a water tower on top—a veritable skyscraper in those days. Edmonton's population was then about ninety-five thousand, larger than any town I had ever visited. The big city life was for us and we stayed. Mother remarried in 1943 and also moved to Edmonton, buying a house directly across from what is today Westmount Shopping Mall.

It was now wartime, and flying took on a whole new meaning for me as Edmonton became a hub for military aircraft of all kinds.

All day long, the sky overhead was filled with low-flying craft on final approach to a runway located just west of where we lived with my father. There were American fighters, mostly Bell Aircobras, on their way to Russia and emblazoned with the Red Star insignia. There were Tiger Moths, Avro Ansons, and Airspeed Oxfords, all painted RCAF trainer yellow, with red, white, and blue roundels on their wings and fuselage.

They were beautiful against the bright blue sky. To an airplane lover like me, they were heavenly!

I attended McCauley School with my friend Sam Cahoon. After grade nine, we applied for work at Aircraft Repair to assist in the war effort. This was the major overhaul centre for military aircraft in Western Canada. We were hired; we were only fifteen years old, but there was a war on. We were employed as "runners," pulling handcarts to move parts from one department or hangar to another. At last, I was surrounded by real airplanes—and I was getting paid for the privilege.

Mother, who was working at the airport, bought a bigger house on 132 Street and persuaded me to return to school. I moved in and started grade ten at Westglen High School.

It was my intention to join the Air Force at age seventeen and become a fighter pilot. Parental permission was required and Father was supportive. I would soon be flying Spitfires, I thought.

My seventeenth birthday fell on 7 May 1945. I was in school when victory in Europe was declared (now celebrated on 8 May). The war was over. Classrooms and corridors were chaotic with overjoyed teachers and students, most with some family member away at war.

I had terribly mixed emotions. On the very day they were to have been realized, my dreams had been shattered. Little did I know I would soon develop yet another passion.

Frank Maguire, my mother's new husband, returned from overseas that December. One of his trophies of war was a folding Zeiss camera taken from a German prisoner. It was a far more complex camera than the Box Brownie I owned. I practically haunted the public library, learning how to use it and reading all I could about photography.

I began to develop film on my own and made a contact printer and then an enlarger from an old camera purchased at Harry Hiller's Exchange on 101 Street. (Hiller's son, Arthur, became an acclaimed film director best known for hits like *Love Story, Silver Streak,* and *Outrageous Fortune.* Arthur is older than I am by a couple of years; I never knew him as a kid.)

After finishing grade eleven, I took a summer job developing and printing for a street camera operation. They shot with thirty-five-millimetre film, which was even smaller than my Zeiss 120 negatives.

Later in 1945, an opportunity came along with a company called Venus Studios, which was located in the basement of the Williamson Building on Jasper Avenue at 97 Street. They were using view cameras, shooting negatives that measured five-by-seven inches, which were huge compared to what I was used to. I was soon learning professional portrait photography.

The studio's main activity was a practice known as "kidnapping." Venus salesmen pushed coupons in Alberta and Saskatchewan towns for $2.95 apiece that entitled the bearer to an eight-by-ten black and white photo. I was the designated photographer.

Arriving in a town by bus or train with a large case containing lights, camera, and tripod, I would set up a makeshift studio in a hall or hotel room. I was paid one dollar for taking a picture, whether it was a portrait, child, pet, or family group. I could sell extra coupons if more than one shot was wanted. This put an extra dollar in my pocket, which was my commission.

Only ninety-five cents from the original coupon went to the studio itself, but the coupon photo was only the "come on." A week after the shoot, a Venus salesman would arrive with rough proofs to sell extra prints. He worked on commission. If he couldn't sell you a print order, then how about hand colouring of the eight-by-ten, or a fancy frame, or both? He would suggest customers pay cash, for quicker delivery; in fact, this only resulted in an instant commission. Ed, the owner of Venus Studios, always sent the cash-on-delivery orders out first. He wanted that money; he already had the prepaid cash.

I met many scoundrels at Venus, but also some good friends, such as artist Meredith "Bunny" Evans, who rented the studio for night art classes, and David Bain, who used it for his School of Creative Photography.

A well-dressed, good-looking character showed up at Venus Studios one day to meet with a salesman friend. He had a camera hanging from his neck. Ed asked

HOLLYWOOD COMES TO ALBERTA

In 1946, Paramount Pictures came to Jasper to film *The Emperor Waltz* in "glorious Technicolor," which starred two of the biggest box office attractions of the day, Bing Crosby and Joan Fontaine. It was the first major Technicolor Hollywood production to come to Alberta.

Billy Wilder was the director and this was his first colour movie, which gave the Technicolor consultant some weight to throw around. The consultant had the paved Jasper Park roads painted in light ochre, and several thousand daisies painted a light blue. Wilder also found Jasper lacking in beauty, importing dozens of bushy pine trees from California to be planted in chosen locations. He had an artificial island built on oil drums, covered with sod, grass, and trees, and floated it on Leach Lake as the set for a love scene between two dogs. An uncle of mine, John Fandrick (who was married to my mother's sister, Faye, and living near Jasper), helped build the island, which cost ninety thousand dollars.

The massive Technicolor cameras and carbon arc lights were cumbersome to set up and operate. The work was slow. They filmed all summer in Jasper, with the major part of the movie still to be made on sound stages in Hollywood. It became a very expensive production and was not released until 1948. A courtesy screening was held in Jasper and, thanks to my Uncle John, my father and brother attended since they were in the area on holidays. Sadly, I couldn't get away from work to be there myself.

Joan Fontaine apparently was not impressed with Jasper or Alberta. In her autobiography, she mentions *Emperor Waltz* only as a film she made in Canada. Bing Crosby, on the other hand, loved Jasper, returning frequently over the years, even establishing a golf tournament there.

The Emperor Waltz was a box office hit in its day, and the spectacular Jasper scenery, in Technicolor, was responsible for increasing Hollywood interest in Alberta. Soon, more big-name productions would come to the province.

Larry Matanski, 1952, Alberta government photographer and movie maker at the age of twenty-four. Only seven years later, in 1959, he became Alberta's first producer of a theatrical motion picture, *Wings of Chance*. Photo: Bill Marsden

him what he did and was told, "I'm on my way to Hollywood to make movies." Ed replied, "You work for me for six months and Hollywood will be coming to you!" His name was Larry Matanski, and he joined us.

I discovered he knew little about still photography or lab work, but I taught him. He did know a lot about moviemaking and offered to teach me. There were no film schools in Canada at that time, and had there been, who could afford to go? Certainly not us.

Larry was self-taught. He studied filmmaking by going to a movie almost every day, be they Hollywood productions or NFB documentaries. He was a keen analyst, once telling me, "When they cut on action like that, it's because they're hiding something."

I accompanied him on his first freelance film assignment: using a rented sixteen-millimetre Bolex camera, he filmed a train steaming across Edmonton's Clover Bar Bridge carrying banners for a Red Cross event.

As Venus employees, we learned about survival, and owner Ed was an expert. In one town in Saskatchewan, where we were unable to make a sale, I discovered I had worn holes in my shoes. Ed moved the bed in his hotel room out from the wall, cut out a good-sized piece of linoleum, and then moved the bed back into place. I was able to cut insoles from it that lasted a week. Ed then sold his Ronson cigarette lighter for two dollars so we could eat. "Always carry something you can sell," he said. We hitchhiked to the next community and did well there, until the local photographer had us run out of town.

An unforgettable lesson was yet to come that would teach me a lot about business and survival. Ed wanted to sell Venus and move to Regina. I was certain I could make the business pay and by the end of the week had worked out a deal. Ed owed me a considerable amount in back pay, so I wrote off what he owed me, then paid him an additional two hundred dollars in cash to become the new studio owner.

That Monday morning, I caught a street car downtown to open my very own studio. It was vacant! No camera on studio tripod, no backdrop, no lights. All the darkroom equipment was gone, and all the cupboards were bare. Only dust and dirt remained. Within ten minutes, the landlord had arrived, screaming about rent owed. At least that wasn't my worry. I told him to locate Ed in Regina. (As it happened, Ed was not in Regina and was never found.) I didn't have a bill of sale. It was a cash deal, with no cancelled cheque, so there was no paper trail to make me liable for the rent or other matters and I walked away. It was my first lesson in business, and a painful one.

After Venus Studios disappeared, there was no work to be found in photography, at least not in Edmonton. I got a job at Northwest Industries, building plywood boats. Larry Matanski, still unemployed thanks to the closure of Venus, heard that a company named Eldorado was looking for prospectors to work in the far north. We applied and were hired.

Wow! I thought. Exploration, adventure, and a paycheque. It was the spring of 1946. I was almost eighteen.

Uranium, False Teeth, and True Love

A Noorduyn Norseman aircraft on floats awaited us at the Cooking Lake air base, just east of Edmonton. We were soon winging our way north in the capable hands of veteran bush pilot "Tiny" Ferris. Naturally, with a name like that, he was a *big* man. There were four other passengers on the plane, older, tough-looking characters who were obviously experienced northerners. In a couple of hours, we landed on the river in Fort McMurray to refuel. It was a desolate-looking hamlet that had once thrived in the days of heavy river traffic. At the time it appeared to have no future. I could not imagine that some thirty years later, there would be an Alberta city here where I would be producing a major film—but I'm getting ahead of myself.

After another two hours of flying, we landed on Beaverlodge Lake— just north of Lake Athabasca in a remote corner of Saskatchewan—and gazed at the tent town that would be our home for the next five months. There were twenty-four men in the camp, a dozen or so A-frame tents, and a large cook tent. The cook was the most important man in camp and was called "Slim." He actually was slim.

Work began the next day. After being shown how to operate a Geiger counter, we were given a territory of forest and rocky hills to explore. A clicking sound indicated the presence of uranium, and a dial reading of the intensity was marked on a wooden stake driven in at the spot. A line of stakes might go from low to high readings in ninety metres. Removing the ore was a pick-and-shovel job, with larger finds blasted out of the rock for us to lug back to camp by the sackful. It was hard work.

Just getting to the sites was hard work, climbing rocky hills wet with dew every morning. Larry noticed that the camp old-timer, Henry, took a different trail. It appeared easier his way, so we followed him for about a week. He carried a large backpack, slipped and fell often, but usually arrived on time. After learning that Henry's backpack contained dynamite and blasting caps, we went back to the old route with everyone else.

Then in his fifties, Henry had lived all his life in the area, alone in a crude log cabin. He was not big on cleanliness or civilized behaviour. After dining, he would take out his false teeth to clean at the table, holding them in his hands as he sucked out stray bits of meat. When I first saw this, he was seated next to Larry, who jumped up and went outside the tent to vomit. He returned with hunting knife in hand, stabbed it into the tabletop, and said, "If you ever do that again, I'll kill you!" Henry calmly replied, "You suck your teeth too; I just take mine out to do it."

We lived mainly on canned goods, like Spam. Fresh meat was rare, no pun intended, but a major "find" resulted in T-bone steaks for everybody, specially flown in for the occasion. Larry and I were present for one of these celebrations. Slim lovingly prepared the steaks, reminding us there was only one each. We were drooling.

First in line, as usual, was Henry. He put *two* steaks on a plate and left them sitting while he went along the buffet with a second plate for other goodies. Before leaving his plate, though, he spat on the steaks! Every man in line then spat on them! Henry took his plates to a table, scraped off the sputum, and wolfed down his meal. He then took out both upper and lowers and, much louder than usual, joyously sucked them clean.

The only reason Henry hadn't been killed by somebody was that he was needed; he was an expert with dynamite. I have a barely visible scar on my head from one of his exploits. One day, we had found a large outcropping, rich with uranium and with a wide crack in the middle. Henry decided to blow it apart in one whack and spent a day prepping the charges.

I was present the next morning when he lit the fuse. I was bellied to the ground in back of a large tree, with my hands covering my ears. The blast was horrific! Trees were shredded, and the air was full of flying wood and rocks, some the size of footballs. The smoke and dust were so dense you could only see a short distance. When it seemed calm, I poked my head around the side of the shattered tree and heard a whistling sound and a "thunk," as something struck my forehead. The camp boss, behind the jagged remains of another tree, ran over and pulled out, from between my eyes, a piece of rock that looked like an Indian arrowhead. There was a lot of blood. Had it hit just a bit to the left or right, I would have lost an eye.

Finally, in October, it was freeze-up time. We were on the last float flight out of the camp, and weather forced Tiny to divert to Fort Smith, Northwest Territories. We bunked for the night in sleeping bags at the Hudson's Bay Company fort. As a result of aerial mapping, Fort Smith was later determined to be in Alberta, as it is shown on maps today.

Curious about the large number of black children in this small northern community, we were told there had been black American troops stationed there a few years before, and much fraternization with local Native girls had taken place. In typical northern style, a pool was put together to pay a substantial sum to the woman who first gave birth to a black child. Apparently it was a close race, with heavy side betting.

Back home in Edmonton, I should have gone back to school, but I had decided that photography was for me—or perhaps employment as a pilot. I was unable to find a job in photography, but found work at Woodward's department store as a draperies stock boy. I was soon made a sales clerk, then section head, and began taking classes in merchandising. But this was just my day job.

Several nights a week, I was at the School of Creative Photography, teaching part time. I purchased a four-by-five Speed Graphic camera, then considered the Rolls Royce of photographic equipment. I also continued to develop my passion for flying, taking lessons at Associated Airways.

When I began flying lessons, I intended to become a professional pilot, but I came to enjoy the freedom of the skies so much, I thought it would be better as a hobby. The cost also became prohibitive after I married.

At the age of nineteen, I was made an assistant manager at Woodward's and they spoke of my having a great future with the company—if I toughened up. I was too easygoing, they said. I quickly became disenchanted with retail and longed to get back into the photography business.

Although I soon realized that retail was not my cup of tea, I will forever be grateful to Woodward's department store for providing me with the most significant and wonderful event in my entire life. They say this sort of thing happens only in the movies, but I'm living proof it can happen for real.

Hustling into the advertising department one busy day, I stopped dead in my tracks. The most beautiful young lady I had ever seen was standing at an elevated, slant-topped table, checking price cards that had been printed for her department. She wore a black skirt, black nylons, and a horizontally striped, black and white wool sweater.

Her lovely eyes glanced my way, then quickly returned to the more interesting price cards. I learned that her name was Sally Masterson and that she worked in Baby's Wear. I worked at getting acquainted and soon discovered that everything about her was as fabulous as her beauty.

I spent a year wooing her, and we were married on 16 April 1949. I was twenty and she was seventeen (she turned eighteen the next day; I was twenty-one three weeks later).

One year later, almost to the day, our first child, Cathy Ann, was born. We were living in a rented house in south Edmonton at the time, with one bedroom converted into a darkroom. I had left Woodward's by this point and was trying to make a living as a freelance photographer. It was tough going, and I could no longer afford to fly.

Little did I know that a whole new chapter of my career was about to start.

Men of the Mountains

In 1948, the Film and Photographic Branch was established by the Alberta Department of Economic Affairs, under Minister Alfred J. Hooke. Kenneth Hutchinson, who had served with the Canadian Army overseas, was appointed the first film commissioner. Hooke was from Rocky Mountain House, where Ken's father had been the United Church minister. Ken and Alf Hooke knew each other well. Hutchinson had no prior knowledge of photography or film; he had been a schoolteacher before the war.

Hutchinson was destined to be more than an administrator. He was ambitious, a born empire builder, and determined to become a filmmaker. Apart from natural ability, he had a major asset—unlimited backing from the minister. He could learn on the job. "Hutch" (as he was called) soon had a film underway, contracted to Ottawa's Crawley Films and directed by Budge Crawley himself, as Ken watched and learned. The movie was titled *Mental Health, an Alberta Public Service*.

C. N. "Chuck" Ross was hired as cameraman/photographer on 1 April 1949. He had served overseas as a combat cameraman and had been employed by the *Edmonton Bulletin* as a press photographer before joining the Branch.

The next Alberta film production used prominent Calgary still photographer Harry Pollard, Jr., as cameraman. Completed in 1949, it was titled *Green*

Acres and told the story of irrigation in southern Alberta. Post-production was done in Ottawa by Crawley Films. I believe this was the first sixteen-millimetre documentary film with colour and sound that was fully Alberta made. The cameraman was an Albertan, as was Ken Hutchinson, who directed.

Meanwhile, Hollywood continued to look at Alberta as an untapped resource of scenery. In 1949, Twentieth Century-Fox came to Banff to film *Canadian Pacific*, starring Randolph Scott and Jane Wyatt. The movie was supposedly the true story of building the Canadian Pacific Railway (CPR) through the Rocky Mountains.

Playing a CPR surveyor, Scott was decked out as a full-fledged cowboy, carrying two six-guns and shooting obstructionists at random. In his book *Hollywood's Canada*, Pierre Berton refers to the movie as "just another transplanted western." From an Alberta point of view, the most interesting aspect of this movie was how it was made.

Most of the Hollywood cast and crew were housed in Calgary's Palliser Hotel. At five o'clock each morning, a special train departed from the adjacent CPR station, taking them to the main location in Banff National Park.

The crew included forty local workers, and breakfast was served on the train. About one hundred kilometres west of Calgary, a three-kilometre spur line was constructed to the west end of Lake Minnewanka, where tents, teepees, and other sets were located. The spur line became part of the movie, where the CPR construction sequences were filmed. It was an ingenious operation and not the last time filmmakers would change the landscape to turn scripts into reality.

Larry Matanski, my friend and fellow refugee from Venus Studios and the prospecting business, was hired by the Film and Photographic Branch in 1950. The first production he was involved with, *Alberta Vacation*, was a fifteen-minute, sixteen-millimetre, colour and sound documentary. The cameramen were Chuck Ross and Larry, with Ken Hutchinson serving as director and editor.

Bing Crosby, who had fallen in love with the Jasper area while filming *The Emperor Waltz* there a few years earlier, happened to be in town playing golf and Larry filmed the event, which was a real coup for the production. Unfortunately, the film was underexposed. The Cine-Special movie camera had a tricky shutter that enabled a fade out, and Larry had accidentally shot with it half-closed. The best correction the lab could make did not bring the Crosby footage up to par—though there was some usable footage of Bing to use in the movie.

The first Alberta-based production to feature a Hollywood star, *Alberta Vacation* was released in 1950, but early TV viewers in Canada and the U.S. would not see it on the small screen. Paramount Pictures advised that showing the movie on television would violate Crosby's contract. The Hollywood studios had declared war on television!

The team of Chuck, Larry, and Ken soon had a second film, *District Nurse*, under their belt, also filmed in 1950. Before long, I would find myself involved in this fast-growing enterprise.

Through Larry, I became acquainted with Ken Hutchinson and when an opportunity came along for a still photographer, Ken asked if I would like the job. In 1951, I was hired as an Alberta government photographer, with a starting salary of $1,920 a year. My career in professional filmmaking had begun.

There were now four people on staff at the Branch: photographer Melvin Petley-Jones, Chuck Ross, Larry Matanski, and myself. Two more were hired, both "mountain men" from Banff: F. W. (Bill) Eley-Round (who preferred to be called Bill Round) and Bruno Engler. They knew each other well, but not as friends. My wife, Sally, and I hosted a welcoming party for them, and Sally was horrified when Bill and Bruno began a fist fight. Bruno's second wife, Angel, hit him on the head with a cast-iron frying pan. When he regained consciousness, he had the good grace to say, "Thank you, Angel."

Bruno Engler had come to Canada in 1939 from his native Switzerland, where he had been a mountaineer and ski instructor. A wealthy student named Molly Nolet had enticed him to move to Banff and paid his way. In a development worthy of a Hollywood romance, they were later married—but not for long.

Although trained by his lensman father as a photographer and motion picture cameraman, Bruno's love for climbing came first. He found work as a mountain guide in Banff, where he made many notable ascents—including the south face of the Banff Springs Hotel, being chased by the RCMP at the time, for some reason. He made good his escape by entering the hotel through the open window of a guest room, on the seventh floor.

Bruno rolled his r's when speaking, and his favourite expression was "Let's have a *parrrty*." Although a courtly gentleman with a charming Swiss accent and delightful sense of humour, he could become nasty when drinking, and he was easily provoked.

Another gathering at our home once resulted in Bruno knocking a guest unconscious. I asked him why. Bruno said, "You don't know much about *parrrties*. He didn't like my necktie, and he's only had one drink. A few more and he won't like my face. Might as well take him by surprise and get it over with now."

There were many other eventful *parrrties* with Bruno over the years. I recall one in Banff that lasted most of the night. Early the next morning, he took Larry and me climbing up a rock face on Mount Rundle. It was terrifying, even though we were roped to Bruno, who said, "You haven't lived until you've climbed an overhang with a hangover."

Bruno was a superb outdoor photographer who would get either a spectacular picture or nothing. In the excitement of a choice photo opportunity, he might shoot with the lens cap on or, as once happened, shoot a large amount of colour movie film through a yellow filter that had been mistakenly left on after filming in black and white. There was never a dull moment with "the mad Swiss," as he was dubbed by Chuck Ross.

Bruno Engler left the Alberta government in 1955, but we kept in touch until his passing in 2001. He had become legendary as a skier, mountaineer, photographer, and raconteur. I treasure a copy of his 1996 book, *A Mountain Life*, inscribed to me with: "My good friend and past colleague, with memories."

Bill Round was an intellectual and likely a genius. He sought perfection in everything, although sartorial splendour was not on the list. He was a big man, with the general look of an unmade bed, and totally unconcerned about his appearance. Bruno Engler was much the same, and this caused Ken Hutchinson heartburn, resulting in a decree that all staff of the Film and Photographic Branch would wear blue blazers, grey flannels, white shirt, and tie!

Bill was an excellent still photographer, who had also studied moviemaking. The Alberta government provided the opportunity for him to apply his theoretical movie knowledge. He was born and raised in Banff, knew the Rockies well, and usually took mountain scenic pictures at ground level, whereas Bruno's spectacular photographs were obtained by climbing. The

Bruno Engler, skiing on Mount Norquay in Banff, 1954. He was one of my fellow photographers with the Alberta government for a few years and my friend for almost fifty years. Bruno was a master mountain photographer, climber, and skier extraordinaire. This picture of him he considered "quite ordinary." Photo: Bill Marsden

ground-level pictures were more frequently used in government publications and in movies because they represented the tourist's point of view. This was a long-time source of friction between Bill and Bruno.

Bill Round was not a flamboyant character like Bruno. He was quiet and reserved and a deep thinker.

He left the Alberta government in the late 1950s and went to work with Lew Parry Films in Vancouver for a few years, before joining the British Columbia government where he became head of the BC Film and Photographic Branch. A heavy smoker, he died of lung cancer in the late 1960s.

In the early days of my government career, darkroom work kept me busy—by demand, not by choice. On the plus side, I had access to the very best camera

(Then) Princess Elizabeth, and her husband, the Duke of Edinburgh, while on a tour of Canada in 1951, visited the Imperial Oil Refinery in Edmonton. A model of a drilling rig is being demonstrated by Calgary oilman Carl Nickle. I was an Alberta government photographer and, after receiving security clearance, I was assigned to cover this event, the only photographer present. Photo: Bill Marsden, Provincial Archives of Alberta

equipment and made good use of it in my spare time, continuing to experiment and learn. I was processing colour film and making dye transfer prints, acquiring what would have been a very expensive education and getting paid.

Others were getting the choice photo assignments—"Ho-hum" jobs were mine: bridge openings, ribbon cuttings, and the like. I was also doing some work for a Publicity Bureau gazette called *Within Our Borders*, a giveaway magazine about Alberta. It was still a fair distance from the "glamour" of the movies.

Princess Elizabeth and Prince Phillip's visit to Edmonton in 1951 resulted in my receiving security clearance and accreditation as a Royal photographer. A reception for them at the Imperial Oil Refinery was my assignment; I would be the only photographer present.

There were about fifty guests in a large room, enjoying refreshments

Combat cameraman Sgt. Chuck Ross shows his Eyemo newsreel camera to Major General Chris Vokes, commander of the Canadian Forces in Holland during World War II. Chuck became an Alberta government photographer after the war, then manager of the film and photographic branch, and finally director of film industry development for Alberta. Photo: Canadian Army

while waiting for introductions. Prince Phillip was in the middle of the crowd, surrounded, as the princess returned from a specially built powder room without her lady-in-waiting. She stood alone, completely ignored, in a large archway for what seemed to me an unreasonable length of time. She is a small woman, and the circumstances made her appear insignificant. It would have made an interesting photograph, but I chose not to take the shot.

I later made several flash photos of the Royals. I felt a heavy hand on my shoulder, looked back, and then looked *up!* A very large Scotland Yard inspector said, "I say, you've taken enough, haven't you?" I said, yes, and departed.

Back at the darkroom, Bruno, who had been assigned to cover comings and goings at the Royal train, was raving about a picture he had taken of the couple on the rear platform of the Royal train car, smiling and waving.

Marilyn Monroe and Robert Mitchum prepare to "navigate" the Bow Falls in *River of No Return* (1954). Photo: Whyte Museum of the Canadian Rockies NA-66-1679

"A *terrrrific* shot!" he said. It was also the only one he was able to get.

The magazine for the four-by-five Speed Graphic held twelve sheets of film. In the darkroom, with only one sheet to develop, Bruno accidentally dropped all twelve sheets onto the floor. Crawling around in the pitch dark, he could only find eleven. Calculating the odds, he gave up the search and processed the eleven sheets. After the film was fixed, he turned on the lights and saw the missing sheet far away in a corner. The eleven sheets in the tank of fixer were all blank. The *"terrrific"* picture was on the floor, exposed to light.

In 1952, the film *Resources for Industry* was shot by Chuck Ross and Bill Round and directed by Hutch. I won two awards for still photography from the Commercial and Press Photographers Association of Canada, including the Eaton's Trophy for the best photograph from Alberta. Chuck, Bill, and Bruno

Engler also made a film called *Wild Animals of Alberta*. The Alberta government's young film unit was starting to get very busy.

Several big Hollywood productions came to Alberta to film during the early 1950s, and Ken Hutchinson would assign one of his two "mountain men"—Bill Round or Bruno Engler—to assist the companies on location.

Bill was loaned to Universal International when they came in 1953 to make a North-West Mounted Police (NWMP) picture, starring Shelley Winters and Alan Ladd. It was shot in Banff National Park, which provided magnificent mountain backgrounds for the scarlet coats that were worn throughout the film. Alberta never looked better—but the film was titled *Saskatchewan*.

In 1954, Twentieth Century-Fox made *River of No Return* in Banff and Jasper National Parks; it starred Robert Mitchum and Marilyn Monroe, who was the world's hottest sex symbol at the time. During the shoot, Marilyn supposedly sprained her ankle, although she was suspected of faking it to spend a few days with her visiting boyfriend, ballplayer Joe DiMaggio. Marilyn was not popular with the crew; an assistant director was heard to remark following the ankle incident, "Too bad she didn't break her damned neck."

The ankle was examined and taped by Bill Round's friend Dr. Pat Costigan. He told Bill he could find nothing wrong, but enjoyed taping what was likely the world's most admired ankle. Costigan was an orthopaedic surgeon in a ski resort, internationally recognized for his expertise with spiral and other complicated bone fractures.

A Twentieth Century-Fox newsletter, however, described the incident like this: "Poor Marilyn in the wilds of Canada, with a terrible ankle injury, and in agonizing pain, had to be treated by a local physician."

Universal International returned in 1954 to film a gold rush epic, *The Far Country*, starring James Stewart and Ruth Roman. Jasper National Park's Columbia Icefields would become Alaska's Chilkoot Pass. It was a dangerous site. Bruno Engler was assigned to the production and convinced director Anthony Mann to change locations for a scene being filmed. A half-hour later, an avalanche—predicted by Bruno—buried the former site.

Bruno was very proud of a photograph he received from actress Ruth Roman, inscribed: "To Dear Bruno, thank you for saving my life." Bruno's wife, Angel, and daughter Mary Jane both had small parts in the film.

Alexandra Falls, on Hay River in the NWT, in 1952. Hugh Dempsey and I were doing a photo story on the opening of the new McKenzie highway from Grimshaw, Alberta, to Hay River, NWT. I was an Alberta government photographer; Dempsey was then a writer for Alberta's *Within our Borders* and later became an esteemed historian with an honorary doctorate, as well as the Order of Canada. He is standing on the lip of the Alexandra Falls, on the Hay River. Photo: Bill Marsden

In 1952, writer Hugh Dempsey and I were assigned to a photo story about the new Mackenzie Highway from Grimshaw to Hay River in the Northwest Territories. We drove for several days from Edmonton, with overnight stops, and obtained some unique material. I took a picture of Hugh standing on an overhang at the top of Alexandra Falls on the Hay River. Virtually unknown, they are thirty-two metres high. The picture received wide distribution, but few people today will believe it is the esteemed historian, and recipient of the Order of Canada, Dr. Hugh Dempsey standing precariously on the lip of the falls.

By this time, Larry Matanski had left the government and was making a film for Associated Airways. He showed up in Hay River, flying a small Aeronca aircraft on large floats. To cap our own story, I wanted some aerial shots. Larry obliged and then flew us 250 kilometres across Great Slave Lake to Yellowknife.

While bar-hopping in Yellowknife, we met a helicopter pilot and an engineer who were flying back to Hay River the next day. A bet was made for a race to the beer parlour there—the loser to buy all drinks, all day. Their machine was a Bell 47 on rubber floats.

Larry Matanski and I, seen standing beside Matanski's Aeronca aircraft, which we flew across Slave Lake to Yellowknife. I am holding a Speed Graphic camera and had been taking still photos for a highway story. Matanski, with his tripod mounted Bolex movie camera, was making a film for Associated Airways. Photo: Hugh Dempsey

Halfway across the lake, the helicopter team sat down to refuel from ten-gallon drums they carried onboard, and Larry circled to jeer when we should have kept going. We were ahead coming into Hay River and landed at the float base. Hugh Dempsey drove us into town. Passing the helicopter landing pad, we were happy to see they weren't there. Our arrival at the beer parlour found our helicopter friends seated at a table loaded with beer, waiting for us to pay. They had landed on the hotel roof and then walked down the fire escape into the bar.

The next morning, a crowd gathered on Main Street to watch the chopper take off. As it revved up, it seemed the two-storey, wood-frame building would shake apart. Larry returned to Edmonton where his aircraft was grounded by the Ministry of Transport; his floats were only approved for a larger aircraft.

Meanwhile, back at the branch, Bill Round was the movie maestro. He would teach me the finer points of filmmaking. The branch had been given more space on the ground floor of the Legislative Building. There was an editing room with synchronizers, rewinds, and upright Moviola equipment. Sound recording and mixing facilities were added in the screening room, including a stock music library. Except for printing and processing, we had all the facilities necessary for film production. Most of our films were made "in the field," other than when we recorded the occasional speech by a politician.

In 1953, Ken Hutchinson's dreams came true with an award-winning film called *Gift of the Glaciers*, a story of the Columbia Icefields. It was Bill Round's creation from day one, with poetic narration written by Bob Cantelon of the Publicity Bureau. Ken took director and editing credits and *Gift of the Glaciers* won the Canadian Film Award for the "Best Film in Tourism" category. It was the production that really put the Alberta Film and Photographic Branch on the map with national recognition, allowing Ken to successfully promote expanding the branch, including the creation of a film and photo unit in Calgary.

Fritz Lang came to Edmonton in 1953 to scout a movie he would make for Columbia Pictures. To my delight, I was assigned to work with him. He was, arguably, the greatest of the German film directors who immigrated to America in the 1930s after the Nazis came into power. His 1926 film *Metropolis,* two years in the making and Germany's most expensive movie to that date, was one of the first great science fiction classics.

"Countdown," a commonly used word today, was originated by Fritz Lang for a rocket launch in a 1920s science fiction film, *Lady in the Moon*. He said, "if I count one two, three, four . . . an audience doesn't know when it will go off. But if I count down . . . five, four, three, two, one, ZERO . . . then they will know."

When I met Fritz he was sixty-three years old. Every photo I had ever seen of him showed him with a monocle in his left eye, which I came to believe was a Lang trademark. He was now wearing glasses. When asked about it, he said, "When I first came to America I could only afford one lens, now they pay me so much money I can afford two."

His movie would be a remake of a 1938 French film by Jean Renoir, based on the Émile Zola book *The Human Beast*, a love-and-hate story with a railroading background. It was the big Canadian National Railway (CNR) steam locomotives that had attracted Fritz to Alberta. They hauled enormous loads on mountain grades to the west coast. These engines were magnificent in form and function.

Fritz Lang, the famous German/American film director, leans out of the cab of a Canadian National Railways steam locomotive to film with a sixteen-millimetre movie camera. He was scouting in Alberta, in 1953, for the motion picture *Human Destiny* and, as an Alberta government photographer, I was assigned to work with him, show him Alberta, and take pictures as he requested. Photo: Bill Marsden, from Provincial Archives of Alberta

Fritz was accompanied by screenwriter Alfred Hayes, who had worked with him on *Clash by Night,* in which Fritz had directed Marilyn Monroe in one of her early film roles. By all accounts, dealing with Marilyn was a nerve-racking experience, as other directors would discover. Nevertheless, Fritz was an admirer. "When she got it right, she had no equal," he said.

The CNR was very co-operative. We toured and photographed its Edmonton rail yards before boarding a private car that was to be our home for the next week. It was hooked onto a mountain-bound freight, pulled by one of the huge steam engines. We each had a private room, and a steward was assigned to take care of our needs. Fritz's first job was to instruct the steward on how to make his special version of a martini.

A CNR executive travelled with us to arrange for stops, sidings, and

This magnificent CNR steam locomotive, designed for mountain use, pulled a large number of freight cars and a posh private car that was the travelling home for famous film director Fritz Lang, writer Al Hayes, and me while scouting for a movie in 1953. Here it is being turned around on the Jasper CNR turntable for the return journey to Edmonton. These mountain engines were what attracted Fritz Lang to Alberta, but his film *Human Destiny* was eventually made in the United States. Photo: Bill Marsden, from Provincial Archives of Alberta

hookups to other engines when required. We would be taken wherever Mr. Lang wanted to go. En route to Jasper, Fritz called for a stop. He was going to walk the long length of the train to ride in the engine cab. The CNR exec yelled, "Wait, Mr. Lang," and had the engineer back up so Lang could climb directly into the engine cab.

Fritz was fascinated with the big locomotives, asking questions, making notes, and filming with a sixteen-millimetre movie camera. He had me shoot stills on the move and while the engine was idle, details like hissing steam and the huge drive wheels, which he stood alongside to show scale. He loved to ride in the cab, seated behind the engineer, leaning out into a storm of smoke and cinders.

The steam whistle was blown at every level crossing. It was ear piercing, blotting out all other sounds.

COLUMBIA PICTURES CORPORATION
1438 NO. GOWER STREET
HOLLYWOOD 28, CALIFORNIA
HUDSON 2-3111

May 26, 1953

Mr. Bill Marsden,
Suite One,
10583 - 108th Street,
Edmonton, Alberta, Canada

Dear Bill:

Just returned from Washington, D.C. and found your pictures at home. I think they are great and will help us a lot. Thank you also for the extra pictures you took from your files of Jasper and vicinity, though it breaks my heart that I will not be able to photograph Maligne Lake.

The film I shot has turned out very well too and together with your pictures, they give a very good impression of how Jasper and surroundings will look on the screen.

Thank you for your "statement of our financial affairs," but as long as you don't increase the forty-four cents to a thousand dollars, I don't want to hear about it any more. What shall I do with a measley hundred dollars?

Contrary to what I had expected, I didn't have a chance to read Alec Gray's book so will have to do it now and then return it to him. I just had a long story conference with Al and he sends you his best regards and thanks you very much for the different photos you made for him (I love mine where I look like a wistful rooster) but where the "double portrait" of Al and me, you should have realized that I was shooting with a covered lens --- fine director you are!

What about your vacation? Give my best to your wife and drop me a line as to how you both are. I hope I will see you in the very near future.

Sincerely yours,

FL/jl

Letter from Fritz Lang, the famous German/American film director.

We parked on a siding at Jasper for three days, shooting the station, rail yards, and scenic locations that Fritz found very attractive—as he did a young waitress at a local restaurant.

"That is the nicest, loveliest young lady I have seen in a long time," he said of her. "In Hollywood, she would get an offer immediately."

"You're a famous movie director, why don't you tell her? It's likely her fondest dream," I said.

His reply: "She is too nice. I would not want to see her treated the way they do in Hollywood!"

American locations had also been scouted for the movie, but Fritz was determined the film would be made on Alberta's CNR with the big mountain engines. But it was not as economical to film in Alberta in 1953 as it is today, and executive producer Jerry Wald of Columbia Pictures ordered the film to be made in the United States, with diesel trains. I believe Fritz felt the soul of the story had been yanked from his grasp with the loss of steam, and he lost heart with the production.

His film, *Human Desire,* starring Canadian-born Glenn Ford, Gloria Graham, Broderick Crawford, and Edgar Buchanan, was released in 1954. A review by critic Bosley Crowther would seem to confirm my thoughts about the movie: "When the story presented in this picture was done some years ago in a French film directed by Jean Renoir (1938's *La bête humaine*), there was, at least, a certain haunting terror, a certain mood of dark malevolence conveyed. The mind of the locomotive driver became an area of agonizing pain, and the pounding of railroad wheels and the shriek of whistles credibly drove the man insane. But even that morbid fascination is missing from this film, which has been directed in a flat lethargic fashion by the usually creative Fritz Lang."

There were no diesel engines where Jean Renoir had filmed in 1938.

I remember Fritz Lang saying, "No movie ever looks as good as the rushes, or as bad as the first cut," and I have seen this proven many times.

Fritz was a hard taskmaster, but we got along very well. He said I should become a cameraman, and he took Sally and me to dinner and offered to help us get established in Hollywood. But we were too fond of Alberta to make the jump.

It is a decision we've never regretted.

As time went on, I became more involved with filmmaking, working closely with Bill Round. Together, we made *Skyline Trails,* a twenty-minute production

MADE IN ALBERTA?

A few famous movies believed to have been made in Alberta actually were not. The 1936 classic *Rose-Marie* is a good example. The 1992 *Alberta Trivia* book states: "On the Maligne River near Jasper is a spot called Rose-Marie's Rock. It was here the famous love scene between Nelson Eddy and Jeanette MacDonald was sung and filmed for the movie *Rose-Marie,* during the first [Alberta] location shoot of a movie by a Hollywood film crew. The pool of water behind Rose-Marie's rock is Nelson's Eddy." But none of this is true.

This classic 1936 movie was made in Nevada, at Lake Tahoe, and on Hollywood sound stages. A brief sequence of real Mounties on parade was filmed near Vancouver, after lengthy lobbying with the Canadian government, but that's the closest Nelson Eddy got to Alberta. In 1953, MGM did a remake of *Rose-Marie,* starring Howard Keel and Ann Blyth and dropping the hyphen from the title. This was also shot in Nevada and Hollywood, except for some second-unit scenes (without principal performers) that were, in fact, filmed in Jasper.

The *Banff Crag and Canyon* newspaper of 24 July 1953 reported: "Seventy Stoney Indians from Morley assisted in making the picture *Rose Marie* in Jasper National Park.... Some scenes were taken at Mount Edith Cavell, Pyramid Lake, Mount Athabasca, Patricia Lake, Windy Point, and along the Athabasca River fifty miles south of Jasper. Costumes provided the Indians were fringed buckskin pants, a blanket to drape over their shoulders, and a headband complete with feathers. Another costume was the loincloth, which is reported to have somewhat dismayed the Indians as they have never worn such dress before." This 1950s version of *Rose Marie* is likely responsible for the Nelson Eddy/Jeanette MacDonald myth in Jasper.

Springtime in the Rockies, starring John Payne and Betty Grable, was made in Hollywood in 1941 on Twentieth Century-Fox sound stages. A second-unit cameraman filmed in Banff and Lake Louise. Many still photos were taken and greatly enlarged to provide backdrops for sound-stage filming. It's easy to believe you're at Chateau Lake Louise when you see this movie.

The 1965 classic *Dr. Zhivago* is also said to have been filmed partly in Alberta. Actually, one quick shot was made from a CPR train near Banff to intercut with a sequence of the family travelling through the Ural Mountains in Russia. Otherwise, most of *Zhivago* was made in Spain and Finland.

about the Trail Riders of the Canadian Rockies, spending two weeks on horseback in the mountains and living in teepees.

The year was 1953. By this time, I had become competent in editing, sound recording, mixing, and negative cutting. I could actually call myself a filmmaker; there were now a handful of us in Alberta who could do the whole thing.

Looking at some of the films we made decades ago, I'm often ashamed of the quality, until recalling the handicaps we faced. The Kodak Commercial Kodachrome film we used was rated at ASA 10, for daylight exposure, ASA 8 for tungsten lighting. Every light we could locate was required for even a small interior scene. Indoors, we were always shooting "wide open," allowing no depth of field (also known as deep focus). There was no such thing as a zoom lens or a gyro mount. If we needed a moving shot, it was done hand-held or from whatever we could use as a crude dolly. Shots were usually static, except for pans and tilts, always from a tripod, and usually a long shot, medium shot, and close-up were taken to provide choices in editing.

It is amazing we were able to work as well as we did, given the limitations.

The Film and Photographic Branch had become very useful in government, and it decided to open a branch in Calgary. To my amazement, I was offered the job of photographer and, after discussing it with Sally, I accepted. We moved to Calgary on 1 April 1955—Sally and myself, daughter Cathy Ann (now five), and baby son Mark, born 27 December 1954. As a bonus to what I considered to be the best job in the world, a government automobile was provided. A studio and darkroom were constructed in the Alberta Office Building in downtown Calgary.

Photographic opportunities around Calgary seemed endless. If there were no specific assignments, I might head into ranching country or the mountains to shoot scenic pictures for our files. They would eventually be used in government or other publications to promote Alberta. I was exposing and processing a lot of four-by-five colour film, and much of my work was in the deep south of the province, including Lethbridge, Waterton, and Medicine Hat. I came to love the south as I had the north. I could hardly believe I was getting paid to do this.

In Calgary, even the rival photographers were friendly. There was usually a drink to be found in a darkroom, if you knew where to look. Shelves were crowded with chemical bottles and most of us used the one labelled "glacial acetic acid" to hold our booze. The uninitiated wouldn't touch it. In a strange darkroom, you removed the cap and took a sniff first. If it actually was

During Banff Indian Days, in the summer of 1954, I took a colour picture for an Alberta poster with an Indian chief and the RCMP sergeant in charge of the Banff detachment as models. This photograph was taken of me hard at work. Photo: Bill Round

acetic acid, a whiff would just about knock you over. Bruno Engler, in his Banff darkroom, used one of several bottles marked "developer" to hold his favourite scotch. Suffering from a cold one day, with his sniffer out of order, he mistakenly poured a measure of scotch into a tray and diluted it with two parts water. When a print wouldn't develop, even after exposure was increased, he realized his error. It would have been the correct dilution for developer, but was too weak for a drink. Bruno simply added more scotch, forgot about printing, and drank the mixture in the tray.

The city of Calgary had become our family favourite. We loved it for many reasons, including its proximity to the mountains and to the American border. An hour's drive on any point of the compass reveals scenery similar to many parts of North America and other parts of the world, which makes it an attractive choice for film locations.

In 1955, Larry Matanski moved to Calgary to establish Master Film Studios Ltd., having found local oil-industry investors. A sound stage, black and white

Alberta's first modern film studio, Master Film Studios Ltd., at 505–5 Street SW, Calgary, was established by Larry Matanski in 1955. (L to R) Werner Franz, Johnny Pfiffig, John Groot, Mary Hundert, Bob Willis, and Spence Crilly. Photo: *Calgary Herald*

film processing, sound recording, and mixing, as well as optical printing, were now available in a former church in downtown Calgary at 510–5 Avenue SW. There was an initial staff of five, a good assortment of cameras, including two 360-metre Auricons, and significant lighting and sound equipment. This was Alberta's first modern film studio.

Television commercials, oil industry productions, and provincial government work were obtained, but the operation was not profitable under Larry's management. He was replaced and he moved back to Edmonton in 1958 to form Matan Productions, in partnership with his brother, Eddie. Larry began planning to produce a feature film.

Master Films struggled on in Calgary with a variety of managers and imported producers. Much of the equipment was sold, but original employee Bob Willis eventually took it over and made it into one of Alberta's successful operations. In Edmonton, Nick Zubko left the University of Alberta to found

WATCH FOR Teenager to become tycoon / Edmonton movie-maker's Hollywood-style gamble

BUSINESSMAN TO WATCH: Montreal's Stephen William Garber, only 17 but already doing $15,000 to $20,000 a year business as boss of his own one-year-old firm, Specialty Ad Sales Reg'd (sales incentive programs, advertising giveaways). He financed his company at 16, with savings and bank credit. Now he's planning to branch out into manufacturing plastic items.

Watch for 28-year-old Edmonton violinist Thomas (Mickey) Rolston to become a national name in music. Born in Vancouver, schooled in California, New York, London and Brussels, he's a veteran of European tours and the London Philharmonic. He'll be heard across Canada as soloist with Vancouver Symphony on a Canada Council-sponsored broadcast over CBC radio December 13.

Scorning his eastern Canadian rivals as "too CBC-ish," Edmonton movie producer Larry Matanski, 31, is out to prove Hollywood techniques can pay off for Canadians too. He's got $200,-000 in Alberta investors' money riding on the box-office success of a frankly commercial adventure yarn filmed in Alberta and due for release soon. In Hollywood tradition, he bought a novel (Kirby's Gander, by Edmontonian John Patrick Gillese), retitled it Wings of Chance, got a Hollywood writer to add love interest and hired three Hollywood performers as leads.

MATANSKI

Only the title and plot were changed

Edmonton movie producer Larry Matanski makes it to the pages of *Maclean's* (1 November 1959). Reproduced with permission.

Cine-Audio Ltd., with black and white film processing and printing. Nick had several employees filming for the Canadian Broadcasting Corporation (CBC). His business thrived and he became a major contributor to the Alberta film industry. When the Alberta Motion Picture Industry Association (AMPIA) was formed in 1973, Nick Zubko became its first president.

The year 1958 became a critical year for me. Ralph Moore, the deputy minister of Economic Affairs, requested that I move back to Edmonton to become assistant film commissioner. It was a promotion with a salary increase, but the job would also involve administration. My family had come to love Calgary. We had bought a house in Calgary. I declined the offer.

Within a week, a memo arrived, ordering me to report for duty in Edmonton in thirty days or submit my resignation. I resigned.

The Ice Farmers

By 1958, Hugh Dempsey, my colleague from the Mackenzie Highway adventure, was involved with the Glenbow Foundation in Calgary. He was also my neighbour and suggested there might be an opportunity for me with the Foundation. He arranged a meeting with its founder, mega-millionaire Eric L. Harvie, who said, "I've been told that you quit your job with the government because you'd rather live in Calgary than in Edmonton."

"Yes, sir."

"I don't need a further recommendation. In the office next door you'll find Hod Meech. Tell him what you want to do, and how much you want to be paid."

That was the entire conversation, and it was the beginning of a very interesting period in my life as the director of the foundation's film and photo department. I would be doing both still photography and movie work, hopefully acquiring help in both categories as we expanded (it didn't happen).

I didn't have camera equipment or a darkroom, but I did have a lovely office in the Hull Mansion, with fresh flowers on my desk regularly from a greenhouse on the estate. A well-known Canadian oil painting, *Canoes in fog, Lake Superior 1869*, by Francis Ann Hopkins, occupied one wall. Smaller paintings and watercolours were changed monthly, all coming from the Glenbow's art collection. Camera equipment was finally purchased when the government said we could occupy its Calgary studio and darkroom, which wasn't being used. The government was beginning to woo Eric Harvie in order to acquire the Glenbow collections.

Subjects to photograph were often of my own choosing, or they were via a request from foundation archivist Hugh Dempsey. A series of portraits I am proud of included elderly Natives and other prominent Albertans—talented individuals such as cowboy artist and sculptor Charlie Beil; Jimmy Simpson, legendary mountain guide and builder of Num Ti Jah Lodge on Bow Lake; Norman Luxton, founder of the Luxton museum; and Edmonton musician Vernon Barford. All were wonderful people, but not wealthy. I also made a portrait of Eric L. Harvie, who was *both* wonderful and wealthy.

Photocopying and printing were contracted to old-time Calgary photographer Joe Rosettis. Using a view camera to produce an eight-by-ten-inch negative, I made a photograph of Calgary at night from the North Hill, exposing at dusk, then again when the building lights came on. From it, I made a sectional print that measured 2.5 metres high and 7 metres wide as background for a Glenbow display. It was the largest print made in Alberta to that time, according to Kodak.

It was wonderful to be working with Hugh Dempsey again. His ideas and causes were always first class. Aboriginal subjects were of prime interest to Hugh. He had been assisting the Indian Association of Alberta when he met the woman who became his wife, a true Blood Indian princess, Pauline Gladstone. Her father, James Gladstone, was Canada's first Indian senator and the subject of one of Hugh's many books.

Hugh was dedicated to documenting Native life and, working together, he and I made a number of films on the subject. The first was titled *Native Pottery*. Archaeologist Dr. Dick Forbis had excavated fragments of pottery on the Blackfoot Reserve, enough to establish their size and shape. Glenbow had a potter on summer staff, and she duplicated these vessels as we filmed. Local clay near Gleichen was used, as was a bonfire kiln, as the Natives would have used. The results were impressive.

The next film Hugh and I made was *Indian Quill Work*. Before the fur-trading companies developed glass beads for bartering, the Indians decorated buckskin garments with dyed porcupine quills. An elderly Blackfoot woman knew how it was done, and Hugh arranged for us to film her in the process, which was fascinating. I was especially impressed with the way it began. She carried a stout stick and a piece of soft buckskin as I followed her into the bush with a hand-held movie camera. She found a porcupine. As she slowly approached, it became defensive, getting ready to turn and flick its tail. The quills were standing straight up as she threw the buckskin, simultaneously clubbing the animal on the end of the nose. The porcupine was unconscious as she peeled off the buckskin, which was loaded with quills. As we left with this treasure, "Porcie" woke up and wandered off to grow more quills. (And we think we originated conservation!) The quills were soaked in natural dyes, cut to length, and then sewn onto buckskin in patterns, much like glass beads.

Okan was another major film we produced. It was an hour-long documentary of the Blackfoot sun dance, made at the Blackfoot Nation's request to preserve the ceremony for future generations. We filmed near Cluny, where the event has taken place for hundreds of years. Hugh worked out an agreement that enabled us to film all events, including secret ceremonies, as long as the movie was shown only to Native audiences and professional researchers. Nick Zubko and Cine-Audio were engaged to provide equipment and assistance. I would direct and operate a second sound camera.

A holy woman was chosen to preside at the sun dance, and a suitable tree was found for the lodge centre pole. It is considered an honour for the tree, and prayers were said before it was cut down, along with thanks for its sacrifice. Hauled into camp by horses and wagon, with drums, songs, and ceremony, the tree was put in place with more fanfare, and the lodge was built around it. Dozens of teepees were erected. From a distance, the sun dance camp looked as it would have a hundred years before, with one notable exception: there were cars and trucks parked in front of many of the teepees. We had to get rid of them in order to maintain the historical authenticity of the documentary, so a parking lot was created outside of camera view. It was announced we would pay five dollars for each vehicle parked there. The camp soon cleared, and our lot was almost full. It soon had to be expanded because every day more powered transport showed up, including tractors!

Filming inside teepees with available light was a challenge that required the use of high-speed colour film. It was very grainy, but the realism it provided was far more valuable than anything we could have achieved with lighting. Only I, with a single camera, was allowed to film an initiation into the Horn

Society, the most powerful and secret of all the tribal groups. Hugh tells me I was, at that time, the only living white man to have witnessed this ceremony. I continue to honour the trust the Natives placed in me.

Every event happened inside, under canvas. Even with bright sunlight, we were filming with the lens "wide open." One evening, as we were getting ready to return to the hotel in Cluny, a tribal Elder said, "See you tomorrow." I told him we wouldn't be there the next day because the forecast was for rain. He was shocked and told me, "It won't rain; we're having a sun dance. When we have a rain dance, it rains. You come tomorrow."

True to forecast, it was raining when we left the hotel the next morning. The crew was not happy; they had expected a holiday, but there we were, braving the downpour to return to the camp. As we peaked a rise and looked down into the valley, we saw sunshine. Dark grey skies were all around, except for a hole where sunlight beamed through, lighting up the encampment like a giant searchlight. The sun shone every day of the sun dance.

I talked with an Elder on the subject of sun worship, as opposed to what the missionaries had come to teach. He said, "The Sun makes grass and trees grow, gives life to birds and animals and us. There would be nothing without the Sun, and when I look up I can see it. Your God I have never seen."

Editing and post-production on *Okan* kept Hugh and me busy for many months. We believed it was a good film. An authority from the Smithsonian Institution called it "the best film ever made of a Native ceremony."

Government employment had provided a technical education and had helped me develop creatively, but the opportunities provided by Glenbow were more aesthetic, interesting, and valuable to me as a human. Involvement with Natives in various projects taught me more than I could have learned from any other source. What I had always believed to be the choicest things in life now seemed less important.

My Indian friends know the best is what our society takes for granted: sunrise, sunset, starry skies, trees, birds, and animals. They know the secret is to harmonize with Nature, not fight Her. Their spirituality is absolute and meaningful. My Sunday School education was narrow and, I would say, bigoted in comparison. I greatly admire their unconditional love of children, no matter what the background or parentage. There is no such thing as an illegitimate child in their society.

Here I am behind an Auricon camera, filming the Blackfoot sun dance at Cluny in 1961, for the sixteen-millimetre movie *Okan*. This Glenbow Foundation film reveals all the mysteries of the ceremonies, but viewing is restricted to Native audiences and professional researchers. Photo: Joe Rosettis, Glenbow Archives

A moving experience was my adoption in 1961 into the Blackfoot tribe, with the name of *Meanistokus*, or "Father of His People," as was the original holder of the name, Low Horn, one of the signers of Treaty Number Seven. It is a huge honour to be given such a name. My Blackfoot brother was Henry Low Horn. We would see or hear from him when he was in Calgary and broke or from the police when he needed bail money. We took care of him on such occasions. Henry was killed years later, run over by a police car at night while he was passed out on a reserve road.

Western Minerals was an Eric Harvie-owned company that had purchased a huge parcel of Arctic land outright from the federal government. Seismic exploration had been conducted and drilling was about to begin. This was an incredible operation to film, and I was given the job.

Nick Zubko is filming the sun dance movie *Okan* at Cluny in 1961. Nick, the founder of Alberta's Cine-Audio Company, became one of the founders and the first president of the Alberta Motion Picture Industries Association. Photo: Bill Marsden, Glenbow Archives

I flew into camp on the Peel Plateau, north of the Arctic Circle, by chartered aircraft from Dawson City. The camp, supplies, and equipment had been hauled in by tractor trains—a 480-kilometre journey through two mountain ranges. This could only be accomplished in winter when the ground, lakes, and rivers were frozen solid.

Bunkhouses and a kitchen were components of each tractor train, because it was a ten-day journey, if all went well. A tractor or sleigh breaking through the ice would hold up the entire procession. This journey was filmed in eight millimetre by one of the crew. I had it enlarged to sixteen millimetre, then edited it with sound for a production titled *Arctic Tractor Train*. The narration was written by a notable Alberta author, my friend John Patrick Gillese.

The drilling rig was hauled to the site in the same manner. The owner/operator was concerned that it might be too costly to move the rig out when the well was completed. Western Minerals purchased the rig and drilling began.

It was difficult to film because of the extreme cold. In camp one morning, every thermometer showed minus-sixty—the lowest temperature they could register. It was likely colder. My movie camera wouldn't even turn over. The "official" Arctic drink is overproof rum because it won't freeze, and I consumed my share—I needed it! Tractors surrounded our bunkhouses, running twenty-four hours a day. After spending two weeks in the camp, I found I couldn't sleep in a Dawson City hotel room. It was too quiet.

In 1959, Larry Matanski began production of a theatrical motion picture. Alberta's film industry has been spattered with colourful characters; Larry was like a painting by Jackson Pollock. While still a teenager, he had bought a Bolex camera and used it to make films as a freelancer, before founding film companies in Calgary and Edmonton. That Bolex was often seen on a pawnshop shelf during lean times. Now at the age of thirty-one, he would undertake Alberta's first homegrown feature-film project, *Wings of Chance*.

Larry could have written the book on how to look like a movie producer. He was not tall, but was definitely dark and handsome and a flashy dresser. He always had his own airplane and drove big automobiles, which like the airplanes were heavily financed and replaced often. His banker, who owned a Volkswagen, told Larry that's what he should be driving. The response was, "I could put one of those in my trunk." He owed the bank a considerable amount at the time.

Matanski was also a pilot/adventurer, flying into northwest Canada's remote Nahanni Valley, spookily called the "Valley of Headless Men," and returning with the first movie footage of the area, including the magnificent Virginia Falls. He was one of the best pilots I ever flew with. In the mid-1950s, while making a film for Civil Defense about the evacuation of Calgary, he piloted a tandem Aeronca with me in the rear seat, shooting with a thirty-five-millimetre Eyemo camera. We were filming cars leaving the city. A built-up section of highway allowed Larry to drop lower, wheels almost touching the grass in the ditch. Our left wing was over the roof of a car travelling at one hundred kilometres an hour. We kept pace and I was able to film a child, hands pressed against the rear side window, looking at us goggle eyed. I could not have shot that scene with any other pilot.

This scene from the film *Okan* shows the "making of a Brave." Skewers pierce his chest on both sides and are attached by leather thongs to a centre pole. Blowing a wooden whistle, the warrior dances around the pole, tugging at the straps until the skewers break through his skin. He is then officially a Brave and carries the scars of the event for life. (We faked this for the film, but there were volunteers who would have done it "for real!") Photo: Bill Marsden, Glenbow Archives

Larry often freelanced for the National Film Board and, on return from their Montreal studios, once told me, "Everyone there has a beard, even some of the guys." There was usually humour in his conversation, not always intentional. After viewing a showplace Hollywood cemetery one day, he said, "They really know how to live down there."

Matanski was an extraordinary promoter and idea man, stimulating to be with but unpredictable. He was cursed with a lifelong inability to live within his means. He was not a drinker; his personal addiction was gambling. When he failed to deliver an assignment or caused heartburn for investors, gambling was usually responsible. This was the reason I never became a business partner with him, although we were always friends. He stood as my best man when Sally and I were married.

Tony Mokry, a friend and business associate of Larry's, remembers stopping in Las Vegas with him while en route to Los Angeles. Larry soon lost the considerable amount of money he was carrying for post-production expenses on a film. He was still rolling the dice when Tony said, "Let's get the hell out of here, where's the car?" Larry said, "It's at the corner service station, and they have the keys. Give me that twenty dollar bill I saw you put in your shoe this morning." At the service station, the Cadillac was high in the air on an outdoor hoist. The manager said, "It comes down when I get the twelve hundred dollars he borrowed." Tony wrote a cheque and picked up Larry, and they left for Los Angeles. The twenty dollars from his shoe had already been lost.

Larry's feature film, *Wings of Chance*, was based on the short story, "Kirby's Gander," by Edmonton writer John Patrick Gillese. The $287,000 budget was provided by Alberta investors. Tax shelters or any forms of government assistance were not available for Canadian films in 1959. Matanski brought in equipment and key people from Hollywood, including the director, department heads, and leading actors. The stars were James Brown and Frances Rafferty, both well known at the time from American television shows such as *The Adventures of Rin Tin Tin* and *December Bride*.

Wings of Chance is about a bush pilot named Kirby who crashes in the northern Alberta wilderness and can't be found by air searches. He lives off fish and other game and befriends some young geese. Using aluminum from his aircraft, he leg bands some of the geese with his name and location; when one is shot that fall, the leg band is given to the RCMP and Kirby is rescued.

Wings of Chance was shot in Edmonton and Jasper and trained many Albertans in the process. I worked on part of the show, learning much from director of photography Leonard Clairmont, who had written several books on the subject.

Filming went smoothly, as did post-production in Hollywood. The end result, released in 1961, was not bad; in fact, it became the first Canadian motion picture to be purchased outright by an American distributor. Larry sold it to Universal Pictures for less than cost. It is reputed to have made nine million dollars for Universal.

During a visit to Hollywood in the early 1960s, Larry and Tony Mokry tried to persuade studios to invest in their next film. Canadian producers were rare in

Key people from Alberta's first "homegrown" theatrical motion picture, *Wings of Chance*, at Jasper, in 1959. (L to R) Hollywood director Edward Dew, Alberta producer Larry Matanski, director of photography Leonard Clairmont, and camera operator Jack McCoskey. Clairmont and McCoskey were both from Hollywood. Photo: Bill Marsden

DISNEY WOLVERINES

In 1960, Walt Disney Studios arranged with the Alberta government to set up a fenced "wildlife studio" in Kananaskis Country. Post-production would be completed in Hollywood. This operation produced many Disney wildlife shows for television over the next decade.

Among their prized captive animals was a wolverine. Wolverines rarely "speak," and a Disney producer said they hoped to purchase some wolverine sounds.

A young entrepreneur, who will remain nameless, overheard this discussion and went to the cage that night with a tape recorder. Poking the animal with a stick, he obtained some great sound effects, which were sold to Disney. Today, he works on films being shot in Alberta in a different capacity.

Hollywood at that time, inspiring one executive to refer to these newcomers as "The Ice Farmers."

In November 1963, as if to confirm the "ice farmer" label, Larry began a winter shoot for a largely outdoor epic titled *Naked Flame*. This being a story about British Columbia's freedomite Doukhobor sect, he believed female nudity could be justified and would be cleared by the censor as a semi-documentary. It was shot in Calgary and Canmore, with Larry producing and directing.

Larry didn't consider film an art form. He admired the basic simplicity of 1960s' movies. Action/adventure in a memorable setting, that's what Hollywood wanted, he thought, and that's what they would get—with some equally impressive female nudity.

The idea for *Naked Flame* was developed by Tony and Larry and then expanded into a screenplay by a Los Angeles writer. Five actors were brought in from Hollywood. Leading man Dennis O'Keefe was a well-known star of film and stage, a song-and-dance performer, comic, and romantic hero who had paid his dues, appearing in dozens of 1930s' films in bit parts before moving up to leading-man status and eventually hosting his own TV series in the late 1950s. Leading lady Kasey Rogers had been absent from the big screen for almost ten years, having changed her name from Laura Elliott and appearing in dozens of television shows. Supporting actors Al Ruscio, Barton Heyman, and Linda Bennett were all relative unknowns at the time. Local artists included Mort Van Ostrand, Jack Goth, Kay Grieve, Les Kimber, and Bruce McInnes—the list included several names that would become prominent in the Alberta film industry in coming years. Department heads were imported, but most crew members were Albertans who had also worked with Larry on *Wings of Chance*

The cameraman's union would only issue a work permit for me as an assistant, although I would eventually perform all functions behind the camera and obtain a Hollywood union card. Gaffer Frank Leonetti and camera operator Jack McCoskey were from Hollywood and had also worked on *Wings of Chance*. The director of photography (DOP) assigned by the union was a cantankerous old rascal named Paul Ivano. Tall and slim, his face sculpted into a pout, we would never see him smile. He first inquired about my astrological sign, and when I said Taurus, he said, "That's terrible, I'm Taurus, too, and that means we will either come to hate each other or become good friends." Like many in Hollywood, he had a personal astrologer with whom he consulted frequently.

Wings of Chance leading man, Jim Brown, at crashed aircraft, in a scene from the film. Two Fairchild 24 aircraft, identically painted, were used in the film—this "wrecked" one and another that was used for the flying scenes. Special permission was obtained to land float-equipped aircraft in Jasper National Park. Photo: Bill Marsden

Ivano had come to Hollywood from Russia in 1919, where he had been a photographer renowned for glamorizing older females. An aging actress had arranged for him to come to America as her cameraman. Paul told me that, in those days, the DOP was expected to sleep with the leading lady, the theory being he would be more dedicated to making her look beautiful if they were lovers.

Paul worked on the 1926 Charlie Chaplin-produced film *A Woman of the Sea*, the negative of which was destroyed by Chaplin in the 1930s. Paul was also involved in Erich von Stroheim's 1924 classic *Greed*, James Whale's *Frankenstein* in 1931, and even a 1951 Three Stooges film, *Gold Raiders*.

Working with Paul was not easy, but it was good experience. Like many old-time cameramen, he had a magic box of tricks that no one was allowed to look into. I became familiar with a few items, like unique gauzes for diffusion and hand-painted graduated filters for difficult situations, like dimming down a

A scene from 1963's *Naked Flame*, the second feature film made by Edmonton's Larry Matanski, filmed in Calgary and Canmore. The story was loosely based on activities of the Freedomite Doukhobor sect, who ritualistically stripped and then burned their houses as a form of protest. Photo: Bill Marsden

bright sky when shooting in a shaded area. One cute, quick trick of his was to stretch a piece of nylon stocking over the lens, burning a hole in the nylon with a cigarette tip to provide a vignette for close-ups.

Ivano and camera operator Jack McCoskey didn't get along, to put it mildly. Perhaps McCoskey was another Taurus. Even in each other's presence, they would speak only through me. McCoskey might say, "Tell that dumb Russian we need an f-stop." Ivano would reply to me with an even nastier reference to McCoskey. This was painful because I liked and respected them both.

On occasion, one or the other wouldn't show up for work. I became adept at performing the work of two men on the big BNC Mitchell camera, and I shot second-unit footage (that is, scenes without the principal performers) with an Arriflex, which was designed for one-person operation. Larry said the reason we weren't shooting the entire movie this way was because "you can't find an actor in

Larry Matanski (seated under the camera) directs Hollywood's Al Ruscio (standing) and Calgary's Mort Van Ostrand (seated) in an office sequence filmed in Canmore in 1963 for the Alberta feature movie, *Naked Flame*. Hollywood cameraman Jack McCoskey is behind the Mitchell camera. Photo: Bill Marsden

Hollywood who'll stand in front of any camera other than a Mitchell." It was a status symbol. (Today, a similar status symbol would be the Panavision camera.)

Naked Flame had script problems. The Hollywood writer who originally developed the screenplay was required on location for rewrites. He was a bearded hippie, who arrived in Calgary in November wearing open-toed sandals, torn jeans, and a weird looking T-shirt. He had no money. Canada Immigration ordered his return to Los Angeles.

Matanski sent him money for a topcoat, suit, shoes, and a shave and a haircut, as well as two hundred dollars in cash and another return airline ticket. This time, he arrived in Calgary looking neat and prosperous, expressing outrage that he had been refused entry into Canada on the previous trip. There was no record of that incident.

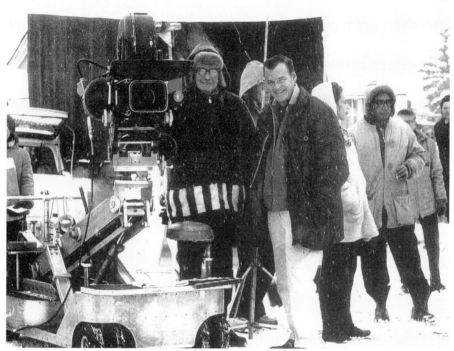

We enjoyed a relaxing moment while filming *Naked Flame* in Canmore, in November 1963. (Winter was not in the script!) Camera crew Jack McCoskey and Bill Marsden stand alongside the dolly-mounted Mitchell camera. Hollywood gaffer Frank Leonetti is to the right. Photo: Larry Matanski

His disclosure made it necessary for an Immigration officer to ask a series of questions that included, "Have you ever been hospitalized for a mental illness?"

"Yes," he answered, almost proudly, "I'm a writer!"

He was returned once again to Los Angeles.

Our leading man, Dennis O'Keefe, also wrote for the movies and took on the task of revising the script. The film credits read "Screenplay by Everett Dennis," O'Keefe's pseudonym.

When Matanski was first promoting the idea of *Naked Flame* in Hollywood, a distributor had said to him, "You mean in Canada you got crazy broads that burn down their houses and tear their clothes off? *Fantastic!*" The opening scene was to be a demonstration of this.

On a cold November night, we set up to burn several farm buildings

Supposedly a summer picnic scene in *Naked Flame* at Banff National Park's Two Jack Lake. We began filming outdoors in November. The Hollywood actors are half frozen (Dennis O'Keefe and Kasey Rogers). What the director hopes the audience will believe to be white sand is actually snow. Photo: Bill Marsden

on the outskirts of Calgary. Two fire engines with crews were present in case things got out of hand. The female extras for the sequence had been picked for their physical endowment. The young woman in the opening shot was a good example. Wearing only a flimsy dress and no undergarments, she was to walk past the camera carrying a torch, throw it into the barn, and then rip off the dress.

A grip had been instructed to use solvent to splash around in the barn, because it doesn't vaporize rapidly and is not as explosive as gasoline.

Unknown to us, the barn was indeed doused with *gasoline*!

I felt sorry for her as she passed my camera. I was wearing snow boots and a parka and was still freezing, but I knew she would soon be warmed up by the burning barn. That was an understatement. When the torch hit the building, there was a loud *whoof* and a huge burst of flame! For a split second,

THE REAL COLONEL SANDERS

When filming courtroom scenes for *Naked Flame* in Calgary, I left during the
lunch hour. On my return to the set, I saw a distinguished-looking older gentleman with white hair, moustache, and goatee. He wore a white suit and shirt
and a black-string bow tie. He was the size and shape of our much younger,
smooth-shaven art director, Bunny Evans. Our makeup lady said, "What do
you think of the job I did on Bunny?"

I walked over for a closer inspection, nose to nose. He gave me a
strange look, then stuck out his hand and said with a drawl, "My name is
Colonel Harlan Sanders." The chicken king was in Calgary to open a new
restaurant, and when he heard there was a movie shooting, he brought samples of his Kentucky Fried Chicken for the cast and crew (along with a
reporter and photographer). I was surprised to discover he was the *real*
Colonel Sanders, but nothing could surprise me about the accomplishments
of makeup artists.

I thought the girl was in the fire. I was closest to her, but the rule is to keep the
camera running no matter what. Two firemen ran over and carried the naked
woman away. They appeared to be enjoying their work. She was okay, but lost
her eyebrows and some pubic hair.

A few days later, we were in Banff National Park, filming scenes at Two
Jack Lake. It was again bitterly cold. Dennis O'Keefe asked if it was normal to
be filming outdoors this time of the year. I had to admit it was unusual. He
replied, "This guy Matanski is crazy! He just might make it."

An actress we suspected of casting-couch activity confirmed the fact
when she loudly inquired with those immortal words: "Who do I have to fuck
to get off this picture?"

Cold or not, production continued. A picnic scene was set up by the
lakeshore, with the foreground swept clear. I could still see snow in the near and
far background. Larry said, "Don't worry, everybody will think it's white sand."

The picnickers, O'Keefe and co-star Kasey Rogers, were turning somewhat blue from the cold. This we fixed with makeup, but their breath showed in
the freezing air. We put ice cubes in their mouths, dubbing in the sound later. There
were many similar problems, but by mid-December 1963, shooting was complete.

Deadline For Murder

THE NAKED FLAME
(Canadian — Melodrama — Color)

A Headliner Prods. release (in 1970) of a Corona production. Produced, directed by Lawrence Matanski. Screenplay, Al Everett Dennis; camera (Eastmancolor), Paul Ivano; editor, Monty Pearce; music, Bernie K. Lewis; sound, Dave Pomeroy; art direction, Meredith Evans; associate producer, Anthony W. Mokry. Reviewed on Video Cassette Recordings vidcassette, N.Y., Oct. 7, 1987. No MPAA Rating. Running time: 81 min.

Paul Ashley . . . . Dennis O'Keefe
Kathy Severin . . . . Linda Bennett
Elena . . . . Tracey Roberts
With: Kasey Rogers, Al Ruscio, Barton Heynan, Robert Howay.

New York, — "Deadline For Murder," currently in homevideo release, is a very odd bird, originally filmed in Calgary in 1963, released unrated (with nude footage apparently added) as "The Naked Flame" in 1970 after the death of its star Dennis O'Keefe and reviewed here for the record.

An interesting and most unusual storyline concerns the real-life sect of Duhobors, Canadians of Russian extraction who include nude rituals among their practices (thus giving the film its ultimate exploitation tag).

O'Keefe plays a lawyer sent by Dominion Mining to investigate problems at a local mine, but O'Keefe left the area three years earlier under a cloud after he testified against the brother of his girl friend, a Duhobor named Elena (Tracey Roberts, now a well-known acting teacher).

Melodramatic story has Elena's batushka (or godfather) Sorkin blackmailing a miner whose son is in love with Kathy (Linda Bennett). Latter was promised to Sorkin as his future wife by her parents when she was just a child. O'Keefe rekindles his affair with Elena, but several cases of arson and murder ensue before a hokey climax in which the surprise guilty party commits suicide in court.

Acting is fine, with the gimmick that whenever a fire or protest occurs, the Duhobor women ritualistically strip. None of the principal actresses appear nude on screen, making the intercut topless footage suspect and most likely added in the 1960s to spice up an unreleased feature.

It's definitely an odd posthumous addition to O'Keefe's filmography, as well as a respectable credit (with attractive location photography) for cinematographer Paul Ivano, whose work includes films by Von Stroheim and Von Sternberg. Director Lawrence Matashki also produced the 1961 Canadian thriller "Wings Of Chance." *Lor.*

Variety magazine reviewed the movie *Naked Flame*, filmed in Calgary and Canmore. Reprinted with permission.

Larry headed for Los Angeles to begin post-production, with a long stopover in Las Vegas, where "it was easier to find females for some of the nude scenes we couldn't shoot in the snow." Of course, there were also crap tables in Las Vegas. Too much time was spent on additional filming and post-production. More investment had to be found.

The film was actually well made, despite the hardships, but by the time it was released in 1964, nudity on the screen was somewhat more common and *Naked Flame* was not a success. It still appears once in a while in the wee small hours on television under the title *Deadline for Murder*, and it was reviewed by *Variety*.

Larry subsequently lost interest in moviemaking. He moved to Vancouver, then to Seattle, and worked in the aviation industry. He developed fibreglass aircraft floats and two new aircraft types. But financial success eluded him. He passed away after heart surgery in 1996. Larry Matanski will be remembered as one of Alberta's pioneer filmmakers.

By the late 1950s, more than a decade after my dreams of flying Spitfires had been dashed by the outbreak of peace, the Militia occupied much of my spare time. I was a junior officer in Calgary's South Alberta Light Horse. Our commanding officer was the appropriately named Lt. Col. Patrick Wilberforce Huntington Higgs. We were known as "'Iggs's 'Orses," originally a cavalry regiment, now equipped with Sherman tanks. It was said our motto had been "Love and Ride," but was now "Screw and Bolt."

One summer, I was a public relations officer at Camp Wainwright in east-central Alberta, where reserve regiments were attending, as was the Commanding Officer of Western Command, a Canadian legend of World War II named Major General Vokes. Honorary colonels were arriving by private rail car for a weekend "bash" at the General's Mess, as well as for a review of the Wainwright troops. Vokes was there to meet his guests, and I was to photograph the event.

First off the train was my boss Eric Harvie, who was with the Calgary Highlanders. General Vokes rushed over to greet him. Col. Harvie saw me and said, "Bill, have you met Chris?" I snapped to attention, shook hands with "Chris," and departed. Over the next ten days, I was invited to several functions in the General's Mess, finding myself the lowest-ranking officer there on all occasions. My "acquaintance" with Eric Harvie was obviously considered significant.

The mess was important to me then, in camp or back in Calgary.

THE ITALIAN CONNECTION

Frank Leonetti, the gaffer (lighting director) on *Wings of Chance* and *Naked Flame*, was the manager of a Hollywood studio after World War II. Since he knew the film industry and also spoke Italian, he was loaned to the United States government to help plan and develop the post-war economic rehabilitation of Italy. The project that employed him was known as the Marshall Plan.

Frank told me how he had deep-sea divers raise generators from a sunken battleship to provide power for a makeshift film studio. And obviously, an immediate filmmaking asset in Italy was the post-war look of bombed-out buildings in city and countryside. Thus, a new style of black and white movie was born. Today, we would call it "reality." Some great motion pictures resulted, such as the acclaimed *Bicycle Thief* and Roberto Rossellini's *Rome, Open City*, and they were soon in worldwide distribution.

Film was the first industry to bring foreign exchange into Italy after the war. It was simple to manufacture and to export. This proven example of instant economic development would become useful many years later in presentations to the Government of Alberta on behalf of Alberta's film industry.

Lunches there were frequent, and sometimes I wouldn't make it back to the office. Booze appeared to have become a best friend of mine. A closer friend was Lou Wener, a self-made millionaire, who told me I was drinking too much. He said I should quit, go into business for myself, and become rich. (I eventually managed to accomplish two out of the three.)

I left Glenbow in 1963. Sally and I formed a film production company called William Marsden and Associates Film Productions Ltd. We were soon busy making industrial films for clients like the UFA Co-op and Alberta Government Telephones (AGT, which is now part of Telus).

We bought a house in the Elbow Park neighbourhood of Calgary. It had been built in 1912, and we began to rewire, replumb, and remodel our home, a project that took ten years to complete. It was a wonderful place to raise our family, which now consisted of three children, with another daughter, Tracy Leah, having arrived.

The house gave me access to a well-equipped workshop. More than twenty years after my banana-crate plane crashed during its test flight, I began to build a real airplane, inspired by my friend Gordon Fryer, who had completed and was flying a "homebuilt" of his own. I purchased plans for a two-place, low-wing monoplane of French design, a Jodel D-11. The wood-and-fabric construction was practical in the age of plastic resin glue and Dacron fabric. It would become a four-year, spare-time activity, but I would someday be able to fly my own plane.

Dreamland

Working alongside Les Kimber was my big bonus on *Naked Flame*. Les had been hired as property master, but did almost everything—he even had a speaking part in the film. We became close friends and worked together for decades.

Big, tough, cigar-chomping Les had an impressive track record in the theatre, as a manager and stagehand and in other jobs, having just returned from a North American tour of *My Fair Lady*. *Naked Flame* was his first film and, after it wrapped, he returned to managing Calgary's Mac 14 Theatre, which was on 2 Street SW and was once known as the Isis movie theatre. There was always work for Les on Alberta-made television commercials and industrial films, and these credits helped him acquire membership in the Directors Guild.

Dreamland was an Alberta tourist-promotion film we made together in 1965. In the film, Les and Molly Whalen played a husband and wife who, in their dreams, appear to tour the world. The twist at the end was that we learn all the wonderful sights and adventures in their dreams really took place in Alberta.

Another "star" of the film was a new candy apple red Pontiac convertible, provided by General Motors, gratis. The Marsden house and Marsden children were also recruited for the production—it was a tight budget! The film was shot in the month of June, including a skiing sequence. We hiked up a mountain to a glacier in Banff—me with camera equipment, Les dressed for winter and carrying skis. I stayed at rock level; Les climbed up the glacier and skied down, with a classic snow-spraying stop! Until he suggested this sequence, I hadn't even known he skied.

Les became renowned as a production manager on big-budget pictures like *Superman*. His grizzly bear image was such that an assistant director passed out cold when Les yelled at him. He once punched out an obnoxious producer —his *employer*—because the man had mistreated a secretary.

My family was privileged to know the gentle side of Les. While attending a Stampede party in our Calgary neighbourhood one time, we had been overserved with food and booze. Les found a shady spot alongside the front porch and was having a snooze, flat on his back, cowboy hat tipped over his face. Our five year old, Tracy, wearing cowboy boots, jumped from the porch right onto his stomach. It was an explosive awakening that almost shook shingles on the house. But the legendary tough guy quietly said, "Don't do that, Tracy!"

By the mid-1960s, my homebuilt Jodel aircraft was taking shape in my workshop. I bought an engine from a crashed aircraft, and Stan Green, a friend who headed the Aero department at the Southern Alberta Institute of Technology, overhauled it as a class project. An aircraft welder made up an engine mount and the landing gear. I would do the fabric covering and install the engine and instruments.

I had started the aircraft project in my basement workshop after I discovered some Sitka spruce planks in a Calgary lumberyard. The spruce was aircraft grade—a rare find, so I bought it all. Birch aircraft plywood and plastic resin glue were purchased from an aviation supplier.

An airplane is thousands of small pieces, flying in formation. Construction was time-consuming, but relatively easy, as the blueprints I had were excellent and I have always enjoyed woodworking. I had a large garage built on our property, and the aircraft was assembled there, piece by piece, from the components made in my workshop over a four-year period.

I moved the aircraft fuselage and wing out into the yard one day to take photographs, which caused a stir in the neighbourhood, but by the time the press showed up it was back in the garage. Everything was approved by a Ministry of Transport inspector before the aircraft was finally covered with fabric and painted.

I hired a truck and trailer to haul everything to a Calgary Flying Club hangar, where I installed the engine and instruments. It wouldn't be long before my handiwork took flight!

In 1965, William Marsden and Associates was producing a film for AGT and was forced to turn down a larger production with a tight deadline; business was just getting too good. Jack Gettles of KVOS-TV in Bellingham, Washington (just south of Vancouver), came along at this point, trying to hustle business for a film company that had been formed. Discovering we were well established in Alberta, the new company, Canawest, offered to buy out our operation.

Sally and I toured the Canawest Studio in Vancouver and were quite impressed, especially with a young staff director named Ken Jubenvill. An agreement was reached. It would lease our company and provide a retainer and commission on business in Alberta, Saskatchewan, and Manitoba. Canawest helped us complete a production that was underway for Rogers Sugar, providing some great animation for us. This became an important part of our business, with forty-five people eventually employed in the Vancouver animation department, which subcontracted animation work for Hanna-Barbera TV productions, such as *The Abbott and Costello Show* and *The Beatles*, as well as for assorted TV commercials for the likes of Saskatchewan Government Telephones, Lowney's, Canada Post, and Alberta Treasury Branches.

I was a cameraman who had been forced to learn other aspects of filmmaking in order to survive in a limited market. Now, as a producer, I could draw on experts in every film craft because we had them on staff. The market was larger and we had resources to take on any project.

James Lovick Advertising was delighted with the film we made for Rogers and commissioned one for their client, Wardair. Lovick, vice-president Dougald Lamb, and I flew to Europe to scout the film. A Canadian in Amsterdam in the early 1960s was treated royally, since our army had liberated Holland only twenty years before. English was spoken everywhere. There was much to see and do in the most wide open city in Europe.

Meanwhile, England of the 1960s was very different from the England of today. A hamburger purchased on the street was actually made with ground ham. The currency, in pounds, shillings, and pence, in no way related to our decimal system, providing street vendors endless opportunities to shortchange

West to the Mountains, a 1966 documentary made for the Alberta government, shows a trainload of settlers arriving in Alberta, filmed at Calgary's Heritage Park train station. About fifty friends and neighbors in period costumes are in this scene and were forced to become members of the actors union because of an agreement just signed between SAG, the American actors union, and Canada's ACTRA. Photo: Bill Marsden

us. Most of the newer buildings we saw were not in districts under development, but scattered in areas where bombs had destroyed existing structures two decades before. In a perverse way, Berlin was responsible for urban renewal in London.

A big shock for me was my first encounter with rough English toilet paper. It made me realize that Hitler *was* mad. Anyone believing he could conquer people who subjected themselves to this torture had to be crazy!

Wardair required broader European coverage than the budget would allow, so stock footage was bought at Elstree Studios near London. Ken Jubenvill, Rod Parkhurst, and I filmed in England and then filmed in-flight activities, showing Wardair comfort and service. It was followed by a Wardair Hawaii production.

Balladeer Burl Ives, the star of *West to the Mountains*, sings a verse of the ballad written specially for the film by Calgarian Wally Grieve. Ives is seated on a wooden oil derrick in Calgary's Heritage Park. Photo: Bill Marsden

In 1966, Gettles was making more acquisitions in order to grow Canawest. He bought Roozeboom Productions in Vancouver and then Master Films in Calgary, which was the company Larry Matanski had created. Bob Willis, who as head of Master Films had been a competitor but a friend, was now my partner. We both became vice-presidents of a new Alberta company, which was called Canawest Master Films Ltd. Bob had been hired by Larry as an animator and artist in the earliest days of Master Films and had developed into a filmmaker, one of the best.

We had a staff of six, plus freelancers, and brought director Ron Brown over from our Vancouver studio. With sixteen productions underway in 1966, we were the biggest film company operating between Toronto and Vancouver.

Relaxing with Burl Ives at Moraine Lake in Banff National Park during the filming of *West to the Mountains*. I made a number of colour photographs of him seated on the big rock (to his right) for the cover of a record album to be called *Joy Unspeakable*; Burl said, "this place certainly is." Photo: Les Kimber

While developing the idea for a film to help celebrate Canada's 1967 Centennial, I made a proposal in 1966 to Russ Patrick, Alberta's minister of Economic Development. It called for the story of Alberta to be told by a balladeer.

Russ seemed skeptical at first, until I informed him that we would be able to get the well-known actor/singer Burl Ives to play the balladeer. That sold him on the idea.

The film, entitled *West to the Mountains,* was directed by Ken Jubenvill and written by Richard Tomkies. The title came from Tomkies's research; an early settler, when leaving Ontario, was told, "Go west as far as you can, but don't cross the mountains." The title ballad was written by Calgarian Wally Grieve.

Our budget was six figures—the most ever spent on an Alberta film to that date. Even so, it was not really adequate for a thirty-five-millimetre film with a major Hollywood star, but it gave us an opportunity to prove our ability, with a wide-screen production and the potential of international theatrical distribution.

The company had a one-week contract with Burl Ives. Shortly after his arrival in Calgary, it began to rain. The Alberta slogan was "Sunny Alberta," which we were obliged to show on the screen. We couldn't film a frame until Mother Nature co-operated.

After three days of heavy rain, I was pacing the floor in the apartment suite we had provided Burl. He said, "Sit down, you're wearing out my carpet. What's eating you?" I reminded him our contract was for seven days of his time, and we hadn't yet shot any film.

He said, "That agreement is between your lawyer and mine. They aren't here. I'm here, and for as long as you need me. Now sit down and let me read to you out of the Good Book." That was just the type of man he was.

Many actors have been renowned for Bible readings, but none could equal Burl Ives. Every Sunday, Burl would attend the House of God that happened to be closest to where he was staying. Denomination didn't matter. And every year he recorded an album of hymns for donation to a church.

Eventually, the rain let up and we got to work.

The opening scenes of *West to the Mountains* were of a covered wagon, drawn by a team of horses, carrying an Eastern Canadian family to Alberta. They pull into a replica 1905 Alberta town, which was in reality a display in Calgary's Heritage Park. The park's recreated village provided us with many of the sets for our production. We filmed in the General Store, North West Mounted Police office and jail, hotel, barber shop, and Hudson's Bay Fort, and on the deck of the wooden oil derrick where Burl sang a verse of the movie's ballad.

We also staged the arrival of a trainload of settlers and had about fifty extras on the station platform in period costumes. Most of them were friends

LES KIMBER, THE PRODUCTION MANAGER

Les Kimber, as production manager, was the centre of every project he worked on. The production manager is the producer's right arm. I wish I had all the money that Les saved me on productions. I also wish I had the money I lost to him over the years in crazy bets, poker games, and dice.

The production manager prepares the budget and is in charge of all expenditures. He has to know the cost of everything and everyone. He is an encyclopedia of knowledge about unions and overtime and where to get the cheapest and best of everything. I saw Les operate as a tough manager, a negotiator, and a psychologist.

Les was awakened in his room at two o'clock one morning in 1980 when a prominent Hollywood star in Les's latest picture, well known for his drinking, was making a scene in the Banff Springs Hotel lobby, demanding they open the bar. Les showed up in slippers and bathrobe with a bottle of whisky. He said, "The man wants a drink, give him a drink!" Within fifteen minutes, the actor had passed out and Kimber helped carry him to his room.

Les once told me of a young director calling for three hundred extras in a scene being filmed in Lethbridge. I asked him where you could get that many daytime extras in a small city. He said, "I gave him eighty, and he [the director] said, wow, three hundred is a lot of extras, isn't it!"

Director Robert Altman frequently went over budget on pictures. When he came to Alberta to film *Buffalo Bill and the Indians* in the early 1970s, Les kept tight control, even refusing to house actors in an expensive hotel partly owned by Dino DeLaurentis, the executive producer of the picture. Although initially a bit perturbed, DeLaurentis was impressed with Kimber's work ethic and never made another picture in Canada without offering the production-manager position to Kimber. To my knowledge, the only DeLaurentis film Les actually accepted was *Orca*, which was shot in Newfoundland in the mid-1970s. Les didn't like to work outside of Alberta.

Les Kimber was a legendary production manager and line producer, longtime chairman of the District Council of the Directors Guild of Canada, and a tireless devotee to the Alberta film industry. AMPIA presented him with the Billington Award in 1993, the year this picture was taken. Les passed away in 1998. The Directors Guild of Canada has established an annual scholarship in his name. Photo: courtesy Jan Kimber

and neighbours. But this is where, as they say, it "hit the fan."

Production manager Les Kimber informed me that the national president of ACTRA (Association of Canadian Television and Radio Actors) was on the set. ACTRA and SAG (the American Screen Actors Guild) had just signed an agreement. Unless our extras and all future performers were members of ACTRA, Burl Ives could not appear in the movie.

Burl Ives was the cornerstone of the production; without him, there would be little attraction for international audiences. Our production team can take credit for helping ACTRA get established filmwise in Calgary; they gained many new members that day—with us paying, of course.

The unions were having a field day, something we hadn't expected or included in the budget. Our director of photography, Osmond Borradaile, was an International Alliance of Theatrical and Stage Employees (IATSE) cameraman, as was camera operator Vic Spooner. The union was insisting we hire an assistant cameraman. I presented my card from the IATSE Hollywood camera local and said, "That's me, producer and assistant cameraman." We were also forced to employ two grips we didn't need. Les had them constantly carrying around some heavy flats we didn't need either. I believe that *West to the Mountains* was Alberta's first fully unionized documentary film.

Burl Ives had received an Oscar in 1958 as Best Supporting Actor for his role in *The Big Country*, co-starring Gregory Peck and Charlton Heston. He wouldn't look at our "rushes" (raw-film footage) as they came back from the lab. He told me he had never seen himself on the screen; he believed it would affect his method of acting if he did.

We arranged for the National Film Board in Montreal to process our film. As a result, the rest of us were able to view the rushes quite soon after filming. There were no customs problems as were sometimes encountered when relying on American processing facilities.

Burl's next record album was to be titled *Joy Unspeakable*. During his stint with us, he asked for suggestions for a cover photograph. At first light one morning, he sat on the big rock overlooking Moraine Lake and the Valley of the Ten Peaks in Banff National Park and said in awe, "This *is* 'joy unspeakable.'" He began to play his guitar and sing that hymn, an experience I'll never forget in that beautiful setting and solitude. I shot several four-by-five colour transparencies and donated them to his cause. Every Alberta MLA received a copy of that album. My family has his album titled *My Gal Sal*, which is inscribed: "To Bill's Gal Sal with love, from Burl."

West to the Mountains was a huge success. The NFB distributed a sixteen-millimetre version worldwide in six languages; they paid the cost of translations and for six hundred prints, which was profitable for us. *West to the Mountains* played in theatres and on television around the world. Burl, Ken Jubenvill, and I discussed doing another film together one day, a pet idea of Burl's that would be called *All the World's Religions as I See Them*. No one could have handled that subject better than Burl, but we could never find a way to finance the project. Burl continued to act well into the 1980s, appearing in such productions as the classic miniseries *Roots*. He passed away in 1995.

Jodel D-11 homebuilt aircraft constructed in my home workshop over four years and test flown in 1967. I flew this plane for eight years before selling it to my brother because I had since built and started flying a special biplane. Photo: Bill Marsden

My Jodel aircraft was completed a few months later in 1967 and test flown at Calgary International Airport on 30 July by professional pilot and aero engineer Gordon Fryer. Before the test flight, I spent several days running up the engine and taxiing the aircraft around the airport, but the first flight of any aircraft should be made by a qualified test pilot, so I wouldn't do it myself. The owner/builder is too close to the project to be impartial in assessment.

An experienced test pilot will have a well-proven routine. After carefully checking normal flight conditions, he performs stalls and spins, recording entry speeds and successful recovery procedures.

Gord did not wear a parachute, which is unusual for the first flight of any aircraft, let alone a "homebuilt." I like to think he was demonstrating confidence in my workmanship. It may also relate to him being told I would have a rifle, and if he baled out, he would be dead before reaching the ground, anyhow.

After a two-hour test flight, a few minor corrections were made to my aircraft before Gord coached me through the same test manoeuvres and then turned me loose as pilot in command.

I first flew my Jodel D-11on 1 August 1967. It was a thrill I'll never forget. I have believed ever since that home-building something you place your very life in is the ultimate test of faith in your own ability.

The Jodel was still flying thirty-seven years later.

Hoping to repeat the success of *West to the Mountains* by spotlighting another province, after several months of trying, in early 1967 I was finally able to get a meeting with Premier Ross Thatcher of Saskatchewan and I made a sale. We would shoot a thirty-five-millimetre film, wide screen, with prearranged theatrical distribution in Saskatchewan. I had pointed out to Premier Thatcher that his appearance on the big screen should help him win the coming election, which no doubt helped swing his decision in my favour.

Bob Willis directed the film, which was titled *Saskatchewan, the New Harvest*. I shot most of the film myself, but on occasion used Bill Roozeboom or Phil Pike from Vancouver.

We were all on hand to film the official opening of the Gardiner Dam on the South Saskatchewan River on 21 July 1967. The dam was named after an earlier premier of Saskatchewan. Tommy Douglas, another former premier, was present, as was former prime minister John G. Diefenbaker, after whom the lake the dam created would be named. Our client, Premier Thatcher, was there, as was the current prime minister, Lester B. Pearson.

The lengthy speeches heard that day might lead you to believe that each of these politicians had single-handedly built the dam. "Dief," who obviously believed the dam should have been named after him, said, "No Gardiner Dam can hold back the might of a Diefenbaker Lake!"

We moved on to film events, industries, and scenery across Saskatchewan, and when the movie was finally released in 1968, we arranged for it to play in every theatre in the province. Ross Thatcher was resoundingly re-elected.

Seeking wider distribution and print sales for *Saskatchewan, the New Harvest*, I later flew to Regina and was greeted warmly by the premier. I explained that National Film Board distribution was available and would mean worldwide coverage at no cost—if we removed a short speech that Thatcher

This biplane, which I also built, was test flown in 1972. It is a ¾ scale replica of the RAF Hawker Fury fighter aircraft of the 1930s. I painted it with the markings of the famous RAF 43 Squadron, although the shark's teeth are not authentic. It is fully aerobatic and is now based in Ontario, after providing me with years of enjoyment and also some tense moments. Photo: Bill Marsden

had done for the film; the NFB considered this to be too political. Thatcher was outraged, and I thought he was going to have me thrown out of his office.

"They can't take me out of my film, no way, forget the damned free distribution!" he said. That was that! Likely, in his view, the film had already proved its value to Saskatchewan by helping his party retain power.

Back in Calgary, I was flying my Jodel at every opportunity and now had my own hangar at the Airdrie Airport. I flew this plane all over Alberta and won a few trophies at air shows.

My passion for aircraft building still strong, I began to build a second aircraft in 1968. This time the project would be an open-cockpit biplane, a three-quarter-scale replica of the RAF Hawker Fury fighter of 1930.

It would have just over a seven-metre wingspan, carry markings of the famous RAF 43 Squadron, and take another four years to complete.

In 1968, Bob Willis and I teamed up for a project in the Yukon. He would direct, and I would be cameraman. The film, for Anvil Mines, was subcontracted to us by a Hollywood producer I will call LeRoy. The script had been written in Hollywood.

Anvil had a significant lead/zinc deposit, three hundred kilometres northeast of Whitehorse. An open-pit mine was to be developed, then a mill to process the ore. An entire town for twelve hundred people, which was to be named Faro, would be built to support the project.

It was a huge project in more ways than one. We would be shooting over a two-year period. When we began, all that existed on the site of Faro was a good airstrip, in foothills country, with DC-3s hauling in supplies and workers. A highway was built to Whitehorse and portable housing was trucked in to become a large camp for a rapidly growing workforce.

When the mill became operational, huge trucks began hauling ore to Whitehorse to load onto the White Pass and Yukon Railroad. Every two or three months we returned there for progress filming, driving from Calgary to Edmonton with a load of equipment, then flying in on a CP Air DC-7.

LeRoy flew from Hollywood to meet us in Whitehorse several times, on one occasion informing us we couldn't proceed to camp until a Tyler mount arrived from Hollywood. This was a special camera rig used for helicopter filming, with a gyroscopic action that prevented shaking. Rarely seen in Canada, I had never actually used one.

Prior discussion of the idea with me would have been helpful; it was a busy time of year, and helicopters were not readily available. While waiting for one to be obtained, I was able to assemble the mount from instructions, but had serious concerns. A door would have to be removed from the helicopter in order to install the contraption. I would be sitting on the mount, most of me outside the aircraft, with feet resting on the skids. The mount would be secured with web straps. It didn't sound like fun.

After a week, a chopper was finally located. I was at the airstrip with the assembled Tyler mount when it landed. The pilot walked over and said, "I'll be damned, that's the first Tyler mount I've seen in years, and way to hell up here!" It turned out he had once been the pilot for a NFB production called *Helicopter Canada*. I would soon learn all there was to know about Tyler mounts, from one of the most qualified people in Canada.

LeRoy was an interesting travel companion. Once, while leaving

Whitehorse together on a crowded flight that would last several hours, we were among the first to board. He took a window seat, and I sat next to him. He said, "Take the aisle seat." I replied that someone would then sit between us. He said, "No they won't, trust me." He removed an air sickness bag from the seat pouch, opened it up, placing it on the seat between us. Passengers would look and then move on up the aisle. One lady seemed unconvinced, so LeRoy leaned over the bag and made gagging sounds. The seat remained vacant all the way to our final destination.

The town of Faro was completed by May of 1969. The mill was finished and machinery was being installed. Houses, schools, and shops were set for a September inaugural ceremony. In June, a lightning strike caused a forest fire that destroyed the young town. At great expense, it was completely rebuilt in time for the scheduled opening. We ended up shooting the building of the town of Faro twice!

Filming interiors, living quarters, kitchen, and dining hall required lighting equipment and crew flown in from Vancouver. The mill had a huge interior, already well lit with mercury vapour lamps. We ran tests with filters and obtained good colour correction, which enabled us to film these important sequences with available light. Every evening, we had dinner in the camp dining hall with miners, carpenters, and electricians, all in their work clothes. LeRoy, very conscious of his status, always wore a jacket and tie to dinner with the common herd and claimed a corner table to be ours exclusively. The mill was operational, tests were being conducted, and there were many new people in camp. The dining room was crowded when a large man wearing grimy coveralls and carrying a food tray plunked himself down on the vacant chair at our table. LeRoy was first outraged, then patronizingly sweet.

LeRoy: "Where are you from?"
Stranger: "Well, I'm from New York, but just moved to Los Angeles."
LeRoy: "I used to live in New York, where did you live in New York?"
Stranger: "I lived at (xxx) Park Avenue."
LeRoy: "No, not where you worked, where did you live?"
Stranger: "Second floor, (xxx) Park Avenue."
LeRoy: (Incredulously) "You had an apartment on the second floor at that address?"
Stranger: "No, we had the second floor."

LeRoy: (choked up) "I live in Pacific Palisades in Los Angeles. Where
    do you live?"
Stranger: "I don't know. I've been away. My wife bought the house. All
    I know is that our next door neighbour is Gregory Peck."
LeRoy was almost in shock.

We learned that the stranger was a renowned metallurgist brought in to
analyze the performance of the mill. (Many years later, I actually met Gregory
Peck and told him the story. He was amused, though I had long since forgot-
ten the stranger's name. Peck said, "That would be Dr. Richard Kennedy,
a long-time neighbour and friend. He was very wealthy, as was his wife. He
passed away two years ago and left me his pre-Columbian art collection.")

The White Pass and Yukon Railroad would carry Anvil-mined ore from
Whitehorse to Skagway, Alaska, to be loaded onto ships. Destination: Japan. This
was the last operating narrow-gauge railroad in North America, which offered
a spectacular train ride through rugged mountains. There were many tunnels,
frail-looking bridges, and sections of track that seemed to just hang on the
mountainside. From the large trestle over Dead Horse Gulch, part of the original "Trail of '98" could be seen—a narrow path dug deep by the heavy boots
of the thousands who hiked the trail during the 1898 Gold Rush.

Skagway is a lovely old town on the Pacific Ocean, with a year-round
harbour and an airstrip covered with private aircraft. At the time I first visited,
boats or planes were the only transportation in or out of Skagway, other than
the railroad. (Today, there is a highway providing a road link.)

This was an American town, but the biggest employer, the railroad, was
a Canadian company headquartered in Whitehorse. It was refreshing to hear
Americans gripe about being "ripped off by those damned Canadians." For the
first time in my life, and likely the last, the Canadian dollar was worth more
than the American dollar—$1.10, in fact! The hotel, restaurants, and shops in
Skagway would not give the exchange rate—it was "par only." When I took a
few hundred Canadian dollars to the local bank to obtain the legal exchange, I
was told, "Par only, take it or leave it!"

On our next trip to Whitehorse, there was an ore train ready to leave for
Skagway to meet a ship coming from Japan. LeRoy wanted aerial shots of the
ship as it arrived in port. He arranged for a helicopter carrying a Tyler mount

to take us to Skagway on 6 December 1969. It would be very cold sitting on the mount outside the helicopter in Alaska in December, and I wasn't looking forward to the experience.

We suggested the location of the ship should be confirmed through the port authority; it might not be on schedule. LeRoy said, "It will arrive in Skagway on December 7 at noon." Asked how he could be sure, he said, "The script says so." The Whitehorse helicopter company didn't believe the script. They required a guarantee of four hours per day, every day we were away, at $750 per hour.

It was not a good day for flying when we left Whitehorse, but we had an appointment with a ship, as LeRoy put it. He and pilot Cliff Armstrong occupied the front seat of the Bell Jet Ranger, with Bob Willis and me in the back. Within half an hour, we were in a heavy snowstorm and soon flying "on the deck," less than a metre above the railroad tracks. We moved ahead very slowly, gazing intently out of the plastic bubble that separated us from the elements. The rails would disappear in a swirl of snow to reappear to our left or right—never where expected. We were like bugs inside a jar submerged in a vat of milk.

The tracks could not be followed for long; we were in the mountains, and there were tunnels ahead. Cliff decided to land. He set down on the tracks, skids perpendicular to the rails—the only way he could land—in the only possible place. Leaving us in the machine, blades revolving, he disappeared into the whiteout, his tracks filling in with falling snow. He was back in ten minutes to say there was a place just ahead where we could set down properly.

We lifted off immediately, landing in a large clearing alongside the tracks, and were still sitting in the helicopter when a White Pass freight train came through! We were spotted by the engineer, who stopped, then backed up the train to talk with us. He suggested we leave the helicopter to ride with him into Skagway. He would drop us off the next day on his return to Whitehorse. With thanks, Cliff said we'd wait for the weather to break.

An hour later, a hole appeared in the cloud cover. We were soon up into a clear blue sky for a lovely flight into Skagway. The next morning, we met the train crew at breakfast in the hotel. The engineer asked if we had gone over or under the new power lines crossing the valley. To this day, we don't know the answer to that one!

For four days, we waited in Skagway for the ship to arrive. It was an enjoyable town and there were worse places to kill a few days. Cliff and I went flying several times, since it was being paid for anyway. During one of these flights, I salvaged an engine from a crashed helicopter that I hoped to use in my biplane. Bob caught up on some reading, while our producer spent his time cursing the scriptwriter.

The ship finally arrived on 10 December at 2:00 AM in pitch-black darkness, so we weren't able to actually film the arrival or the loading. That afternoon, we shot the departure of the loaded ship and left Skagway at dusk for the flight to Whitehorse. There was heavy cloud cover, but we were soon on top where visibility was unlimited. The higher mountain peaks poked up through the rolling cloud blanket, illuminated by a large full moon, so bright it cast shadows. It was among the most beautiful sights I've seen in some fifty years of flying.

Our only handicap was a headwind, and fuel supply became a concern. Cliff contacted Whitehorse, requesting that his engineer meet us at the Carcross Highway junction with a barrel of fuel.

Descending to follow the highway for many kilometres, we were soon hovering over the junction. It was a very cold night and there was no traffic on the icy road, so it seemed logical that the approaching headlights we spotted would have to be the engineer with our fuel. Cliff landed in the middle of the highway. We sat there, rotors creating a small blizzard, navigation lights and a bright red flasher highlighting our presence. The approaching vehicle loomed larger and was not reducing speed. We were going to be hit head on!

LeRoy, sitting up front, pushed open his door and dived into the snow-filled ditch. That very instant, a dilapidated old car veered off into the same ditch, just missing LeRoy. We scrambled out of the helicopter. The driver of the car, who was intoxicated, staggered onto the road. Pointing to Cliff, he said, "Wot chew doin' down here?" then raised his arm skyward, "Yer s'posed to be up 'dere!"

We helped get his car out of the ditch and got him on his way. Cliff lifted off. There was another vehicle approaching, which he looked over carefully before landing on the highway again. We were soon refuelled and away, arriving in Whitehorse about 10:00 PM. As it happened, this was our last trip for this show.

Post-production work was done in Hollywood without our participation. The completed film, released in 1970, was called *New World in the Yukon* and was narrated by Canadian actor Lorne Greene, who was starring in *Bonanza* at the time. It received wide distribution, likely resulting in an increase in value for Anvil shares.

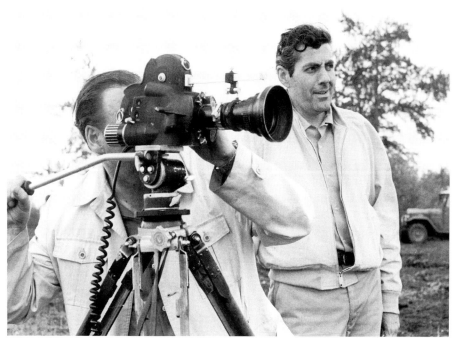

Bob Willis and I (behind camera) were near Whitehorse, in 1969, filming for *New World in the Yukon*, an industrial film for Anvil Mines, at Faro, YT. It was narrated by Lorne Green, star of *Bonanza*. Photo: Cliff Armstrong

Alberta continued to draw in big-ticket Hollywood productions. In 1969, *Little Big Man*, starring Dustin Hoffman and Faye Dunaway, came to Alberta. The show was filmed on the Stoney Indian Reserve at Morley, west of Calgary, with many of the tribe as performers. Chief Dan George, a great Canadian, played a major role in the movie and became somewhat of a celebrity down south, receiving an Academy Award nomination for best supporting actor.

Little Big Man was extremely important to the Alberta film industry because Les Kimber was employed as unit manager, a big position for him on a production this large. Also, a man named John Scott provided horses for the show and was hired as wrangler. This was Scott's first picture. Scott, along with Kimber, would become prominent in the Canadian film industry, but despite wide recognition and offers, both remained in Alberta. More about John Scott later.

I am posing, in 1969, with a crashed helicopter near the US–Canada border on the White Pass and Yukon railway. This was an American helicopter that crashed in Canada. After contacting the owner in Haines, Alaska, I was able to import the wreck into Canada and salvage the engine for an aircraft I was building. Photo: Bob Willis

Chuck Ross and I visited the impressive set at Morley one day. "Dusty" Hoffman was an interesting young man to meet, and we were dazzled by his performance with a "six-shooter," which seemed out of character. In only a few years, this young man had gone from shilling Volkswagens in TV commercials to film stardom with his roles in *The Graduate* and *Midnight Cowboy*, and his acting career was just starting. In this film, he would be required to play both a young man fighting with General Custer and a man of more than a hundred years old. The makeup artist was Hollywood's famous Dick Smith, who used several pounds of latex rubber to create a very ancient face—though one still recognizable as Dustin Hoffman.

Director Arthur Penn informed Chuck that he really needed snow. We were in the mountains, and there was a chill in the air, so Chuck said, "You will have snow tomorrow." It did snow overnight, and the producer told everyone that Chuck Ross "had great connections upstairs." Unfortunately, it was only a

Bob Willis and I are unloading camera equipment at the Faro, YT, airstrip, where we were filming *New World in the Yukon*. We had flown in from Whitehorse in this DeHavilland Otter aircraft. Photo: our pilot

brief miracle. Within two days, the snow was gone, and Chuck's "upstairs connection" didn't work a second time.

Inexperienced with chinooks as he was, the smart thing for Penn to do would have been to shoot the wide scenes with the snow, but the director had shot only close-ups, so the crew and some cast members had to return to Morley the next January to film more snow scenes, including a cavalry charge. It was very cold, and to ensure continued attendance of the local Indian cast members, a hot breakfast was served on the set each morning for them and their families. During the cavalry charge, a Colt revolver was lost in the snow. All weapons brought in from the United States had to be returned, as the RCMP would be checking every serial number, so Les Kimber bought all the garden tools he could find in nearby hardware stores and had the Morley flats hand-raked until the gun was found.

Alberta Gets a Prime Cut of the Movie Industry

In 1971, Peter Lougheed's Progressive Conservatives replaced the Social Credit provincial government that had been in power since I was a child. Ron Brown had left Canawest-Master, moved to Edmonton, and formed Century Two Motion Pictures with Tommy Banks. He was doing well.

As much as we loved Calgary, Sally and I had received a good offer for our house. It seemed logical we should move to Edmonton and build up contacts in the new government. Both Jack Gettles and KVOS-TV president David Mintz agreed. In August 1971, we said goodbye to Calgary and relocated to Edmonton.

Television commercials were an important part of our business, as were corporate films. Edmonton offered more opportunities in both categories, as well as government work. With Bob Willis and staff still in Calgary, I would be operating more as a salesman.

Canawest-Master Films had several projects underway in Alberta, and we were still finding work in Saskatchewan and Manitoba, although local TV stations were setting up film production companies of their own, using the "we employ people and pay taxes here" argument as a very effective sales tool to government and others. Volume was down in Vancouver, and this large operation needed a constant stream of work to keep it going.

We were losing employees; the best weren't waiting to be laid off. Richard Tomkies departed to become a freelance writer, and Ken Jubenvill quit and partnered up with cameraman Maurice Embra to form J&E Productions in Vancouver. Richard would write their scripts.

In 1971, the movie *Prime Cut* came to Alberta to shoot. This tale was an orgy of drug trafficking, prostitution, extortion, loan sharking, and shootouts, with rival gangsters being ground up into sausage meat. (I am not making that up!)

The film starred movie tough guy Lee Marvin, who was noted for his boozing and was somewhat hung over when Chuck Ross visited the set with his teenage son Jim, who was a Marvin admirer. To everyone's surprise, Marvin was most gracious in conversation with the youth. The nature of this film may have been the inspiration for young Jim Ross to later make his career with the RCMP.

Prime Cut was a costly movie. Les Kimber found a nice farm near Rockyford for the main set. A white rail fence was constructed on both sides of the long driveway, then about a kilometre of frontage as well. A new wing was built onto the house for a massive kitchen, with two large walk-in freezers. A swimming pool with cabana was added. The fortunate owner gained several hundred thousand dollars of home improvements, as well as a special sunflower crop that was planted for the film and left for him to harvest.

In 1972, shortly after Ken and Richard quit and I moved to Edmonton, I left Canawest-Master to form a new Alberta company, JEM Film Productions. I continued to maintain working ties with Ken and Richard, and we soon had a film underway for Alberta Forestry, which Ken and Maurice Embra began shooting in Grande Prairie.

Ken wanted to film a lightning strike causing a forest fire. Maurice achieved the effect by electronically exploding black powder, discovering in the

ALBERTA ON THE NORTHSIDE

One job of a filmmaker is to open the eyes of viewers to places and ideas they might never have considered before. In 1971, Canawest-Master Films made *Alberta on the Northside*. Filmed mostly north of Edmonton, it portrayed what had been considered the least glamorous part of the province. Rod Parkhurst and Ron Orieux, with superb cinematography, revealed it to be a land of beauty. Richard Tomkies's script stressed the area's industrial importance and potential. An original music score written and performed by the Brothers Bogart made it an audio treat as well.

"This film reflects the earthy pioneer camaraderie you find up there, not the desolation so many people think exists," said Bill Bogart. He ensured that his music accented that quality, and Ken Jubenvill's direction and editing artfully blended all ingredients.

Alberta on the Northside received worldwide distribution. It was awarded the Chairman's Special Gold Camera award at the U.S. Industrial Film Festival in 1972, judged to be the best among six hundred competing films from fifteen countries. This was one of many awards that this team received over the years, including three other Gold Cameras. I was privileged to work with Richard and Ken for fifteen years.

process that a condom was the best container for hanging gunpowder in trees. Preparing for the next day's shoot, he loaded up a dozen condoms, dropping the empty packages in his motel room wastebasket. A week later, I was in the same motel with my son, Mark, working on another show. Mark dated one of the maids, who told him about the remarkable Mr. Embra, who had used a dozen "safes" in one night!

Meanwhile, in government, Premier Lougheed had vowed to reduce Alberta's dependence on the sale of non-renewable natural resources. Alberta trade offices were being established worldwide, and incentives were provided for the expansion of industries that could export manufactured products around the world. Film production became part of this policy when Chuck Ross was appointed to manage such an office in 1972. His new title would be Manager,

Film Industry Development, Department of Business and Tourism. This was also the first government office in Canada to promote locations for the production of Hollywood movies.

When shooting in Alberta, productions like *Prime Cut* had been assisted by Chuck Ross as head of the Film and Photographic Branch, but the government was not yet promoting Alberta as a film location. This would change after Chuck's new appointment.

The indigenous Alberta film industry was small, but ambitious. The biggest producer of films, documentary and educational, was Alberta Education's ACCESS TV. We believed this work should be contracted out, rather than produced "in house." Chuck agreed and urged us to form an association. Nick Zubko's Cine-Audio film lab suffered when ACCESS began to ship film out of the province for processing. As a result, producers who supported Nick met and decided to follow Chuck's advice.

The Alberta Motion Picture Industries Association (AMPIA) was founded in 1973. The articles of incorporation were signed by the legally required five members: Nick Zubko, Ron Brown, Gerry Wilson, Dale Phillips, and myself. Nick became AMPIA's first president. Len Stahl, a freelance writer and public relations adviser, helped establish the association and became our executive secretary. Len also provided me with secretarial and other assistance for many years. Once, in Hollywood, at a round-table lunch with some film types, I was asked, "Does your secretary have big tits?" I replied that I had a male secretary, which prompted the question, "Oh, are you gay?" I said no. Another of the group said, "Wow, classy!" Hollywood is a classy place, eh?

Chuck Ross, with his new mandate that included attracting Hollywood productions to Alberta, first checked out the competition—American states that were luring film crews out of the Los Angeles area. University of Alberta drama professor Ben Tarver and I were recruited to accompany Chuck to New Mexico in 1974. At that time, this state was the most successful in acquiring film production from Hollywood.

Like Alberta, New Mexico has a wonderful variety of scenery. It also has proximity to Hollywood and a year-round outdoor shooting climate. There was a rustic western town, which had been home to thirty-four movies, and New Mexico had a full-time representative in Hollywood. It was tough competition, with more of the same to be found in Texas and Arizona.

Undaunted, Chuck began actively promoting Alberta in Hollywood. At least he had no competition in Canada. At the time, Alberta was the only province to see potential in attracting film production from Hollywood.

By 1972, I had completed my homebuilt Hawker Fury biplane. The Fury is a single-seater and was first flown by airline captain Jack Johnson in October 1972. His comprehensive test pilot report, written on a cigarette package, said, "It flies real good."

Now it was my turn to take flight. I was qualified to fly twelve different aircraft types, having had familiarization flights with instructors. The Fury, being a single-seater, allowed for no check ride. There were just a few words of advice from the test pilot, get in it, and go! The aircraft had a rudder bar instead of rudder pedals; it was a bad design and ground handling was difficult.

Once airborne, however, it was a nice airplane to fly. The open cockpit allows a pilot to *feel* all the sensations of flight. You can tell if you're slipping or skidding in a turn by the rush of air on your cheeks. Speed can be estimated by the humming of the wing-bracing wires; they play different tunes at different speeds. If they ever become silent, you are about to fall out of the sky. This bird could even be flown without instruments.

Coming back to earth was a task I found difficult in the Fury. My first landing was a nervous experience and so was almost every one thereafter. An emergency landing in a farmer's field with an overheated engine one day prompted me to make new engine cowlings and, while at it, to modify the narrow undercarriage. It was my hope I could now land the airplane without "cutting washers out of the seat cushion," as we say.

It was a calm day in July 1974 and I had been flying the Fury for about eighteen months when I took off for a test flight with the modification. After flying for an hour, my return was greeted with a strong crosswind—real nasty for a biplane. I should have flown to another airstrip with favourable wind direction, but it would have been a long hike back to where my car was parked.

Due to the crosswind, I was landing at a higher speed than usual and, just at touchdown, was hit with a gust that put the aircraft cockeyed to the runway. I hit hard! The landing gear was torn off and the wooden propeller literally exploded, filling the air with flying debris and dust as the plane skidded down the runway on its belly! Before the Fury was completely stopped, I unhooked the life-saving shoulder harness and was out of the cockpit running, fearing fire.

A scene from the movie *Locusts*, an American "made for TV" show that filmed near Lethbridge in 1974, starring Ben Johnson, Ron Howard, and a number of Alberta performers. Puffed wheat, wind machines, and peanut shells were used to simulate "locusts." Photo: Chuck Ross, Government of Alberta

The dust was still settling as I cautiously returned to see that, in addition to the extensive damage, a piece of Plexiglas had been knocked out of the windscreen. It was determined that the brass-bound tip of the propeller had hit there and been deflected to pierce the upper wing, with enough momentum that we never did find it. Without that deflection, I would have been killed. That damaged windscreen now hangs on my workshop wall.

I eventually rebuilt the Fury and sold it to a very experienced pilot, whom I thoroughly warned. He also wrecked it while landing. My half-brother from Mother's second marriage, Butch Maguire, and I bought an old "bush" aircraft, a 1946 Stinson 108, which we completely rebuilt, installing new radios and instruments. It would outperform any contemporary aircraft in its category, and the registration, C-FLIK, seemed appropriate for a filmmaker. It flew me to various film locations for many years.

Ron Howard, a young *Locust* star in 1974, was later featured in the TV series *Happy Days* and is now a prominent motion picture director. Photo: Chuck Ross, Government of Alberta

In 1974, the made-for-TV disaster movie *Locusts* came from Los Angeles to film near Lethbridge. Youth in the area had been encouraged to collect grasshoppers all summer long, but the insects didn't photograph realistically. Puffed wheat thrown into a wind machine and peanut shells dropped from a helicopter, filmed in reverse so they appeared to fly up, did the job much better.

Young actor Ron Howard, soon to become a TV icon with *Happy Days* and later a noted director, was a big hit with the locals, as was real cowboy Ben Johnson, who had ridden in the Calgary Stampede. As an actor, Johnson had received an Oscar for his role in *The Last Picture Show* a few years earlier. Several Calgary performers were in *Locusts,* including Jack Goth, Bill Speerstra, Bill Berry, and even Les Kimber. This movie-of-the-week was filmed in a record eleven days, with Lethbridge's weather having been perfect.

Chuck Ross accompanied me to England in 1975, where, a co-production agreement having been signed, I was hoping to negotiate a feature-film partnership. We both made excellent contacts at the famous Pinewood Studios. I

EDMONTON'S FILM PRODUCTION INDUSTRY

Edmonton's domestic film production industry had begun in the early 1950s with Larry Matanski's short-lived Western Canada Films. His principal investor was former bush pilot Edgar T. Jones, who would benefit from the experience only by becoming a leading wildlife cameraman and bird artist who received the Order of Canada in 2000. Nick Zubko launched his Cine-Audio company in Edmonton in the mid 1950s, and in the 1960s, Mark Dolgoy, Reeven Dolgoy, and Allan Stein founded Barnyard Films International, while Tom Radford and Bob Reece formed Film Frontiers. In 1971, after spending a year in India, Dale Phillips established FilmWest Associates with Ken Pappes, Harvey Spaak, and Anne Wheeler. Like me, they were all seeking sponsored films to produce. It was very competitive.

In 1975, the National Film Board opened its North West Studio in Edmonton, which would prove very beneficial to filmmakers, providing regional contract work and encouraging them to do "their own thing." Tom Radford, Anne Wheeler, and Dale Phillips became prominent NFB producers, along with Graydon McCrea and Jerry Krepakevitch. Meanwhile, Kicking Horse Productions was set up in 1975 by Arvi Liimatainen and Peter White and would soon include Grace Gilroy, Doug Cole, and Mark Slippe.

Alberta's indigenous film industry was well underway, but it was still dependent on sponsored films.

formed Londalta Film Productions with offices in Edmonton and London, but was ultimately unable to finalize a project.

But even as we found little success in Europe at this time, Alberta promotion in Hollywood began paying off handsomely when Robert Altman's *Buffalo Bill and the Indians, or Sitting Bull's History Lesson* came to Alberta in the summer of 1975. This major film starred Paul Newman, Burt Lancaster, Joel Grey, and Geraldine Chaplin. It had a big budget, although Altman was noted for ignoring budgets as well as scripts. He preferred to let his actors do their own thing. Les Kimber was hired as production manager on the film and maintained tight control.

Buffalo Bill and the Indians, or *Sitting Bull's History Lesson* was filmed on this set on the Morley Reserve in 1975. The film starred Paul Newman, Joel Grey, Burt Lancaster, Geraldine Chaplin, Shelly Duvall, and Morley's own Frank Kaquitts as Sitting Bull. Photo: Bruno Engler

The entire cast and crew occupied Calgary's International Hotel, where general manager Sam Wong always provided exceptional treatment for the people who made films. Even rushes were screened in the hotel; a third-floor suite had been converted into a small theatre.

Altman had developed a fondness for Canada after making *That Cold Day in the Park* and *McCabe and Mrs. Miller* in British Columbia a few years earlier. He chose Alberta for *Buffalo Bill,* he said, "because we needed really good cowboys and Indians." He also found Alberta unions to be less rigid, though that changed during his production.

American film companies usually brought many of their own crew to these location shoots, employing few Canadians. IATSE (International Alliance of Theatrical and Stage Employees) sent a delegation to Ottawa that included Calgary's Mel Merrells and Vancouver's George Chapman. They met with senior federal officials and obtained a ruling that affected many of Altman's crew. The ruling was that foreign crew members would require a work permit issued by the Government of Canada and that no foreign worker could be employed if a qualified Canadian was available from anywhere in Canada. This ruling exists to this day, and the policy has been of continuous benefit to our unionized film craftspeople ever since.

Buffalo Bill was filmed on the Morley flats of the Stoney Indian Reserve, with ten Canadians in key roles, including Stoney Frank Kaquitts as Sitting Bull. The production would briefly employ five hundred Stoney Indians and two thousand extras from Calgary.

The main set consisted of six large circus tents, a small log fort, and an arena large enough to seat three thousand. Bruno Engler, one of Ken Hutchinson's "mountain men" from years earlier, was employed as production still photographer and became a friend of Paul Newman's during the shoot.

Newman was well known as a practical joker and was also known to be fond of popcorn. Early in the production, he found his motor home filled with fluffy popcorn—hundreds of litres of popcorn. Altman was the admitted culprit, and Newman declared war.

Bob Altman, after an exhausting day, found several hundred baby chickens had been turned loose in *his* motorhome. It was evident they had been there for some time. There is no record of Altman's retaliation. I suspect it may have been quite personal and effective, because Newman's next move was to offer the special effects supervisor ten thousand dollars to cut Altman's prized Mercedes automobile in half. He refused to do it, in spite of Paul's assurances, "You don't have to worry; I'll buy him a new one!"

Paul Newman's contract called for twenty-four cans of Coors beer to be provided every day of the shoot, a product that was not available in Alberta at the time. Chuck Ross was able to persuade the Alberta Liquor Control Board to import sixty-three cases. Only Mr. Newman was allowed to drink beer on the Indian Reserve, but of course there was a party at the International Hotel every night. The whole experience was joyous for all from beginning to end. The production finished on time, not too badly over budget, and it achieved both critical and box office success, including winning the Golden Berlin Bear Award at the 1976 Berlin International Film Festival.

PINEWOOD MODELS

My favourite movie studio is England's Pinewood. If you're looking for an ornate plaster ceiling for a European castle, they likely have one in stock. Their plaster-casting department is considered to be the best in the world, as is their miniature work.

The model expert at the studio, the late Derek Meddings, and his crew once built dozens of radio-controlled model cars, with brake lights that worked, for a disaster scene on a bridge for the first *Superman* film. They built a bridge model, about thirty metres long, on the Pinewood back lot. The switch from shots of full-size cars on the real bridge to the models on the much scaled-down replica is done flawlessly and we never realize the difference. If you recall the 1974 James Bond film *The Man with the Golden Gun*, the villain flies away in a car that becomes an aircraft, after extending retractable wings. The airplane model for that sequence was jet powered, with a three-metre wingspan, which was built and flown by the same crew.

Pinewood's 007 Stage, the world's largest, was designed by Ken Adam and built in 1976 to house the interior of villain Stromberg's supertanker in the Bond film *The Spy Who Loved Me*; it housed millions of litres of water—and three submarines. It has been the home of the spectacular sets for many subsequent Bond films and countless other big-budget productions. Its value to Pinewood and the film world was demonstrated in 1984 when, after a fire during production of Ridley Scott's *Legend* destroyed the facility, it was rebuilt in only a few months, in time to host the production of the next Bond film, *A View to a Kill*. Later, it would be renamed the Albert R. Broccoli 007 Stage in honour of the long-time producer of the Bond films.

The Bond producers are keen on realism. During *A View to a Kill,* an office set was decorated with what appeared to be priceless antique furniture, *objets d'art*, and masterpiece paintings. I believed it was a work of art in duplication when I saw it, before learning that everything on the set was real. It was insured for millions of pounds, and security guards surrounded the "office" on a twenty-four-hour basis until filming was completed, days later.

For this same movie, a scene was shot in Arizona with a twin-engine aircraft. It was to be dismantled and shipped to Pinewood for additional filming. "Too time consuming," said the production manager. He hired a pilot to fly the plane across the Atlantic and land in a field alongside the studio. A waiting crane lifted it over the fence onto the Pinewood back lot. There was a hefty fine to pay—for an illegal, non-airport landing—but they still saved money on the deal. That's what a good production manager does.

Days of Heaven, Nights of Hell

I became the second president of AMPIA (Alberta Motion Picture Industries Association) in 1976, succeeding Nick Zubko. AMPIA persuaded the provincial government to develop a fairer film-tendering process and conceived a new system of completion guarantees for government contracts, which was accepted. AMPIA would now earn fees that had been going to bonding companies. AMPIA also asked the government to minimize its ACCESS TV production and contract the work to private-sector film companies.

On 6 April 1976, *Edmonton Journal* business editor Pete Brewster reported: "After a series of meetings extending over more than a year, the Alberta Motion Picture Industries Association feels it is no closer to an answer than it was in the beginning. The filmmakers contend they have no dispute with the avowed objectives of ACCESS. In fact they contend if the government crown corporation would stick with its mandate, it would provide them with a firm base on which to build a major industry in Alberta. They say, 'This is absolutely contrary to the avowed government policy of supporting private enterprise and small business, and the contention that Alberta is the bastion of free enterprise.'" That last quote came from me.

ACCESS was hiring staff and making films that could have been contracted out to Alberta filmmakers, with ACCESS providing only scripts, creating
work for AMPIA members, and saving money for the government. We needed
the work. The ACCESS organization was building a production empire, when
distribution should have been its only function, in our view.

The media were supportive province-wide, and chambers of commerce
became involved. The Alberta chamber wrote to Premier Lougheed in support
of AMPIA. A freeze on hiring was finally put in place at ACCESS. By then, there
were nearly three hundred employees. It would be many years before any substantial benefits would accrue to the private sector from ACCESS.

In 1976, prominent Hollywood director and past president of the U.S. Academy
of Motion Picture Arts and Sciences Arthur Hiller returned to his native
province to direct a major motion picture, *Silver Streak,* starring Gene Wilder
and Richard Pryor. This was a train picture, and the CPR was co-operative with
the production team. A chartered passenger train roamed southern Alberta during the shoot, which was based out of Calgary.

Arthur grew up in Edmonton, where actor Leslie Nielsen was a neighbour and school chum at Victoria High. Memorabilia of both are displayed at
"Vic." It was at his father's store where I bought some of my first camera equipment years before. Arthur had served overseas with the Royal Canadian Air
Force during World War II and then worked with the CBC in Toronto, and in
television in New York, before moving to Los Angeles and feature-film production. His credits are impressive, as is his devotion to industry causes.

In recent years, Arthur has been very active with the Victoria School of
the Performing and Visual Arts in Edmonton. He generously provides time and
effort to inspire students in theatre crafts and filming. An adjacent street was
recently named Arthur Hiller Way.

Silver Streak was a huge commercial success, and the Wilder and Pryor
comedy team would make a number of popular films over the next decade.

Days of Heaven, known to the crew as "Nights of Hell," began filming in the
Lethbridge area in 1976. It took two years to complete because director Terry
Malick wanted to shoot in all of our seasons.

The film starred Sam Shepard, Richard Gere, Brooke Adams, and Stuart

LESLIE NIELSEN

Leslie Nielsen is considered to be one of the most popular Hollywood comic actors of the last twenty-five years, with hits such as *Airplane* and the *Naked Gun* films to his credit, but the Saskatchewan-born actor has never strayed far from his Western Canadian roots. Nielsen was raised in Edmonton, where his father was an RCMP officer.

In 2003, Nielsen was presented with a Lifetime Achievement Award from AMPIA. Although much in demand in Hollywood, Leslie has always made it a principle to assist productions in Western Canada. In 1992, he hosted the Alaska Highway film *The Great Road*. He has appeared in documentary films made by Alberta producers Bob Willis and Denny Ranson, as well as in Wendy Wacko's 1985 feature film *Striker's Mountain*.

If you were an Alberta producer and needed him, Leslie made himself available. Edmonton's Grant MacEwan College recently named its new division The Leslie Nielsen School of Communications in his honour.

Margolin, and told the story of a young couple, posing as brother and sister, who go to live with a wealthy farmer. The movie gained its "Nights of Hell" reputation because of the many evening shoots that were required and for its rough production meetings.

Director of photography Néstor Alemendros received an Oscar for his beautiful cinematography that one critic described as: "Too artfully arranged, like a series of slide entries in a photography contest." For years afterward, whenever the word "Alberta" was uttered during meetings in Hollywood, I would often hear someone say, "Isn't that where *Days of Heaven* was filmed?"

The big film event for Alberta in 1976 was the launch of Fil Fraser's "home-grown" feature film *Why Shoot the Teacher?*, based on the novel written by his friend Max Braithwaite. Fil formed a company with his own financial group in Edmonton, engaged Jim DeFelice to write the script, and then spent six months looking for an Eastern Canadian partner. The CTV network finally came into the project, as well as the Canadian Film Development Corporation (CFDC).

CTV assigned Larry Hertzog as line producer. Canadian-born, England-based Silvio Narizzano of *Georgy Girl* fame was hired as director, while Hollywood's Bud Cort and Samantha Eggar were cast as principals in the film. *Why Shoot the Teacher?* was filmed northeast of Drumheller in the town of Hanna. The budget was set at $1.2 million.

Prominent Alberta crew members included Les Kimber as production manager, Wendy Partridge as head of wardrobe, and Jim Long as assistant director. Many Alberta actors were in the cast.

Jim DeFelice had written the script for a winter shoot, with snowball fights and street hockey played with frozen horse turds, but filming began in March—an unusually warm and snowless March for Alberta. DeFelice was soon on location, rewriting the script to fit the mild weather.

Filming eventually wrapped in Hanna on time and within budget, despite weather problems. But post-production in Toronto became a nightmare, with confrontations between director, editor, producer, and others on CTV's home turf. Post-production costs skyrocketed. CTV ended up selling the completed film to a tax-shelter operator. Fil and his group only recovered their investment. Nonetheless, *Why Shoot the Teacher?* was a box office success and remains one of Canada's top rated and most famous films. The learning experience of making it would be valuable to Fraser for future productions.

Alberta Culture minister Horst Schmid was very supportive of the film industry, providing funding for the first Alberta Film Festival and helping us in many other ways. He was ready to commission a study, but the appointment of Chuck Ross as the manager of Film Industry Development, in a business department, would overrule him.

In 1977, Robert Dowling, minister of Industry and Tourism, announced the appointment of a committee to study all aspects of the film industry. The committee was made up of economic consultant W. G. Brese, film exhibitor Brian McIntosh, feature-film producer and broadcaster Fil Fraser, and myself.

The study required wide travel, and we were accompanied by Chuck Ross, who remained neutral in any of the discussions. Chairman Bill Brese was also neutral, very analytical, and a sharp questioner of our conclusions. McIntosh concentrated on exhibition, distribution, and marketing issues, which were his specialties. Fil and I, dealing with production issues, launched our effort in Montreal.

THE BANFF TELEVISION FESTIVAL

Fil Fraser founded Alberta's first film festival at Red Deer College in 1974. During our visit at Canadian Film Development Corporation (CFDC) headquarters in Montreal, we met with their director of film festivals, Jean LeFebvre, to promote a film festival in Edmonton in conjunction with the upcoming 1978 Commonwealth Games. Jean agreed to help, and Fil presented his idea for a Banff Film Festival "that would rival Cannes." Jean was impressed, but said, "There are too many film festivals; what's needed is a television festival."

Fil soon had his lawyer at work, as well as Len Stahl, who had tirelessly assisted with the first Alberta festival. The New Western Film and Television Foundation was incorporated in 1978 for the purpose of funding a Banff Festival. Fil was president, I was vice-president, and board members included Dr. David Leighton (president of the Banff School of Fine Arts), Neil Armstrong, Vic Rogers, and Jeanne Lougheed.

In the earliest stages, Fil and I agreed that the ideal executive director would be Banff resident Carrie Hunter, a public relations adviser we both knew, who was recommended by Dr. Leighton. Dr. Jerry Ezekiel, assistant director of Film and Literary Arts in Alberta Culture under director Ruth Fraser (then married to Fil Fraser), left the government in 1984 to become the festival's full-time program director. Jerry had been active from the first days of the festival, after being seconded to it by Alberta Culture. He became president and festival director before tiring of administrative duties. He is now senior vice-president.

Carrie and Jerry, with assistance from David Leighton, were largely responsible for the success of the Banff Television Festival. Although I was asked to stay on as a director after joining the government in 1981, I saw it as a conflict of interest, believing I could be of more assistance to the festival in government (which I was).

The festival, which celebrated its twenty-fifth anniversary in 2004, is the most respected event of its kind in the world. In 2003, even though attendance was down because of the SARS scare, there were nearly seventeen hundred delegates from forty countries. *Entertainment Weekly* proclaimed, "The movies have Cannes. Television has Banff."

THE WORDS OF SAM GOLDWYN

The chance to visit Goldwyn Studios during the 1977 sojourn to Hollywood was of particular interest to me. Samuel Goldwyn, an idol of mine, had passed away a few years earlier. Our host had been his executive assistant, and I asked him many questions about the great man.

I was aware that Goldwyn hired the best writers in the business but was often in conflict with them. I asked about, and was shown, the second-floor window that Goldwyn would lean from to yell at writers who were sauntering through the main gate, usually late. They argued that they were being paid to think, so they were working all the time.

Sam said, "Do your thinking in the office starting at 8:00 AM from now on; even the president of my bank is working at 8:00 AM."

A gutsy writer replied, "Why not have your bank president write the scripts?" But they complied.

Months later, during a post-mortem session about a film that had really bombed, the writer said, "I can't understand it, Mr. Goldwyn. I was here every morning at eight."

Coincidentally, at Disney Studios, my friend Bill Bosche, whose office was near the front door of the animation building, told me that Walt Disney himself would sometimes make a surprise visit to this, his favourite department. Bosche would send a warning to fellow workers if he spotted him: "There's a bear in the woods—pass it on."

Quebec had a thriving French-language film industry in the 1970s. This success was due to combined assistance from the CFDC and the Institut Québécois du Cinema, established by Quebec's Department of Culture to aid in the preservation of the French language and way of life in Quebec.

Our motivation for requesting assistance in Alberta would have to be based on economics. We called on the CFDC (now known as Telefilm), where CEO Michael Spencer showed interest in assisting Alberta. He and Chuck had served together in the Canadian Army film and photo unit in World War II.

Fil and I next met with producers and production managers in Toronto and Montreal, before moving on to Ottawa to meet with federal officials. Crossing the country, our entire group later checked out Panorama Studios in Vancouver, a facility that was considered a costly failure because there wasn't enough film work coming into Vancouver. In order to recover some of their investment, the owners were renting it out for fertilizer storage.

Later, we met with senior executives at several Hollywood studios, including Columbia, Warner Brothers, Walt Disney Studios, Twentieth Century-Fox, Universal, and Goldwyn Studios. They were all co-operative; there were no "runaway productions" of any significance at that time, so no one thought we might ever cause them a problem. They were helpful in telling us what would be necessary to develop a film industry. I think they were amused with us, and I doubt many of them could have found Alberta on a map.

Tucson, Arizona, was next on the itinerary, where the state film commissioner, Bill McCallum, was helpful to our study. We toured the Old Tucson western town, which was much like the one I had seen in New Mexico during a similar reconnoitre a few years before. Old Tucson was established in 1940 and has been the base for some 180 western movies (or parts thereof) since then. Shows like *Gunfight at the OK Corral, The Mark of Zorro, Little House on the Prairie,* and *Tombstone* have all made use of the facility.

It is significant that these towns are located where the western stories actually took place, in a year-round filming climate that is dry and allows for simple and inexpensive construction. I always knew that Alberta could service westerns, as long as only our natural scenery was required. The province looks very much like Montana and Wyoming, after all.

We don't have, nor are likely to have, a permanent western town set, although John Scott's ranch maintained a western set from *The Virginian,* and the *Lonesome Dove* town was retained on the Copithorne Ranch west of Calgary, where several other shows have filmed. It will be interesting to see how long they last. For construction to survive long term in our climate, it is necessary to follow our building code, which would make it expensive. A western town set is not like a "Field of Dreams"—build it and they will come. Low-budget westerns will use an existing town in California, Arizona, or New Mexico where they can shoot year-round. Big-budget films like *Unforgiven* will build where they find scenery that hasn't been seen before. The towns they build are minimal in construction, the roofs often leak, and the structures are covered with tarps when shooting interiors. As a result, the film towns built here are not expected to last longer than the length of the production.

A principal objective of our study group was to examine incentives in a country that had been most successful in developing its own film industry—Australia. In Sydney, we received a very warm welcome from the Australian Film Commission.

In some respects, our investigation in Australia was ironic. Many years before, that country's movie industry had studied Canadian film resources and then patterned its Film Australia and Australian Film Commission after our National Film Board and the Canadian Film Development Corporation, respectively. No significant success resulted, until some of the Australian states set up their own agencies. First, and most notable, was South Australia, a "have-not" region where virtually no film activity existed before the founding of the South Australia Film Commission in 1972. Within a few years, a number of successful films had been produced there, resulting in the states of Victoria and New South Wales also establishing their own film commissions. Within five years, Australian films, such as *Picnic at Hanging Rock* and *Don's Party*, were being seen worldwide.

This was significant. We had reached some conclusions based on other findings, but based on what we were seeing Down Under, were more excited than ever about the potential for an Alberta film industry, if we combined that knowledge with what we learned in Australia.

We flew from Sydney to Hong Kong to visit the famous Shaw Brothers Studios, one of the most prolific producers of Asian film. Here, the employees were almost captives. Performers and other key people lived on the studio lot in barracks-like buildings, on twenty-four-hour call.

Production of a martial arts film was underway when we visited and it was very interesting to watch. Our guide informed us they were behind schedule and would likely be working until midnight. Fil and I were amused at this, as we were accustomed to working with unions with limits on how long "artistes" could work during any given day. The sound stages at Shaw Brothers were tin roofed and noisy, but we were told that this didn't matter as dialogue would be dubbed in later. As a young female production assistant explained, "Shooting is much simpler and good acting not required; voice over will fix."

We were shown their latest big-budget picture, *Hsing Hsing wang*

AMPDC IS BORN

In the mid-1970s, governments and corporations were the sources for documentary and industrial films, the mainstay for Alberta filmmakers.

By 1976, producers in Ontario and Quebec were becoming active in speculative television and theatrical production. The CFDC was there to assist, as was a federal program of tax shelters for investors in motion pictures.

Established Alberta film producers, good businessmen, were sticking to the sponsored work because of the high risk and the expense of preproduction in television and feature films (such as the cost of a script). Chartered banks would not loan money for speculative films. If you had a good script, the CFDC might invest, and tax-shelter money was available. Alberta investors, looking for tax shelter, were providing a large portion of the funds for films that were being made in Ontario and Quebec.

In a 1979 follow-up to the Film Industry Study, an AMPIA presentation to the government stated that millions of our dollars were going east and that we should keep those investments in Alberta. Assistance for preproduction loans could soon have our filmmakers moving eastern money to Alberta. Hugh Planche, the minister of Economic Development, was sold on the idea and began planning for the establishment of the Alberta Motion Picture Development Corporation.

(*Mighty Peking Man*), a well-made takeoff on *King Kong*, starring a mix of Asian and Western actors, led by Russian-born Evelyne Kraft. But by far, the most impressive item on the lot was studio owner Sir Run Run Shaw's gold-plated Rolls Royce.

We had some time to ourselves in Hong Kong, and Fil and I explored this fascinating city together. He is adventurous and a lot of fun. We ended up in places where we shouldn't have been, though, some ominous, and one area we labelled "Suzie Wong Country." We saw no other tourists there, only crowds of locals on their own unique turf where strangers were not welcome. We were a black individual and a white, amidst a swarm of yellow complexions, prompting Fil to remark to me, "Now you know what it's like to be in a minority."

We eventually found our way back into tourist territory and happily went shopping.

When travelling in a foreign country, I like to purchase art on the street, from the artist. It's easy to pack, duty free, and a wonderful souvenir, and I believe in supporting artists. In Hong Kong, I bought an oil painting on canvas that featured a Chinese junk, other boats in the harbour, and the Hong Kong skyline. It looked good and was reasonably priced. Largely by gesture, the artist persuaded me to follow him to his studio.

He led me into a small windowless room, switching on a bare bulb in a porcelain socket that hung from twisted wires. It revealed an easel, brushes, and a crude palette covered with dabs of colour. The grimy walls had shelves that supported paintings, all on canvas, all the same size, all the same scene—the one I had purchased! There were slight variations in colour of boats, sails, and sky on each canvas. I liked mine best and bought no other. At home, after a few months, the oil paint cracked and curled.

It hangs today on a wall in my woodworking shop, a one of a kind original that brings back pleasant memories.

The film study group submitted a two-volume report to Alberta Economic Development in December 1977. Our principal recommendation was the establishment of an Alberta Film Development Corporation to become operational by 1 April 1979.

Chuck Ross retired as the director of Film Industry Development in 1978 to spend half of each year at his second home in Arizona, after serving the people of Alberta and our industry very well for many years. His replacement, Glenn Ludlow, had been teaching film in Ontario and first had to become familiar with Alberta and its film industry, which required travel around the province. During Glenn's absence, I was sometimes called in as a consultant by his executive director, Dr. Alan Vanterpool.

Meanwhile, at JEM Films, Ken Jubenvill, Richard Tomkies, and I were working on a major film for Syncrude Canada. We were often able to combine work and fun. Meeting in Fort McMurray on one occasion, Ken rode all the way up from Vancouver on his motorcycle. It was just a short hop for me in my refurbished Stinson aircraft. Richard, for his part, bemoaned the fact that he was unable

HOW MEMOIRS MIGHT BEGIN

Inspired by *Terry and the Pirates*, a popular comic strip of years ago, it was always a childhood ambition of mine to sail on the South China Sea. Now, at age forty-nine, it had finally become a reality.

I thought if I ever wrote a novel, it might begin like this: "I stood at the bow of the Chinese junk *Golden Dragon,* my feet planted against the motion of the teak deck. We were on the South China Sea. I felt a warm evening breeze bearing the musky aroma of Kowloon, which was far behind us in the setting sun."

Fast-forward to Beverly Hills, June 1979. I was dining with a British actor and writer who had left his homeland rather hurriedly, "under a bit of a cloud," as they say. I told him of my junk trip two years earlier and how I might use it in a book, which inspired the actor to consider how his memoirs might begin.

He said: "As I sat amidst the splendor of the Beverly Hills Rangoon Racquet Club, munching chocolate-coated strawberries dipped in Chantilly cream, my thoughts turned briefly to my creditors in England, and I wondered how the fish and chips were on Fulham Road."

to use his twelve-metre boat for the trip.

Making industrial and documentary films is an enjoyable way to make a living, and it can pay well. Someone once said, "Given an opportunity to create is the meat and potatoes of life. Money is the gravy."

I have credits on more than one hundred films, covering a wide range of subjects in several countries. Each was exciting in every phase of production, but one film was exciting in ways I'd rather forget. That experience could best be described by quoting the master of mixed metaphors, Hollywood's late Samuel Goldwyn, who said, "A verbal agreement isn't worth the paper it's written on."

A producer finds the work or creates it by developing an idea he sells to the client. Documentary and industrial films usually begin production with a story outline, and the director has control over all artistic elements. The writer, after extensive research, creates the outline. He will let visuals tell the main story, using narrative only where required. His knowledge and participation when editing are essential.

While Richard Tomkies was working with us on the Syncrude film, he was also writing a story for *Reader's Digest* about a mutual friend, high rigger and lumberjack Geordie Tocher, who had spent two years carving a thirteen-metre Haida war canoe from a huge fir log. Tocher was now sailing it from Vancouver to Hawaii with his girlfriend, Karen Lind, and navigator Gerhard Keisel.

Geordie wanted to prove the Haida/Hawaiian theory of explorer Thor Heyerdahl, who believed that Native dugouts had once sailed from the Pacific Northwest to Hawaii. Geordie and his crew had been on the ocean for twenty-eight days when they put into harbour at Santa Cruz, California, because of gale-force winds and crew dehydration. Richard went there to interview them for his article.

A few days later, I heard from Richard's wife, Valerie. Karen had decided not to continue the voyage, so Richard was going to take her place as a crew member.

I was on the next flight to California.

Geordie and crew were lodging in a waterfront motel in Santa Cruz, where we argued for half the night. They were planning to leave in two days, and Richard, who was vital to our Syncrude film, was adamant; he *was* going to Hawaii in the dugout. Needless to say, our Syncrude client was extremely displeased.

The dugout canoe, named *Orenda*, was berthed at a nearby pier. Decorated with carved and painted Haida figures, I had to admit she was a floating work of art, with outrigger and sails, primitive, but well equipped. A marine supplier had provided the crew members with custom-made survival suits that would keep them afloat for a week if necessary—but there was no suit available for Richard. Geordie took me aside to say, if disaster threatened he would give his suit to Richard: "You have my word."

The *Orenda* was on the ocean for thirty days through some very rough weather, and radio contact was lost with the crew. They were spotted just out of Honolulu by a CP Air flight. I flew to Hawaii and found them as guests at the posh Ilikai Hotel in Waikiki, being treated as heroes by the populace, who had proclaimed their arrival by parading on the beach, blowing into large conch shells.

Richard said the voyage reminded him of driving a small car through

Geordie Tocher's dugout canoe *Orenda* off Diamond Head, Hawaii, in 1978, after sailing from Vancouver to Hawaii in 58 days. Tocher carved this boat from a large fir log over a two-year period. Photo: Geordie Tocher

the deep coulees of southern Alberta, except, "on the ocean, the walls were higher and constantly moving." He said it was most terrifying when the canoe began to break up in a fierce storm. The outrigger float, whipped by waves five metres high, was dangerously loose. Geordie was going to crawl out on the slippery, heaving boom and attempt to lash it down, but first he got out his survival suit. True to his word, he handed it to Richard and said, "You'd better put this on."

Richard finally returned to the continent with me to complete the Syncrude film, which was to premiere at the official opening of the company's Fort McMurray plant. The deadline became really tight because of Hollywood lab problems.

We had some special effects we felt could best be accomplished in Hollywood. Also, our narrator was actor Richard Basehart, who lived there. I was recording with him at a Hollywood sound studio only a few days before the deadline, so the proximity of a laboratory for final printing was also a factor.

The day before the grand opening, I left Los Angeles with the first print of the film, catching the last flight to Edmonton. Arriving at about midnight, a chartered aircraft flew me on to Fort McMurray, where at 3:00 AM the airport was covered with executive jets of attending VIPs, all presumably getting a good night's sleep.

In the early afternoon, along with a distinguished audience of oil executives and federal and provincial politicians, I saw for the first time the completed film, which was titled *Sand Barrier*. It received tributes galore, but in all my years in the business, there was never a closer call on a deadline.

It now became our ambition to produce a feature film from Hugh Dempsey's marvellous book *Charcoal's World*. This is the story of the greatest RCMP manhunt in the history of the Canadian West and provides a deep insight into the Native psyche. I obtained the film rights because I believed it could become the finest Canadian western ever put on the screen. I still think the story has that potential.

Ken Jubenvill and I spent a lot of time and money trying to develop this project. The Canadian Film Development Corporation favoured proven feature-film writers for the project, even if they were not Canadian. We had the script written by British actor and writer James Booth, who had appeared in many English feature films, the American TV miniseries *Wheels*, and the theatrical hit *Airport '77,* and was set to play a leading role in *Charcoal's World*.

Every scene would be shot where it had actually happened: in the Waterton–Porcupine Hills area of southern Alberta. This beautiful, rugged country had enabled Charcoal to evade the largest force of mounted police ever marshalled in the West. His crime was killing a man whom he had found making love to one of his wives. When pursued shortly after, he killed a Mountie, which sparked the manhunt. Charcoal travelled with two wives and three children, moving camp frequently in a radius of less than sixty-four kilometres, eluding the Mounties for thirty days. He was spotted and shot at several times, but no bullet ever struck him.

Charcoal was the owner of a Bear Knife, which was believed to keep the owner from harm. While we were trying to develop the film, a famous American knife maker, Walter Kneubuhler, was handcrafting replicas of the

Silence of the North, filmed near Fort McMurray, Alberta, in 1980, starred Ellen Burstyn and Tom Skerrit. Based on a true story of wilderness pioneering, it also starred Canadian actor Gordon Pinsent. Photo: Chuck Ross, Government of Alberta

Bear Knife, a large dagger blade, with a handle made from a bear jawbone and a beautiful beaded buckskin sheath. I had three made: one for Hugh Dempsey, one for Ken Jubenvill, and one for myself.

Ultimately, we were not able to make this film, nor have other producers who have tried since. Our problem, in the tax-shelter years of filmmaking, was the required participation of a broker. They all believed the story lacked "essential box office sex appeal." True, there were no big-boobed blondes in the actual event, and there was no way we could work any in, even if we so wished.

The Bear Knives serve as souvenirs of this blockbuster that never was, and they continue to keep us from harm.

FILM PROCESSING IN ALBERTA

I never thought we would have thirty-five-millimetre film processing in Alberta, since there are good labs only hours away in Vancouver, Toronto, and Montreal. Labs are very expensive to set up, and it takes years to build up trust. Even today, many American cameramen shooting in Canada will insist their film be processed in Hollywood, "where the experts are." No one is opening new labs today; it is only a matter of time before everything will be shot on tape.

Let Music Be the Message

It had been some forty years since the American Eagle biplane flown by Bert Wallis had first launched me into the air over the grassy airstrip near Wetaskiwin. A lot of memories came back to me as I landed my antique 1946 Stinson for a refuelling stop at the airport not far from the site of that first flight.

I was having a coffee at the airport when an elderly gentleman came in. He said I'd flown over his house on my approach, "and it's at least twenty years since I've seen a 108 Stinson, and I'd like to take some pictures."

He stuck out his hand and said, "My name's Bert Wallis."

I proudly gave him a tour of our nicely restored airplane, and we had a wonderful chat over several cups of coffee. I told him of his impact on my life and how much that very first flight had meant to me.

Bert told me about his son, who was a major in the Canadian Armed Forces and the leader of the Snowbirds aerobatic team. He was very proud of his son.

It was a big surprise to see Bert again—it was an enjoyable meeting with a man who had been my childhood (and later) idol. Sometime after, I read of Bert's passing, but I'll never forget how he helped me first take wing so many years ago.

It was now 1980, and the government had not yet acted on our film industry study a year after the Alberta Film Development Corporation was supposed to be in place, although AMPIA (Alberta Motion Picture Industries Association) president Eda Lishman was really pushing them. It was also the seventy-fifth anniversary of the Province of Alberta, and Culture minister Mary LeMessurier had a seventy-five-million-dollar fund to honour the occasion. Grants would be awarded to a variety of Alberta artists, and we happened to have a pet project that would qualify.

The subject was to be the Calgary Youth Orchestra on a tour of England. We would film the concerts, interweaving those visuals with Alberta scenery and events, as a musical tribute to the province. My company, Londalta Film Productions, was awarded a grant to make the twenty-minute production in thirty-five-millimetre wide screen. Although obligated only to provide one print for the Provincial Archives, we planned to obtain wide distribution that would benefit Alberta. The print sales, of course, would be of benefit to us.

Ken Jubenvill and I set out to scout locations on 19 April 1980, flying to Amsterdam to connect with a flight across the English Channel to Norwich in England. We had four seats on a KLM Boeing 747, with lots of room, although there was a bulkhead directly in front of us.

After a nice sleep and a good breakfast, the captain's voice came over the sound system: "Good morning ladies and gentlemen, this is your captain speaking. The time is 9:05 AM Sunday morning. We are one hour out of Amsterdam and I have an announcement I wish to make. We are in very serious trouble!"

This is *not* what you want to hear at ten thousand metres on a lovely Sunday morning. I began taking notes.

"When we took off from Montreal, we heard a very loud bang. It could have been a bird strike, but we believe it was a blowout of a nose wheel tire. We will therefore have to put in effect full emergency landing procedures. We will make a low pass over the runway while people on the ground check the nose wheel. You will be advised. Perhaps we have no problem; however, I have always found it wise to be prepared."

We had enjoyed the spacious seating, but were now concerned about being so far forward, with a bulkhead in front of us. The cabin crew was asking passengers to remove false teeth, sharp objects from pockets, et cetera. A steward asked if we would exchange seats with a young couple, both of whom were holding a baby and now required four seats. Our new location was right next to the rear emergency exit. I was given the seat alongside the door and told Ken he would be the second person off the aircraft (actually, I would have let him go first, honest).

The 747 made a low pass over the runway and we could see emergency vehicles standing by. The captain announced they had been unable to determine if there was nose-wheel damage. We would attempt a landing.

Two stewardesses sat in a fold-down seat opposite us, both quite pale, knowing they would be the last to leave the aircraft. We admired their calm courage. The landing was uneventful, and as we came to a stop in the middle of the runway, tense silence erupted into cheers and applause.

Not really in the mood to take another plane right away, we cancelled our connecting flight to Norwich in order to spend the night in Amsterdam. We checked into a hotel at the airport and were provided a large room with twin beds. Ken opened his suitcase. To my amazement, there on top was his big Bear Knife from the ill-fated *Charcoal's World* production! His daughter Shari, aware of the legend surrounding it, wouldn't let him leave home without it!

The next day, we flew to Norwich, checked out requirements, and then caught a train into London to finalize arrangements with World Wide Pictures. They would provide additional crew and equipment for our filming in Brighton and Norwich, including interior lighting for the massive Norwich Cathedral.

We returned home to a surprise. Our director of photography, Ron Orieux, irreplaceable as far as we were concerned, had decided to marry. He would work with us in England only if he could take his bride. There was but one possible solution, and that's why producers get the big bucks; we would take our wives, too! These expenses could not be charged to the film. We would be paying, but we would show our ladies a wonderful time. We took in a couple of good plays in London, as well as the superhot musical *Annie*, for which a well-placed friend had found us tickets.

When we were in London ten years earlier, Ken and I had dined at a Knightsbridge roof garden restaurant where, with an orchestra on stage, six white-jacketed violinists strolled table to table, playing classical and show music. We had vowed to do it again one day with our wives. Now was the time.

Reservations were made and, as prearranged, the six violins were around our table a good part of the evening. The setting was gorgeous, with white linen and silverware, fresh flowers, and rose-coloured velvet settee and chairs. The music was incredible—our wives were moved to tears. So were Ken and I; it was a costly evening! I later discovered that Sally had "snitched" a small silver spoon and presented it to Ken's wife, Sheila, as a memento. I was quite annoyed.

Ken and I had also found a great restaurant in Norwich while scouting locations. Reservations were made for our first night. I had managed to meet with the maitre d' earlier. He now escorted us to their best table.

We had been served drinks when he returned to look directly at Sally and said, "Are you Mrs. Marsden?" She was naturally startled and replied, "Yes."

He said, "Well, we've been warned about you from London and want you to know that we count the silverware here."

Sally was stunned, as were Ken and Sheila. He was back several times with comments like, "I used to scoff the odd bit of silver myself, no big deal." It became a really fun evening when everyone realized it was a set-up.

Now it was time to go to work. The gaffer crew and equipment arrived from London and began to hook up and test the lights—many lights. The camera and sound crew arrived. We had rented a large vehicle and hired an off-duty policeman as driver. The eighty-piece youth orchestra began rehearsing as we checked lighting and acoustics.

That evening, we filmed the concert. The kids were great! I had promised to pay our crews in cash, and having our driver/policeman accompany me to the bank for a briefcase full of money was very comforting.

Our next set was a village church at Starston, Norfolk, with a limited number of orchestra members, since it was a small church. The audience was wildly enthusiastic when a seventeen-year-old fiddler played "Orange Blossom Special." It had never been heard in the church before, or likely since, or likely in any other church!

Brighton then became our home base. We came to love this seaside city, and a group of us, including Ken, myself, our wives, and an executive from Calgary's

THE GAFFER

The gaffer, working with an electrical crew, is in charge of lighting, in consultation with the director of photography. The ancient and massive Norwich Cathedral where we filmed *Let Music Be the Message* was a big problem for our gaffer. The interior, like the exterior, was of a sandstone colour. There were no walls or ceiling in the huge area that would reflect light back onto our orchestra. They had to use many intense lights to give us the look we wanted.

An interior scene, even if brightly lit for filming, should retain the appearance of natural room lighting. A scary scene will get a "horror" look with lights placed low to cast big shadows on dark backgrounds, giving a freaky "monster" look to an actor. Exterior night scenes get hard backlight, while bright daytime scenes require "fill-in," with large reflectors or filtered lights.

The gaffer and his crew look after it all.

Mount Royal College named John Fisher, and his wife, enjoyed a special dinner at a small restaurant favoured by local resident Lord Laurence Olivier.

We filmed and recorded the orchestra on the grounds of Brighton Pavilion, an oriental-style castle built by King George IV, which was said to be connected to the home of his mistress by a tunnel. We filmed in the central square with Brighton's Town Crier, and Ken shot and recorded a group of our fiddlers on the famous Brighton Pier. It was a very enjoyable project, and one that our wives loved, even though we put them to work on occasion, helping to organize musicians and moving equipment.

We returned to Alberta to finish shooting, as the footage in England was less than half of what we required for the twenty-minute film. A print was delivered to the Alberta Archives, and *Let Music Be the Message* was distributed worldwide to theatres by Cannon Films.

The film has no narration, only the Brighton Town Crier announcing the concerts of the Calgary Youth Orchestra "to help celebrate the Seventy-

Fifth Anniversary of the Province of Alberta." It then becomes a filmic treat of Alberta, punctuated with the music and visuals of the concerts. With Ken Jubenvill's direction and editing, Richard Tomkies's concept is uniquely brilliant.

It is fitting that this would be the last film I would be involved with as a producer. It brought me more enjoyment than anything we ever did. Fil Fraser took a print with him to Russia, along with films of his own, and he tells me that *Let Music Be the Message* was warmly received.

A few years later, while travelling to England with Orv Kope, the film appeared on the aircraft movie screen. He said, "Hey, that's your movie."

I said, "It's a deal I have with Air Canada; when I'm on one of their airplanes, they put on one of my films."

In 1980, Glenn Ludlow left the Alberta government to form his own production company and would soon produce a feature film in Alberta called *Firebird 2015 AD,* starring Darren McGavin and Doug McClure. People in the industry, as well as my wife, Sally, urged me to take over Glenn's job. The clincher was when the minister of Economic Development, Hugh Planche, told me they were finally ready to act on the recommendations of the Film Industry Study from several years earlier.

Planche said, "Take two years out of your private sector life to set up the programs, and we'll take care of you."

The job was still advertised and it became a competition, but I was nonetheless appointed director of Film Industry Development in Alberta Economic Development, effective 5 January 1981. The position would be reclassified as film commissioner some years later.

An immediate priority was to prepare legislation for the establishment of a Motion Picture Development Corporation, and I began working with senior civil servants and legislative counsel. Hugh Planche impressed me from our first meeting. He was very supportive, saying, "You strike me as a guy who isn't going to follow the rules, and I like that, but you're going to get into trouble. When you do, call me direct."

To my good fortune, Larry Shaben, who succeeded him as minister in 1986, was from the same mould.

The Calgary Youth Orchestra in concert on the grounds of the Brighton Pavilion, in England, 1980, for our Londalta Film Productions documentary film about Alberta, *Let Music Be The Message*. The movie played in cinemas around the world. Photo: Sheila Jubenvill

By 1981, Chuck Ross was working with a Calgary group, headed by Alan Waldie, called Tri Media. They had purchased 320 hectares of land on the western outskirts of Calgary and were proposing to build film studios on this Happy Valley site. They were generating a lot of media coverage as "Hollywood North."

The government helped get the land annexed to the City of Calgary, at Tri Media's request, believing that the increase in land value would finance the studio. Tri Media then also requested a fifty-million-dollar loan guarantee. A meeting was held, which I was asked to attend.

Alan Waldie made a very good presentation to the minister and a group of senior civil servants, all of whom had read the Film Industry Study, which strongly advised against any government involvement in studio facilities. Hugh Planche refused to consider a loan guarantee, resulting in an eruption of

THE TRUTH ABOUT DEATH HUNT

Not every film shot in Alberta is a classic, and some are controversial. *Death Hunt,* supposedly based on the true story of the Mad Trapper of Rat River, is a monstrous distortion of history.

The film, which was shot in the Canmore area in 1980, portrays Albert Johnson, a.k.a. the Mad Trapper (Charles Bronson), as an unjustly accused murderer who pits his knowledge of the Canadian wilderness against incompetent RCMP pursuers and eludes them, even when an airplane is brought in to assist. Lee Marvin and Angie Dickinson also starred in this travesty.

The actual event occurred during midwinter of 1932, when Albert Johnson shot and wounded an RCMP officer who was making a routine call. Several Mounties were sent to Johnson's cabin to make an arrest and a fifteen-hour gun battle ensued, ending in a 965-kilometre, four-week pursuit over rugged Arctic terrain. A Mountie was killed and another wounded during the pursuit. The police called in a ski-equipped airplane, flown by famed pilot "Wop" May. His aircraft was a Bellanca cabin monoplane, capable of hauling supplies and several passengers. The movie producers, however, used a single-cockpit biplane, perhaps because it was available, and cast the pilot as an erratic air force officer who machine gunned the "good guys."

"Wop" May was a hero in reality, as were the RCMP involved. Albert Johnson, the Mad Trapper, was killed in the final shootout. Two thousand dollars in cash and a hoard of gold teeth were found on his person, the latter believed to have been taken from the mouths of murder victims.

My family had a personal connection to "Wop" May. My mother worked for him when he was operating the No. 2 Air Observer School at the Edmonton Airport during World War II. She often told me what a fine gentleman he was, in addition to being a great pilot.

Death Hunt set near Canmore, Alberta, in 1981. This film upset many Albertans because it was a travesty of an actual historical event that had involved the RCMP and Alberta pilots. The film starred Lee Marvin, Angie Dickinson, and Charles Bronson. Photo: Bruno Engler

anti-government press comments in "Hollywood North," with frequent Tri Media statements about losses to the province, to the film industry, and to the City of Calgary. This could be considered government's first public recognition of the Film Industry Study. Perhaps it had just paid for itself.

The wheels of government turn slowly, as best expressed in the British TV series *Yes, Minister,* when Sir Humphrey Appleby stated, "It takes a number of people a long time to make something happen in government, but there are those who have power to shut it down instantly. The system has the engine of a lawn mower, and the brakes of a Rolls-Royce."

Truer words were never spoken, as I and the Alberta film industry would learn in later years.

Brighton Town Crier, discussing opening scene of the film *Let Music Be the Message* with (L to R) me, the producer, and director Ken Jubenvill. Photo: Sheila Jubenvill

A Corporation Is Born

Dozens of lengthy sessions with bureaucrats, over many months, finally resulted in a draft Motion Picture Development Act in 1981. The Alberta Motion
Picture Development Corporation (AMPDC) would have a board of directors
and a chairman. We decided the chief operating officer should be the executive
director in order to establish a pay scale and benefits relative to a civil service
position. Dallas Gendall, the deputy minister of Economic Development, insist-
ed the corporation should have a president. The directors would be lay people,
so we recommended an advisory committee, with the president of AMPIA
(Alberta Motion Picture Industries Association) as chairperson.

Bill 24, the Alberta Motion Picture Development Act, was passed in the
legislature in the 1981 fall session, establishing a corporation with a fund of
three million dollars. Loans and guarantees could be made for up to sixty percent of the money required for the pre-production stage of a film—the most
difficult money to find. The corporation would not be able to make grants,
only loans. Regulations would now have to be written and approved in the legislature. The process indeed moved along at "lawn mower speed." It was very
frustrating.

The corporation was set up in a manner that placed it further from
government than any similar body had ever been. A concern was possible

Official opening of the Alberta Motion Picture Development Corporation in Canmore, Alberta, 7 December 1982. (L to R) Chairman Orville Kope, Canmore Mayor Pat Byrne, Alberta director of film industry development Bill Marsden, and AMPDC President Lorne MacPherson. Photo: AMPDC

embarrassment to the government because of a film's content. The board of directors would be assuming full responsibility and would likely be picked from government supporters. They could be replaced at any time, individually or entirely, at the minister's discretion. The three-million-dollar fund covered loan activities, but was retained by treasury to be dispensed as required, when authorized. The operating expenses for the corporation were kept separate in my budget, which was certainly under government control. Nevertheless, in time, the president of AMPDC would seem to believe the organization was independent of government.

Incentives for the development of a film industry in Alberta consisted of more than forming AMPDC. The government was committed to developing an industry. The Departments of Education and Advanced Education would provide

academic and on-the-job training programs. The Department of Culture would
be involved in many areas, including the Banff International Festival of Films
for Television, which was to receive two hundred thousand dollars annually. The
minister of Culture failed to get support in caucus for this expenditure, and
Premier Peter Lougheed asked Hugh Planche to take it on as part of his film
package. The festival was stressed as a marketing opportunity for Alberta filmmakers in order to justify Economic Development support.

It had become government policy to locate its agencies in smaller centres. Red Deer would have been an ideal location for AMPDC head office, but
we were instructed to locate in Banff. Board members were being appointed,
and Planche advised me the chairman would be a Medicine Hat television
executive named Orville Kope.

I met with "Orv" in Calgary and was impressed with his openness and
ability (and several good stories I hadn't heard before, which would soon
become several hundred). Our first task was to find suitable office space in
Banff, which proved impossible. We received permission to look in nearby
Canmore and found good space there.

I had been impressed with the appointed AMPDC board of directors,
after expecting some "good old boys and girls" of the correct political persua-
sion and not much else. Surprise number one had been Orv Kope. Board members like Calgary economist Helen Hammond, Edmonton lawyer Ken Chapman, Lethbridge chartered accountant Rex Little, and Waterton and Pincher
Creek theatre owner Larry Becker were all excellent choices, as was drama professor and celebrated actor Thomas Peacocke, who had recently been acclaimed
for his role as Père Athol Murray in the 1980 film *Hounds of Notre Dame*.

The corporation advertised for a president and received many good
applications, mostly from Eastern Canada. An Albertan was preferred. Edmonton
lawyer Lorne MacPherson applied and was accepted, which required him to
move to Canmore, where AMPDC finally opened for business on 7 December
1982, only three and a half years after the target date set by our study.

Helping to develop a film industry was my main responsibility, but with AMPDC
now operational, I could devote more time and attention to attracting foreign
production to the province. Alberta is promoted as a film location through
advertising, attending trade shows, and travelling to international film centres
for personal contact with producers.

Alberta advantages include experienced crews, a wide variety of choice locations, lots of sunshine, and no provincial sales tax. Its disadvantages are a shorter outdoor filming season, a smaller labour pool, and a lack of film-processing laboratories. Our major competitor in Canada is British Columbia.

Currently, most other provinces also have tax incentives for film. The needs of a film company on location are many, and immediate. A feature film production will spend as much as a quarter of a million dollars a day and can't afford delays. In the United States, many film commissions work directly out of the state governor's office in order to cut red tape quickly.

Productions from Hollywood were used to help train Albertans in film crafts. In co-operation with unions, a program was developed in which government would pay salaries for up to six trainees on a production. Albertans now account for an average eighty-five per cent of the crew on any foreign production that is filmed in the province; all are well-trained, highly skilled technicians. This business is very beneficial to our province, bringing millions of foreign dollars into our economy and employing hundreds of Albertans for weeks or months in a manufacturing process that is environmentally pure. They occupy hotels and rent cars and trucks and other equipment, which spread dollars through wide sectors of our economy, and Alberta scenery in the movies helps to promote the province worldwide.

When attempting to sell Alberta as a film location, the mark of a successful meeting with a producer is being rewarded with a copy of his script. It is then reviewed before assigning an appropriate location scout. The scout will determine likely locations, photograph them, and assemble a portfolio to send to the production company. Union rates and other budgetary information are included in this all-important document. As many as a half-dozen film commissions may be making submissions for the same project, at the same time. The low Canadian dollar also gives us an advantage over American competition.

Many film commissions have location scouts on staff. We would engage private sector scouts, paying a good rate. If they were successful, the production would come to Alberta and they would likely be hired as location manager for the film. This opportunity inspired effort that no film commission employee could duplicate.

Film promotion offices originated in the United States in the 1960s—the first one opened in Colorado. When I visited the New Mexico Film Office in 1974, there were only twenty-four such agencies: twenty-three in the US and one in Alberta. Today, there are about three hundred worldwide, including one in every Canadian province and in every American state; most are known as film commissions. It is a very competitive business.

Chuck Ross and Glenn Ludlow both recommended that I become a member of the American-based Association of Film Commissioners (AFC). I did join and I attended my first AFC convention in Puerto Rico in 1981. At the time, annual meetings were held in member jurisdictions, some of them exotic locations. Now all meetings are held in Hollywood.

When I joined the AFC, it was headed by Arizona film commissioner Bill McCallum and his chairman, Arthur Loew, Jr. Its purpose was, and is, to help members become more competent as film commissioners to better assist the motion picture industry. Leading producers and directors are regular resource people at AFC gatherings. Problems are discussed and solutions suggested. Ways and means of attracting production from Hollywood are revealed to competitors, including Canadians, who have benefited substantially.

It always amazes me that our American friends help us, even though Alberta continues to double for American locations such as Wyoming, Montana, and Colorado. But the Americans still welcome us as association members and help new film commissioners learn the job. I believe it is very important that Canadian film commissions maintain a co-operative relationship with American film commissions, although antagonism could be more logically expected since we are devastating competition for them, given our low dollar.

I became devoted to this remarkable organization, always encouraging new membership in my travels. I was elected a director and became its first non-American executive member when I was elected vice-president in 1986. The president will always be an American, however; it's in the charter.

The AFC has continued to adhere to its principles while expanding worldwide. Since I joined, it has been renamed the Association of Film Commissioners International (AFCI), and members now include Australia, France, Bahamas, Chile, Austria, Germany, Jamaica, Hong Kong, Israel, Mexico, England, and Scotland. It is still expanding. Many of the newcomers to the AFCI had no film experience at all; they were simply appointed to a position that had become vacant in their city or government. There were also political appointees.

Our primary concern in helping to train our members was to gain the respect of the industry, and we succeeded. We regularly had top directors at our seminars, telling us how we could be more helpful to them—directors such as Robert Wise (*The Sound of Music*), Arthur Hiller (*Love Story*), Hal Needham (*Smokey and the Bandit*), John Badham (*Blue Thunder*), Michael Apted (*Gorillas in the Mist*), and others.

It was nice to become acquainted with the high-level directors, producers, and actors who became regular participants at our annual symposium. We held one such gathering in Washington, DC, in 1982, where the head speaker was the president of the Motion Picture Association of America, Jack Valenti.

A former adviser to two American presidents, Valenti hosted a party for us in his lavish headquarters, which was attended by prominent senators and congressmen. For a follow-up banquet at the Kennedy Centre, we were to have been addressed by then-President Ronald Reagan, because of his long association with the film industry. A situation developed that prevented his attendance. Washington Mayor Marion S. Barry spoke, as did a leading senator whose name I don't recall.

The benefit of AFCI to Alberta and Canada is considerable in that the AFCI is staunchly in favour of the principle of "runaway production," even if it goes out of country. The organization has developed high-level friendships and respect in the industry and in government. I believe Canadian film commissioners should support the international association. It is a powerful voice and on our side, in principle.

Les Kimber accompanied me to Los Angeles in 1981 to introduce me to his many contacts there and also to England, where we met with many producers, including the group he had worked with in Calgary a few years before, filming the first two *Superman* films. They would soon be back in Alberta with *Superman III*.

To establish an Alberta base in Hollywood with film expertise, an agreement was made with Gerald K. Smith, a former business agent for the Hollywood cameraman union. He had been a good friend to the Alberta film industry ever since coming here in 1977 to address an AMPIA convention and equipment show. Thereafter, his IATSE (International Alliance of Theatrical and Stage Employees) Hollywood camera local included two Albertans in each two-year, free training course for assistant cameramen, which was an enormous boost for our fledgling industry. Now retired from IATSE, he represented cameramen as an agent and was making regular calls at the studios. Equipped with a supply of our published materials and his knowledge of the province, Gerry now had Alberta as a non-conflicting addition to his portfolio.

Both Canadian and American film commissions were dependent on Hollywood production. Having all our eggs in one basket, and an American basket yet, seemed risky. There was the danger of the American government heeding union cries to stop "runaway productions" and "Keep American Jobs at Home." It seemed desirable to also have Alberta representation in Europe, perhaps in London.

Frank Poole, retired vice-chairman of Rank Distributors, was recommended by a friend of Eda Lishman. No one in the business had a bad word to say about him, which was most unusual! His industry contacts were high level and worldwide. He could represent Alberta film interests for all of Europe and also assist our producers with distribution and co-production deals. He was put under contract.

The combined fees for Smith and Poole were less than the overall cost would be for one additional staff member. They were located where we needed them, both had other non-conflicting income, and both were devoted to promoting Alberta for film locations. It became our policy to have Gerry Smith and Frank Poole attend the Banff Television Festival to be available for consultation with Alberta filmmakers.

All these efforts have paid off. From 1981 to the present, Alberta has been successful in obtaining productions from the United States, England, France, Germany, Belgium, Norway, Sweden, Holland, Hong Kong, India, and Japan.

The crew of *Superman III* came from England to film in Calgary in 1982. The film was directed by the legendary Richard Lester, a co-producer of the first *Superman* film, which had shot a number of scenes in Alberta; Lester had later taken over the director's chair on *Superman II* from Richard Donner. Les Kimber was hired as Canadian production manager. Department heads and key film craftspeople like special effects and the flying unit were from England, inspiring the large Calgary crew with their enthusiasm and pride of craftsmanship.

Much of the action took place in downtown Calgary, which was standing in for Metropolis, disrupting traffic on many occasions, but with no complaints from citizens. The co-operation from the city and the residents "was beyond belief," stated Lester, who would return there the following year to film *Finders Keepers*.

Seeing Superman flying over downtown Calgary was a real traffic stopper! Actor Christopher Reeve, wearing a special harness under the famous red-and-blue costume, was suspended by a cable from a large crane. Swinging up and through the air while he assumed an appropriate flying position, it was realistic and scary to watch! Stunt doubles had been tried as flyers, but none could perform as gracefully as Chris Reeve. He would do more flying back at Pinewood Studios in England, against a blue screen, with those shots to be superimposed over backgrounds filmed in Alberta.

This was a very British production. Ken Jubenvill, my JEM Films colleague, had been hired as an assistant director and told me how some traditions die hard.

"I'll never forget being in a large wheat field in the middle of nowhere with a small crew, prepping for background shooting," he said. "A van appeared suddenly. The rear doors opened. Table and chairs were removed and set up, then a white tablecloth, cups with saucers, silverware and baskets of sweets. It was tea time!"

Ken was—and is—a very good film director. Several Canadians were chosen to work as assistant director on *Superman* and I was not surprised to see him included, knowing Ken to be one of the best there is. His name can be seen on such well-known Canadian-made TV series as *The Beachcombers*, *Airwolf*, *Lonesome Dove*, and *Mysterious Ways*, and features such as *Promise the Moon* and *Ebenezer*.

The Columbia Icefields was to have been the perfect location for a *Superman III* arctic sequence, but Parks Canada initially refused permission. Premier Lougheed's office phoned Prime Minister Pierre Trudeau's office and filming was quickly authorized, with a Parks Canada proviso: building the set on the Icefields was okay, as well as filming from a helicopter, but "under no circumstances can the helicopter land on the Icefield."

When shooting the aerials, the pilot saw an individual he believed was signalling him to set down. Assuming an emergency, he landed. The RCMP were on site and made an arrest. Assistant director Michael Steele was taken to Jasper in a police car and put in jail. In court the following day, he was found guilty. The company paid a fine of ten thousand dollars and Michael returned to work. There were no more landings on the Icefields. We never did find out what the person who caused the pilot to land was really doing.

Superman (Christopher Reeve) "flying" in downtown Calgary in 1982 during the filming of *Superman III*. Suspended by cable from a large crane, Reeve performed all the movie's flying scenes himself. Stunt men had tried, but none was as graceful as Chris Reeve. Photo: Government of Alberta

A highlight for me during the production of *Superman III* was the chance to become acquainted with Christopher Reeve, the finest young actor it was ever my pleasure to meet.

Chris was a pilot who had flown the Atlantic solo several times, a pianist, yacht racer, and horseman. Yet unlike many actors, he never carried that "movie star" aura about him. After performing his high-wire stunts on the set, he would stand in line with the crew for lunch.

He returned to Alberta for several more productions over the years, most notably a trio of *Black Fox* TV movies in 1994, before the tragic riding accident that paralyzed him in 1995. Since then, he has devoted his life to giving hope to people with spinal cord injuries and has raised tens of millions of dollars for research. I believe, as he does, that he will walk again one day. If anyone can do it, Chris will.

Christopher Reeve as Superman. Photo: courtesy Chris Reeve

Working with Richard Lester was also a great experience. He is a rare, good-natured genius, with a keen sense of humour.

In the late 1960s, a "new look" was established in movies by four films that made an enormous impact: *The Knack, A Hard Day's Night, Help!*, and *A Funny Thing Happened on the Way to the Forum*. All, funnily enough, were directed by Richard Lester.

I told him how his 1964 Beatles's film, *A Hard Day's Night,* had affected me. Our daughter Cathy, as a teenager, was a Beatles devotee. The Fab Four seemed to have taken over our home with posters, pictures, and records constantly playing at full volume. I came to dislike them and their music. But when *A Hard Day's Night* screened in Calgary, I was delegated to accompany Cathy to the show. Despite being surrounded by screaming teenagers, I thought the movie was wonderful. I saw it several times and came to admire the Beatles and their music.

The film closed the generation gap for me, enriching my family's life.

126

Richard's twinkle-eyed response was, "It changed my life too, Bill."

More major Hollywood film productions followed *Superman III* to Alberta. *Running Brave,* an Ira Englander film for Walt Disney Productions, was shot in Edmonton and Drumheller in 1982. It is the story of Sioux Native runner Billy Mills (played by Robby Benson), who won a gold medal at the 1964 Tokyo Olympics. It was directed by Canada's Don Shebib, with a Canadian crew and a cast that included Tommy Banks, Bill Berry, Bonar Bain, Tantoo Cardinal, Francis Damberger, Thomas Peacocke, and Maurice Wolf. The film was financed entirely by Hobbema's Ermineskin Band.

Also in 1982, writer-producer Eda Lishman, working with co-writer and director Kevin Sullivan, made *The Wild Pony,* shooting in Calgary's Heritage Park and Pincher Creek. They started much later in the season than I would have dared. Winter does come into this western film and simply adds to the excellent quality. Lishman put the financial package together before the Alberta Motion Picture Development Corporation (AMPDC) came on stream. This is a very good film, and Sullivan Entertainment became one of Canada's most successful companies, best known for their TV adaptation of *Anne of Green Gables.* They got a big start in Alberta, thanks to Eda Lishman.

Although the film office was very busy in the early 1980s, I was determined to remain a one-man operation, with a secretary and private-sector, part-time help when needed. I considered my job a twenty-four-hour commitment. Everyone had my home phone number, and a 3:00 AM phone call was not unusual, since it was 10:00 AM in London. I worked hard because I believed in what I was doing, but there were also many fun occasions and some lavish events I vividly recall.

In 1983, after meetings in Tokyo and Hong Kong, I proceeded to the Manila Film Festival. Founded by Philippines First Lady Imelda Marcos, this was a gathering of Asian film executives, with important representation from the United States and England. American producers David Brown and Richard Zanuck (*Butch Cassidy and the Sundance Kid; The Sting*) were there, as were actors Robert Duvall and Chuck Norris, among others. Sir Richard Attenborough premiered his film *Gandhi,* which would win eight Oscars, including Best Picture.

Jake Eberts and his London-based Goldcrest group were also present. I had been trying to meet with them for two years; here, it was no problem. This

WHAT ABOUT SUPERGIRL?

The first three *Superman* films of the late 1970s and early 1980s were successful enough to prompt producers Alexander and Ilya Salkind to make *Supergirl* as a spinoff project in hopes of expanding the franchise.

After hearing it was in development for a 1984 release, I called in at their Pinewood Studio headquarters while in England, hoping to convince them to film once again in Alberta. Art director Terry Ackland-Snow was at lunch, but three walls of his office were plastered with colour photos of High River, Alberta. It appeared to me that we already had this show "in the bag."

When Terry returned, I learned the photos had been his inspiration for a North American town he had already built on the Pinewood back lot. He gave me a tour. It looked like a typical Midwest American small town with some definite High River-like features. A large crane was in place, off camera, to allow lead actress Helen Slater to perform flying stunts. Terry explained the Salkinds were not sure enough of this picture to warrant the expense of location filming in Alberta.

The Salkinds' instincts proved to be correct. Ultimately, the film was not a success and there was no *Supergirl II*. *Superman IV: The Quest for Peace* followed in 1987, but plagued by cuts in both budget and running time, it also failed at the box office and the franchise folded.

affair was the best I ever attended for making contact with individuals who were virtually unapproachable elsewhere.

After receiving an invitation from Mrs. Marcos to attend the closing banquet at the Philippines International Convention Centre, I was glad I had packed my tuxedo. Arriving alone, I was escorted to a table where a number of lovely young debutantes were seated and told to choose one for a dinner companion. I declined and was taken to a table where two couples were already seated. The gentleman nearest introduced himself and his wife and the other couple. He was the New Zealand ambassador, the other was the ambassador from India. Joined by another ambassadorial couple, we were all seated near the head table, as yet unoccupied.

The New Zealander said, "You don't have a lady; I'll get you one," and was gone before I could respond. He returned with an older lady, who was attractive, elegantly attired, and wearing diamonds. She was introduced as Mrs. George Hamilton. I came to know her as Ann. She was actor George Hamilton's mother. President Ferdinand Marcos and the First Lady arrived to a fanfare, followed by head-table guests that included George Hamilton himself. He was seated next to the First Lady, with her husband, the President, on the other side.

The meal was exquisite, as was the decor, table settings, and music. I've never viewed a classier event on the movie screen. There were four liveried servants standing at every table, and each guest was provided with a gift from President and Mrs. Marcos.

I learned that Ann and her famous offspring were staying at the Marcos Palace. Her dinner conversation was delightful. George visited our table frequently; he was a doting son and a charming man. We were interrupted often by her friend Christina Ford, a well-known jet-setter who finally showed up with two handsome young Italians, with whom they left.

George Hamilton and Imelda Marcos spent half the night on the dance floor, and the President went home. So did I—it had been a great night!

The Manila Film Festival showed great potential for promoting the film industry in Asia, although I believe it was founded by Mrs. Marcos as part of her passion to mingle with film stars. The Philippines government paid all expenses for the notables in attendance. From my point of view, it was an opportunity to meet with some significant industry leaders in a relaxed atmosphere.

The festival disappeared with the downfall of Marcos in 1986. It had been a huge expenditure for a poor country and was of no benefit to the people of the Phillipines, who never even got a glimpse of the celebrities attending.

In 1983, Toronto's Lauron Productions teamed up with Alberta's King Motion Pictures to make the feature film *Isaac Littlefeathers* in Edmonton. Directed by Les Rose, the film starred Lou Jacobi, Scott Hylands, William Korbut, Fred Keating, and Mark Schoenberg. AMPDC invested two hundred thousand dollars in the production. It was a well-made, interesting film, but not a financial success. Nonetheless, it would make a big contribution to the development of a film industry in Alberta because it inspired Toronto producer Ron Lillie to develop a project with Alberta's Anne Wheeler—the film *Loyalties*, to be filmed at Lac La Biche.

By 1984, AMPDC had been involved in twenty-two projects. *Draw!*, a $4.2 million western, had been completed the year before. Starring Kirk Douglas and James Coburn, it had been filmed at Fort Edmonton and Drumheller. This project got underway with an AMPDC loan of $168,000, which was repaid within a few months. In 1984–85, $1.3 million in AMPDC loans were responsible for $17 million worth of production in Alberta. Several Ontario companies filmed here, with the required Alberta partner, and some were considering moving to Alberta, such as Robert Cooper Productions.

One of America's most prolific producers of television series, Stephen J. Cannell, attended the Banff Television Festival in 1984 to showcase his *Greatest American Hero* series, with stars William Katt and Robert Culp in tow. He was impressed with Alberta and said he would return one day with a film or a series. Cannell Productions was based on the Paramount Studios lot, and I called on them whenever I was in Hollywood. Stephen's impressive office had once belonged to Howard Hughes, and Stephen had added an authentic English pub to entertain guests.

Two Hollywood movies shot in Calgary in 1985 were linked together. Both were produced by Jack Schwartzman, a lawyer/producer who was married to Francis Ford Coppola's sister, Talia Shire—and Talia would have a starring role in both films.

Legendary stuntman Hal Needham of *Smokey and the Bandit* fame directed *Rad*, a BMX bike-racing film with Talia and Jack Weston. Meanwhile, Keenan Wynn and Talia starred in *Hyper Sapien: People from Another Star*, a story about two cuddly aliens befriended by a farm boy. The two shows weren't exactly classics of filmmaking, but they left about twelve million dollars in Alberta.

Three Alberta productions were also made that year with assistance from AMPDC. Wendy Wacko produced *The Climb* in Jasper and Pakistan, with director Don Shebib, and then she produced *Striker's Mountain* in Jasper, with actors Leslie Nielsen, Thomas Peacocke, and Francis Damberger. Ann Wheeler, with Dumbarton Films, made *Loyalties* in Lac La Biche with Susan Wooldridge, Kenneth Welsh, Tantoo Cardinal, and Tom Jackson. This was turning into Alberta's best year yet for film production.

Loyalties was important to Alberta film development because it was an Alberta story, an original screenplay by Wheeler and Sharon Riis, and it became a successful award-winning movie for Wheeler, helming her first feature film as director. From a film commission point of view, it proved the importance to the economy of a single motion picture. Almost two million dollars was spent directly in the community for hotels, meals, rentals, locations, and extras. I was frequently asked by Lac La Biche residents afterward, "When will we get another film here?"

With the success of Alberta's homegrown film industry, it wasn't long before other provinces wanted a bigger piece of the action. Ontario's minister of Citizenship and Culture, Lily Munro, told her legislature in October 1985 that she was forming an Ontario Film Development Corporation (OFDC), stating, "Ontario's position has slipped." Only six years earlier, Munro had told her colleagues that the province accounted for half of all production in Canada; by 1982, this had slipped to thirty-five per cent, costing Ontario an estimated five thousand jobs.

The OFDC came on stream in late 1985, with a twenty-million-dollar fund; it was able to invest in production, as well as provide pre-production assistance. Similar agencies were established in British Columbia and Manitoba. Other provinces would follow later, all with investment capability.

This wasn't exactly good news for our efforts in Alberta. One problem was that the Alberta Motion Picture Development Act contained a sunset clause, which called for the expiry of AMPDC on 31 March 1989. The Film Industry Study had not considered the possibility of copycat competition; AMPDC clearly needed a broader mandate, increased funding, and the ability to invest.

In 1986, Hugh Planche retired from politics when Peter Lougheed stepped down as premier. After the election, under the new premier, Don Getty, Larry Shaben became minister of Economic Development and Trade. He took a keen interest in film, planning to broaden the mandate of AMPDC, move its office to Edmonton, and, even though times were tough, seek another seven million dollars for the fund.

Stephen J. Cannell made good on the promise he made in Banff and sent an NBC television series, *Stingray,* to Calgary for filming in 1986. Cannell's vice-president, Steve Sassen, brought nineteen people from Hollywood and employed seventy Albertans. The action series starred Nick Mancuso. Warehouses were used for cover sets and for interior filming, but this show mostly required exterior shooting. This meant a move to Vancouver, after four months of Calgary production, when winter arrived.

Once settled on the coast, it was understandable why *Stingray* wouldn't return to Alberta. Why move twice a year? We would have to find a television series that could film in all of our seasons—most likely Canadian, and with AMPDC involvement.

By late 1986, AMPDC had forty projects in various stages of development, with budgets totalling about seventy million dollars. When they went into production, investment would come from other sources. At this point, AMPDC provided loans to develop projects—pre-production. This money had to be repaid when the film went into production.

In 1987, Andy Thomson and Patricia Phillips came to Edmonton from Toronto to form a partnership with Tom Radford. The company they founded, Great North Productions Ltd., would become one of the great success stories of film in Canada. Thomson had eighteen years experience with the National Film Board. Patricia Phillips, who would become his wife, was an actor, writer, and dramaturge. Tom Radford had worked with them during his ten years with the NFB in Edmonton. These three formed a dynamic group.

Their first project, *In Search of the Dragon*, was a ninety-six-minute film about an archaeological expedition to China's Gobi desert. AMPDC would ultimately invest $326,000 in the $1.3 million production, directed by Radford. It was an immediate success critically, and eventually financially, with sales to sixteen countries.

Their second film, *Life After Hockey*, also directed by Radford, had AMPDC participation for one-fifth of the half-million-dollar budget. The film told the story of an amateur hockey player's one shot at the big leagues and featured an appearance by hockey legend Maurice "Rocket" Richard. It garnered six AMPIA awards, including Best of Festival.

Great North's production efforts expanded in many directions, and Tom Radford found himself involved in administration, as well as filmmaking. But he was a filmmaker, and he left Great North amicably after about five years to return to directing.

Andy and Pat established Great North Releasing to market their films, and others, internationally. Not only were they enriched, so were other Alberta producers. During a ten-year period, with freelancers and a staff of twenty-eight, Great North produced 165 hours of documentary and dramatic television from their Edmonton base, resulting in tens of millions of dollars in revenue. Their output included high-profile TV series, such as *Destiny Ridge* (26 one-hour dramas), *Jake and the Kid* (twenty-six hours), and *Acorn, the Nature Nut* (91 half-hour episodes), and many more documentaries and educational programs. Great North Releasing succeeded in marketing Canadian programs to fifty-six countries around the world.

Destiny Ridge remains popular internationally in several languages. This was an Alberta/Canada/Germany co-production, a contemporary drama series about the community of Argent (played by Jasper), where four park wardens patrol and protect the wilderness area. The first season starred European film star Elke Sommer, who was an attraction for the German audience. She was replaced by Canadian Rebecca Jenkins in season two, I know not why. *Destiny Ridge* followed the lives and loves of the inhabitants of Argent, a place of intrigue, drama, and passion.

The Great North saga would not have happened without the Alberta Motion Picture Development Corporation. This alone would have made the AMPDC program one of the great success stories in government.

Film production in the late 1980s provided Albertans with jobs and pumped millions of dollars into the economy. In 1987, United Artists produced *Betrayed* near Lethbridge, directed by Costa-Gavras and starring Tom Berenger and Debra Winger. That same year, CBS made the first of several *Gunsmoke* reunion TV-movies, *Return to Dodge,* with the original TV cast, including James Arness and Amanda Blake, near Canmore (later installments would be shot in our western movie rivals: Texas, New Mexico, and Arizona). CBS also made the TV feature *Body of Evidence*, with *Superman*'s Margot Kidder, in Calgary. All told, these productions left about twenty million dollars in Alberta.

More important, there were several Canada/Alberta projects made that year, such as *The Gunfighters*, an Alliance production, ITV's *The Littlest Detective*, which was shot in the Allarcom studio in Edmonton, and Anne Wheeler's *Cowboys Don't Cry*, filmed near Calgary, with Arvi Liimatainen as producer.

One show that neither my office nor AMPDC was involved in listed

The Virgin Queen Of St. Francis High

(CANADIAN-COLOR)

A Crown Intl. Pictures release of a Pioneer Pictures production, in association with American Artists (Canada) Corp. Executive producer, Lawrence G. Ryckman. Directed, written and edited by Francesco Lucente. Camera (color), Joseph Bitonti, Kevin Alexander; editorial consultant, Rick Doe; incidental music, Danny Lowe, Brad Steckel, Brian Island; location sound, James F. Baillies; additional sound, Per Asplund; associate producer, Alex Tadich; assistant director, Anisa Lalani; casting, Olimpia Lucente, Angela Bitonti. Reviewed at the Egyptian Theater, L.A., Dec. 4, 1987. (MPAA Rating: PG.) Running time: 94 MINS.

Mike	Joseph R. Straface
Diane	Stacy Christensen
Charles	J.T. Wotton
Judy	Anna-Lisa Iapaolo
Randy	Lee Barringer
Diane's mother	Bev Wotton

Hollywood — When tradesters talk of a glut on the market, stuff like "The Virgin Queen Of St. Francis High" is of what they speak. Non-exploitative exploitationer from Canada possesses such shockingly subprofessional production values that members of the opening day audience in Hollywood cussed out the awful dubbing, and one rebellious soul asked all other patrons to join him as he stormed out to the lobby to demand a refund. Two did, the rest paid the price both in lost money and numbing boredom.

It must have been the opening scene that put the fellow in such a mutinous mood, since nothing quite so technically bad has been foisted upon unsuspecting audiences since the heyday of Yugoslavian-Italian-German coproductions of the 1960s.

On film that looks like it's been run through an automated cotton-picker, a nerdy guy bets the stud of the barroom $2,000 he'll get the stuck-up blond of the title out to Paradise Bungalows for a night of hanky panky by summer's end. Dialog and acting seem bad enough, but it's distractingly hard to tell since lines sound as if they were recorded on a battery-operated tape recorder in a phone booth with actors who didn't speak the same language as those onscreen.

Not only that, but throughout the picture there is virtually no ambient sound, only the dialog and a continuous background of inane and arbitrary rock music.

Clever directors sometimes can turn such liabilities into assets, but such is not the case with first-timer Francesco Lucente, who appears to have been aiming for a clean, respectable teenpic in this tale of a dimwitted guy trying to win the heart of a girl intent upon "saving" herself for marriage. Suffice to say the lady's honor, as well as the film's utter lack of talent and interest, remain intact at pic's end.

— Cart.

There were no kudos for made-in-Alberta *The Virgin Queen of St. Francis High* in this *Variety* review, published in 1987. Reprinted with permission.

Calgary's Lawrence G. Ryckman as executive producer—that's Larry Ryckman, one-time owner of the Calgary Stampeders football club. A *Variety* review of *The Virgin Queen of St. Francis High*, published on 9 December 1987, does not identify Alberta as its filming location. That's probably just as well.

Heaven and Alberta

Edmonton's Dr. Charles Allard, encouraged by the growth of the Alberta film industry and with production commitments in regular and pay TV, opened a state-of-the-art film and television studio in Edmonton in 1988. The federal government assisted with a two-million-dollar grant, arranged by MP Jim Edwards, another solid supporter of the Alberta film industry. The fourteen-hundred-square-metre Allarcom Studios sound stage, with offices, dressing rooms, and carpenter and paint shops, was then the largest in Canada and certainly the best. Its post-production facility, Studio Post and Transfer, was also Alberta's first. Dr. Allard and his family would invest more in the Alberta film industry than AMPDC. Dr. Allard's son Tony, a lawyer, became a film producer, and a good one.

During the Banff Television Festival in June 1988, Larry Shaben, the minister of Economic Development, announced the government was expanding AMPDC's mandate to enable it to invest in motion pictures. Seven million dollars would be added to the fund, the corporation would be moved to Edmonton, and the "sunset clause" would be eliminated, meaning it no longer had a 1989 expiry date.

Alberta, which had originated provincial assistance as an economic boost for film production, would now have to catch up with Ontario, British Columbia, and Manitoba, all of which had forged ahead by investing in films for several years.

In 1988, as AMPDC grew, there was considerable activity by Alberta film producers. Eda Lishman wrote, produced, and directed *Primo Baby*, starring Art Hindle, Janet-Laine Green, Jackson Cole, and Esther Purves-Smith. Calgary's West Sky Productions made two movies: *Personal Exemptions*, starring movie veteran Nanette Fabray, and *The Ranch,* featuring Andrew Stevens, which was directed by his mother, Stella Stevens. CBC produced *Getting Married in Buffalo Jump,* with future *Due South* star Paul Gross and Victoria Snow.

One of the biggest productions that year was *Bye Bye Blues.* Written and directed by Anne Wheeler, it was a continuation of her family history that had begun with the 1981 docudrama *A War Story,* which was based on her father's diaries as a Japanese prisoner in World War II. *Bye Bye Blues* tells the story of her mother's life as a "wartime widow," while her husband was serving overseas.

Bye Bye Blues starred Rebecca Jenkins, Michael Ontkean (later to star in *Twin Peaks*), Luke Reilly, Stuart Margolin, Kate Reid, and Francis Damberger and was produced by Arvi Liimatainen, with Tony Allard as executive producer. It was budgeted at $4.2 million, including some funding from AMPDC. An international production, part of the movie was filmed in India, part in Edmonton, and part in Rowley, Alberta.

The town of Rowley is located thirty-five kilometres north of Drumheller, via a quiet gravel road off Highway 56. Hundreds of cars pass by the junction every day, unaware of Rowley's existence. Tom Payne of Central Western Railroad, who had purchased a rail line through the area, was running a 1930s steam train as a tourist attraction, and he wondered if the combination had potential for film locations. It certainly did, as Murray Ord agreed when scouting for *Bye Bye Blues.*

Rowley had almost become a ghost town after the closure of the Canadian National Railway line years before. The station still existed, along with three grain elevators and a 1940s-style main street, which then served a population of sixteen. There were many vacant buildings and a service station still equipped with the old-style glass reservoir gasoline pumps.

Production designer John Blackie brought the town back to life with

Scene from *Bye Bye Blues*. The orchestra and the piano are on their way to a dance engagement. Actor Stuart Margolin is driving the truck, with Wayne Robson standing on the other side. Michael Ontkean and Rebecca Jenkins are seated in the back and Francis Damberger is standing, leaning on the piano. Photo: Douglas Curran

alterations, additions, and paint. The streets were dressed with period artifacts and antique automobiles. An impressive set resulted and was soon active. Residents enjoyed their time in the spotlight and erected a large billboard on a hill overlooking Highway 56, proclaiming their town to be Rowleywood.

Production of *Bye Bye Blues* then moved to Edmonton, becoming the first production to film in the new Allarcom Studio, where set construction had been underway for weeks. Its huge sound stage accommodated sets for a radio station, "Blitzers" ladies washroom, and five dance hall interiors. Other locations around Edmonton included the Princess Theatre on Whyte Avenue and the Seba Beach dance hall. Including studio time, production in Edmonton lasted about three weeks.

The next move for the production was halfway around the world, to India, where Anne and Arvi had scouted locations months previously. They now had to deal with a nightmare of complications, despite the local expertise they had engaged. *Bye Bye Blues* was the first Canadian movie to shoot in India, and it attracted large crowds in a country that has one of the most prolific film industries in the world.

Filming on a street in the city of Pune required two hundred extras, an elephant, two camels, a 1929 Austin convertible, and thirty-five water buffalo. It had been arranged for the streets to be closed, but crowd problems came from every direction, ruining many takes. It took police two hours to get a crowd under control, and to Anne's dismay they used their batons against the bystanders. Filming in India was completed within two weeks, and the team returned to Edmonton for post-production.

Bye Bye Blues received critical acclaim everywhere and a standing ovation at the Toronto Film Festival in 1989. It was nominated for a record thirteen Gemini Awards, and it is one of the best Canadian feature films of all time, in my view, and the only Canadian film to get a three-star review in *Playboy*.

Anne Wheeler has received more awards than any other Canadian female film director, including honorary degrees from six universities and the Order of Canada. Ever modest, Anne says, "A movie camera is no more complicated than a zigzag sewing machine. You don't need a penis to run it."

Bye Bye Blues, along with Anne's earlier productions—such as her first feature film, *Loyalties*, the television movie *Cowboys Don't Cry*, and her documentaries—are wonderful portrayals of Alberta and Albertans. Her films deserve to be considered as historical treasures of Alberta.

In the summer of 1989, Alberta hosted the largest film production ever mounted in Canada, when Japan's Kadokawa Productions began to film *Ten to Chi to* (*Heaven and Earth*) at Morley on the Stoney Indian Reserve, west of Calgary. Scouting for the project had begun two years earlier, and prominent independent Alberta film producer Doug MacLeod was engaged to work with the team.

Within ten days of the start of scouting, a suitable location was found on the Stoney Reserve, which closely resembled the site of the sixteenth-century Battle of Kawanakajima, on which *Heaven and Earth* is based. We were dealing with line-producer Takashi Ohashi, known to all as "Tak." He spoke and wrote excellent English and, among his many film accomplishments, he had been co-producer of the 1970 American/Japanese production of *Tora! Tora! Tora!* and production manager of Akira Kurosawa's acclaimed 1985 film *Ran*. Tak had

AN UNEXPECTED GLITCH

In 1988, a large American production confirmed it would be filming in Alberta. Preparations were underway when I received a phone call from the producer. The production's major star had just learned of the location and told them he could not work in Alberta because of a warrant there for his arrest.

Before becoming a big star, he had played a minor role in a film made in Banff. When confronted by an RCMP officer while intoxicated, he had punched out the Mountie and had been put in jail. The production company needed him to finish the picture and posted bail. He skipped, returning to Hollywood.

The issue was discussed with Alberta's attorney general, who provided a letter that stated: "There is no record of this alleged incident." The response from the actor was: "But is that Mountie still around?"

The answer being no, the show filmed here as planned, pumping about ten million dollars into the local economy or about several thousand times the likely fine that would have resulted from the brawl years earlier.

The actor was Don Johnson of *Miami Vice* fame; the film was called *Dead-Bang*.

also been a Zero fighter pilot in World War II and was shot down twice by the Americans. ("I never got to shoot anybody down!" he said.)

The production also scouted sites in China and Korea, but Tak and his group were impressed with Morley and with Doug, to the extent that they hired him as the Canadian production supervisor, which was a wise choice.

There would be many pre-production meetings over the next year, in Calgary, Morley, Edmonton, Los Angeles, Montreal, and Tokyo. Tak and I became friends, and I treasure a rare crew crest he gave me from *Tora! Tora! Tora!*

The executive producer and director of *Heaven and Earth*, Haruki Kadokawa, is one of Japan's leading film directors, its second-largest publisher, a renowned Haiku poet, and a Shinto priest, as well as being famous in Japan as an adventurer. At the time, Kadokawa was a slightly built, unassuming, forty-seven-year-old multi-millionaire, who followed the disciplined regimen of

Heaven and Earth, a huge Japanese production filmed in Alberta in 1989 on the Morley Reserve, employing more than four thousand Albertans. These mounted warriors are Alberta students, male and female, completely disguised with the masks and armour they are wearing. Photo: Chris Large

Shintoism, beginning every day with prayer and meditation. His staff credits him with phenomenal spiritual ability—to the point they claim he can stop a train with his willpower. He once sailed an outrigger canoe from Japan to Chile, and they say he ordered a fierce storm to desist, which it did.

Kadokawa is a man of great ideas, with the money to back them up. While working on *Heaven and Earth*, he was having a replica of the *Santa Maria* built in Spain at a cost of four million dollars. It was his intention to sail from Spain to America in 1992, the five-hundredth anniversary of Columbus's voyage, which he eventually did with a crew of twenty-one.

Pre-production planning was progressing well until we were informed that Tak had become seriously ill. The replacement producer questioned the merits of filming in far-away Alberta when there were possible locations nearer, in Korea. Doug MacLeod and I flew to Tokyo to once again stress the

141

Five thousand suits of armour were made for the *Heaven and Earth* production by Calgarian Wendy Partridge and her Momentum Design crew. Here they are stored on racks in the arena on the Morley Reserve, ready for action. Photo: Chris Large

advantages of shooting in Alberta. It was painstaking work, and we had to use an interpreter, but we succeeded. We then took the 250-kilometre-per-hour bullet train from Tokyo to Kyoto to visit Tak in the National Cancer Hospital. He was doing well after surgery. We would see him again in Alberta, but not during the filming.

MacLeod finalized his Alberta production team, and work commenced in earnest in 1988 under production manager Tom Dent-Cox. Wrangler John Scott began to deal with the daunting horse requirements for the film; 1,000 would be needed. The horse population around Calgary was about 30,000, none of them considered suitable for the production. To be historically correct, the horses had to stand sixteen hands high, with full manes and tails. John and his crew bought 700 wild and unbroken horses from all over Western Canada and the United States. Forty-seven cowboys were employed, bronco-busting for several months. Another 250 suitable horses, already broken, were also rented for

F&D SCENE CHANGES

F&D Scene Changes occupies the old Dominion Bridge plant in southeast Calgary, a huge workshop that is ideal for theatrical and motion-picture set construction. Movie sets for productions shooting in Alberta have been a mainstay in their twenty-year operation. Their expertise has become so well known that large volumes of work come from afar.

Sets for the New York and Toronto musical productions of *Show Boat,* as well as the numerous travelling versions of the show, were all made in F&D's plant.

One project handled by F&D that could not be built anywhere else was for the 2002 Harrison Ford submarine movie *K-19: The Widowmaker.* They had 165 people working six days a week to build the replica submarine, and twenty flat-deck trailers were required to transport the components to Toronto, where actual filming took place. If there had been an available facility in Alberta that was large enough to house the set, the movie would likely have been filmed here.

the filming. The movie set a world record for the highest number of saddled horses (800) ever used in one sequence for a motion picture.

After being broken, the wild horses used for *Heaven and Earth* were graded, with a brand on each left front hoof. An "A" horse could be ridden by anyone; "B" horses were assigned to experienced riders; "B-minus" horses were for professionals only.

Wendy Partridge, as wardrobe head, designed and supervised the production of five thousand suits of armour and costumes. The numbers were not intimidating to her; she had designed and manufactured the thousands of costumes for Calgary's 1988 Winter Olympics. Doug MacLeod had been supervising producer of the official film of the Calgary games, so both had learned much there that was valuable to dealing with the masses of extras in *Heaven and Earth.*

Calgary's F&D Scene Changes increased their staff from four to twenty-three as they began making weapons and building sets. They produced four

For over 20 years, F&D Scene Changes Ltd. has been internationally recognized for their creative talent in creating sets for film, theatre, and television. Their credits include *K-19 Widowmaker*, *Mystery Alaska*, *Lonesome Dove*, and *Shanghai Noon*. Photo: Bill Marsden

thousand lances, fifty-eight hundred swords with scabbards, and hundreds of muskets and bows and arrows. They built a fort on the Morley Reserve that occupied two hectares, surrounded by a moat with more than two million litres of water, tinted a lovely turquoise colour with vegetable dye.

Heaven and Earth had a Japanese and Canadian crew of four hundred, a large Japanese cast, and three thousand Alberta student extras. Ultimately, forty-one hundred Albertans would be employed, including five hundred Natives from Morley.

Haruki Kadokawa and I became well acquainted. When he first viewed the Morley location, Kadokawa said, "I like this land; let's buy it instead of rent-ing." He developed great respect for the Indians and became personally involved in negotiations with Stoney Chief John Snow. They were very com-patible, both being slow and thorough deal makers. When Chief Snow spoke of guards for the horse corrals, Kadokawa said that guards would not be required. Chief Snow said, "Mr. Marsden, did you not tell Mr. Kadokawa that Indians like to steal horses?" I replied, "If I had told him that, he wouldn't have believed it."

Before the beginning of filming, Kadokawa held a ceremony on the "battlefield." He flew in four Shinto priests and spiritual leaders of an Ainu Tribe from the island of Hokkaido in Japan. Key members of the film crew and the cast in their colourful sixteenth-century wardrobe were participants. Kadokawa, in his Shinto robes, and the other priests made offerings to the gods at a cedar altar.

Kadokawa explained through an interpreter: "We call upon the Gods of the Stoney Indians and the Rocky Mountains to help us make this film safely."

It was a memorable experience to enter the Chief Goodstoney Arena afterward and see stacks of weaponry and six 75-metre rows of costumes and armour hanging on racks, ready to go into battle—on schedule and all made in Alberta by Albertans.

Rehearsals on the battlefield with foot soldiers and rider sergeants last-ed four weeks, then another week was spent training massive numbers of extras, who had to be taught to move, fight, fall, and die like samurai warriors.

The filming of *Heaven and Earth* in Alberta began on 8 August 1989. Seven cam-era crews were provided with high platforms and a crane where they could be stationed. The battle scenes involved thousands of warriors on foot or horse-back, in red or black armour, and were fascinating to watch. Nothing of this magnitude had ever been filmed in Canada. The set was so vast and impressive, as were the warriors, it was hard to believe you were not five hundred years back in time.

Heaven and Earth is the story of a conflict between two sixteenth-century military heroes. The victor would shape the history of Japan. Kadokawa said it was his intention to make a movie that "was so real, when you cut the film it bleeds." The lead actors were two of Japan's most celebrated stars: Ken Watanabe and Masahiko Tsugawa. Watanabe was diagnosed with leukemia during the shoot and had to be replaced by stage actor Takaaki Enoki

(Watanabe would recover and in 2004 be nominated for a Best Supporting Actor Oscar for his role in the Tom Cruise film *The Last Samurai*). Many sequences that had been filmed in Japan with Watanabe would have to be reshot with the new actor, but fortunately only one Alberta scene was affected.

The production had many interesting sidelights. For example, eighteen interpreters were required to keep lines of communication running smoothly between Canadian and Japanese crew members. Another eighty people took care of the horses, who consumed twelve tonnes of hay and more than eleven thousand litres of water every day. Thirty-three of the horses, which had cost as little as five hundred dollars apiece before being broken, were flown from Calgary to Japan for additional filming, at a cost of five thousand dollars each.

There were two kitchens for cast and crew—one for the Japanese, one for the North Americans. By the end of the shoot, most North Americans were eating in the Japanese dining room, and most Japanese in the North American diner.

The majority of the samurai warriors were played by students, primarily from the Calgary area. Later, Kadokawa took twenty hand-picked young Albertans to Japan to help promote the film. They would appear in full costume and then remove their helmets and masks, revealing them to be blonde Caucasian females. It was a very effective promotion stunt!

Heaven and Earth's production team ultimately spent eighteen million dollars in Alberta—more than what several single productions combined would normally spend.

Haruki Kadokawa was back in Calgary the following year to debut a specially created English version of the film. Hosting a lavish party, he thanked cast, crew, and the citizens of Calgary for "my most happy experience." He privately presented me with a gold medal bearing the Kadokawa crest and said it was the second one he had ordered made. "The first one I gave last week to the King of Spain," he said.

By 1989, the upscale Phipps-McKinnon Building in downtown Edmonton had become the new home of the Alberta Motion Picture Development Corporation (AMPDC). The sixth-floor offices, in natural finished oak, were a far cry from the old walk-up in Canmore.

It had become a high-profile agency that was now directly under the noses of government and bureaucrats, and it was inevitable that an uneasy

JOHN SCOTT—CANADIAN STUNT PERFORMER

John Scott is renowned in the Canadian film industry as a stunt performer, supervisor, and production manager. As a horse wrangler, he is acclaimed internationally. Few, if any, have equalled his accomplishments.

Director Haruki Kadokawa planned to make the horses fall during the battle scenes of *Heaven and Earth* by actually tripping them. To the director's amazement, John had horses and riders trained to fall on cue. There were no injuries during the massive cavalry charges. John has never caused injury to a horse. He resigned as wrangler for Michael Cimino's big 1980 western, *Heaven's Gate*, because of the director's lack of concern for the safety of horses.

Many dangerous stunts involve horses and use tricks that were developed in the early days of moviemaking. A rider falling out of the saddle and being dragged, with his foot apparently caught in the stirrup, is a cute trick. A leather strap is firmly attached to the stirrup and threaded up the stuntman's trouser leg, where he holds onto it. This eliminates strain on his leg, and he is able to let go if it becomes dangerous.

Seeing someone holding onto the reins and being dragged by a team of horses is scary to watch, but actually the actor is wearing a ski, much like a small snowboard, strapped to his stomach. The camera can then be "under cranked" to make the action look faster than it really is.

In his thirty-five-year career, John has serviced productions around the world and doubled in stunts with horses or for fight scenes for actors such as Paul Newman, Burt Lancaster, Kirk Douglas, and Gene Hackman. John was the founder of Canada's professional organization, Stunts Canada, and hosts a popular television show, *John Scott's World of Horses*.

Scott was once hired to supervise a stunt for a western called *Samuel Lount*, which was being filmed in Ontario. A horse and rider were to jump through the window of a burning store.

"No problem," said John.

The usual procedure is a careful choice of animal, then several hours of training—first jumping the horse through a bare window frame, then doing so again with strips of plastic hanging from the frame. The eventual fire and "glass" will be a surprise to the animal, but success is inevitable. This stunt is considered impossible to do any other way, unless you happen to have a blind horse. (continued on page 148)

JOHN SCOTT—CONT.

Upon arrival in Toronto, John was told there was no time for training. The stunt would have to be performed the next day.

The store, on the main street of a western town, was a long building. John had sheets of plywood laid to cover a length of floor in front of a candy glass window mounted in a balsa wood frame. The plywood was covered with grease, then sand.

Horse and rider entered at the rear of the building. Once the cameras were ready, the fire pots were lit. "Action!" was called and the horse spurred. When it saw the "glass" in front of it, the animal put on the brakes, skidding through the window onto the main street, unharmed.

"Just another day's work," said John.

relationship would develop. AMPDC had requested a substantial boost in operational funding during a year of restraint in government, but received only a modest increase, the powers that be asking it to "bear with us."

This did not sit well with AMPDC, which announced it was "cutting back on programs and curtailing new investment." This was considered not only unco-operative, but also unreasonable. The fund, now at ten million dollars, had not been affected.

Later in 1989, a complaint written by the president of AMPDC was directed at my office by way of a memo to the deputy minister. "We have felt a movement in your department to shorten our arm's-length relationship," the memo read. "Our operating funds have gone from a grant to a line item in the film division's operational budget without consultation or even formal advisement."

Actually, the AMPDC operating grant had always been in my budget, and I had supported its escalation from $224,176 in 1982–83 to $468,000 in 1989–90. I had joined the government in 1981 to set up the corporation and had been AMPDC's supporting voice in government ever since.

Politics aside, 1989 was another eventful year for film production in the province. Hollywood's John Frankenheimer, who had directed *Dead-Bang* here the year before, came back to Calgary with another feature film, *The Fourth War,* starring Roy Scheider, Jurgen Prochnow, and Harry Dean Stanton. England's BBC made a TV movie, *The Reflecting Skin,* in Calgary and Airdrie, with Les Kimber as production manager. In Edmonton, Allarcom Studio was occupied with a major TV miniseries, *Small Sacrifices,* starring Farrah Fawcett, Ryan O'Neal, and Tommy Banks. Great North Production's *Tom Alone* was filmed near Banff, and was directed by Randy Bradshaw; it starred Hollywood's Ned Beatty and Nick Mancuso, as well as Albertans Bill Meilen, Paul Coeur, and Walter Kaasa.

On 7 November 1989, AMPDC president Lorne MacPherson, addressing filmmakers and the press in Calgary, blasted the policies of Telefilm Canada and criticized the Alberta government for not spending enough to advertise filming in the province. The latter was my responsibility, and I was annoyed.

It was a year of reduced budgets and I had been faced with the choice of eliminating our foreign representatives—Gerry Smith in Los Angeles and Frank Poole in England—or my advertising budget. I chose to eliminate the advertising budget. It is impossible to determine advertising effectiveness, but I knew very well what Smith and Poole were accomplishing, which involved answering inquiries about Alberta, calling on the producers they knew with Alberta film literature, and responding to tasks that I assigned them.

The provincial Departments of Economic Development and Federal and Intergovernmental Affairs were also perturbed at MacPherson's remarks, perceiving more damage to a deteriorating relationship with Telefilm and the federal government. There seemed to be no concern on the part of the AMPDC executive that, with the word "Alberta" in its corporate title, anything said or done by it would reflect on the government. Bureaucrats were urging action. One senior bureaucrat suggested that AMPDC be abolished and its function moved directly into the Department of Economic Development.

With my own retirement looming on the horizon, I believed it was time to acquire an assistant-cum-successor, and I had several prospects in mind. Larry Shaben, the minister of Economic Development and Tourism, decided not to run in the 1990 provincial election, and he asked me to consider his executive assistant, Lindsay Cherney, as my successor. After careful consideration, this seemed to be a very good idea.

Lindsay is one of the most capable people I know. She was the person I dealt with in the minister's office when heavy-duty help was required. My needs—usually urgent, often strange, and always challenging—were dealt with immediately and successfully. With many years experience as an executive assistant to a senior cabinet minister, she was known and respected at all levels in government. She knew the province well and would have almost three years before my scheduled retirement to learn about filmmaking and to meet with Albertans in the business, as well as key individuals in world film centres. It seemed likely that the main problem facing our film industry in the future would be the life or death of AMPDC. I believed that Lindsay's experience, resourcefulness, and influence would be invaluable.

Peter Elzinga became the new minister after the election. Lindsay, with her extensive knowledge of the department, was assigned temporarily as his executive assistant. It would be months before she joined me full time in the Film Industry Development office, with the title of Manager, Cultural Industries. The job description predated AMPDC and included association with the recording industry, job printing, publications, and the graphic arts industry, as well as with film. AMPDC claimed she was invading their turf.

Advertising in Economic Development was supervised by the department's director of Public Affairs, reviewed by the minister, and then turned over to an advertising agency for placement. Minister Elzinga was fastidious about advertising. AMPDC had enjoyed complete freedom in this area but, in co-operation with a group of film companies, was about to place an ad the minister didn't like. He ordered it cancelled. I don't know how it came to his attention, nor do I recall the content of the advertisement, except that I too considered it to be in poor taste.

The minister requested that future advertising be cleared through the director of Public Affairs; AMPDC considered this a major intrusion into its autonomy, but the minister was adamant. Shortly after, AMPDC announced it "could no longer afford to advertise" and shut down its Calgary office "because of budget restrictions," even though this office had been provided free of charge by Economic Development Calgary. The minister assumed the AMPDC board had approved these provocations. The resignation of a board member, coupled with two other terms expiring, including that of the chairman, enabled Elzinga to appoint three new board members, including Lindsay Cherney "to represent the department."

Understandably, AMPDC president Lorne MacPherson viewed her appointment as the elimination of the corporation's last vestige of independence.

He advised that unless the autonomy of the corporation was restored, he could no longer perform the job he had been hired to do. He resigned on 31 July 1990, Lindsay Cherney became president, and Garry Toth, who had been an extremely competent vice-president, became general manager. New board member Douglas Shillington was appointed chairman.

By December 1990, AMPDC had provided $4.6 million worth of equity investment in twenty film and video projects. This included seven theatrical films, two drama series, five TV movies-of-the-week, two television information series, a one-hour TV drama, and three documentaries. This $4.6 million investment had triggered $30.7 million in private and out-of-province investment. Nearly all of this activity originated during Lorne MacPherson's presidency, under the chairmanship of Orv Kope. Six of these films and videos were nominated in thirty-four categories and received sixteen awards at the Emmy and Gemini Awards and at international award presentations in New York, Houston, and Seattle. There was still money left in the fund.

Unforgiven

In the early 1980s, Les Kimber and I were in Los Angeles, visiting Charlton Heston at his Coldwater Canyon hilltop estate. Les had been production manager on the Heston film *Mother Lode,* which had just finished shooting in Canada.

During our visit, Chuck, as the one-time *Ten Commandments* star likes to be called, took a phone call from his friend, Clint Eastwood, who was in the middle of making the action film *Firefox* and wanted to know if there were lakes in Canada that would still be frozen at that time of year—it was early spring. Photographs of Alberta's solidly iced Waterton Lake were in the hands of David Valdes at Clint's Malpaso Productions three days later. They liked the location. Learning that it would be only a two-day shoot and recalling that the Canada–US border runs through the middle of the lake, I suggested they film on the American side; it would be simpler. They were appreciative of the idea.

It was the summer of 1991, nearly ten years later, when I next heard from David Valdes.

"You did Clint and me a favour," he said. "We have a film that might work in Alberta. I'll get a script to you and come up next week for a look."

The film was to be called *Unforgiven.*

Murray Ord was engaged to scout the picture. He showed possible locations to David Valdes, who returned a week later with Clint Eastwood in a Warner Brothers Gulfstream jet. By pre-arrangement, Immigration boarded the aircraft to clear Clint and David into Canada, allowing them to step directly onto the government Bell 222 helicopter parked alongside on the tarmac. With talent of this magnitude, you don't waste a minute of their time. Clint is a licenced helicopter pilot. I discussed this with our aviation department, and government aero mechanics installed an extra set of controls in the Bell. Clint was given the right-hand "pilot in command" seat, with our pilot, Roger Tessier, on the left.

Within a couple of hours, a site was found for the fictional town of Big Whiskey, southwest of High River on the EP Ranch, which was once owned by Edward, Prince of Wales, and was now the property of the John Cartwright family.

Scouting continued all the way to the Crowsnest Pass and Waterton. Our pilot radioed the Warner Brothers jet in Calgary to have it meet the helicopter in Lethbridge, and it was there within twenty minutes. Clint and David boarded the Gulfstream and were back home in California in time for their evening meals after seeing more of Alberta than many Albertans get a chance to see in a year.

Ord worked out an agreement with the Cartwrights, but had to turn down the position of location manager for *Unforgiven* because of a verbal commitment he had made to another local production. Executive producer Valdes was disappointed, but very impressed with Murray's commitment; such fidelity is rare in the film industry, and he vowed to work with Ord on future projects.

Unforgiven was, by any reckoning, a major studio project. Its importance became evident when Warner Brothers sent not one but two of its vice-presidents to Calgary to check us out. Renting the boardroom at an airport hotel, I set up meetings with unions, sat in on the negotiations, and answered inquiries in other areas. It was a lengthy but cordial session, and Alberta received the green light—*Unforgiven* was on its way.

The town of Big Whiskey was created by Henry Bumstead, the Oscar-winning production designer of such classics as *To Kill a Mockingbird* and *The Sting*. It was built by Calgary's F&D Scene Changes, in what "Bummy" said was a record forty-three days.

Production of the film was underway immediately (the last week of August) at the relatively remote and restricted location, with visitors by invitation

The 1991 town of "Big Whiskey" was built on the Cartwright ranch, (formerly the EP Ranch of Edward, Prince of Wales.) southwest of Calgary, for the Clint Eastwood movie *Unforgiven*. It was a remote site chosen personally by Clint, by surveying with a government helicopter. The town was built in forty-three days. A surprise September snowfall that lasted only two days was worked into the story by Clint. *Unforgiven* was nominated for nine Oscars and received four. Photo: Bill Marsden

only. One day I toured the set with Al MacDonald, the deputy minister of Alberta Economic Development and Tourism, and his wife, June; we had left our car in the main camp to board a horse-drawn buggy that took us into the town, where modern tire tracks were not allowed. Big Whiskey was a cluster of about twenty one- and two-storey buildings, with the majestic Rocky Mountains to the west. The view was unobstructed in all directions. The main camp, where we had left our car, was hidden by trees.

Every building on the set had a dual function. Valdes settled us in the town's drug store where craft services provided coffee and pastries. We were soon joined by actor Gene Hackman, wearing his costume of Sheriff Little Bill Daggett, which was covered in fake blood because Clint had just shot him. After

Main Street of Big Whiskey, the site of *Unforgiven*, 1991. Many of the buildings had a dual function: the drugstore contained "craft services," a high-class coffee shop for cast and crew, for instance. Other buildings were used for functions like equipment storage and wardrobe. The agreement with the owner of the Cartwright ranch called for the complete removal of the town and for the site to be restored within thirty days after completion of filming. Photo: Bill Marsden

an entertaining discussion, he left for wardrobe as we moved to the hotel next door where filming was underway. The main floor was crowded with cast, crew, and equipment. Clint exchanged pleasantries with us before returning to directing. He would also be acting in the lead role of William Munney.

Director of photography Jack Green had been with Clint on twenty-one previous pictures. They both believe in dark images with rim lighting. On average, eighty per cent of an Eastwood film is backlit, and Jack is a master of the art. Green delivered exposure information to the operator, and his assistant set the T-stop on the Panavision camera.

We heard, "Camera Ready!" "Sound Ready!" Then Clint said "Roll 'em," stepped in front of the camera in character as Will Munney, and quietly said "Let's go" as the film's final shootout began (Clint doesn't call "Action").

As a director, Clint Eastwood had impressed the industry with his memorable 1976 film *The Outlaw Josey Wales* and the many others that followed. In *Unforgiven*, David Webb Peoples's script did not indicate Will Munney's friend Ned was black, and as cast by Clint and played by Morgan Freeman, this made a major contribution to the film.

Few directors move as swiftly and surely as Clint, even if he's also playing a role in the film. Most of the crew had also worked with him on twenty or more pictures—they operate smoothly and quietly as a team. Clint never raises his voice, and more than one take of a scene on his watch is rare. If a rehearsal is requested, he typically films the event. During the *Unforgiven* shoot, even a surprise snowstorm was not allowed to disrupt the schedule. Clint simply worked it into the story.

Horses were once again cast by wrangler John Scott. This process is much like casting an actor, and Clint's horse presented a problem. An intelligent animal with a pleasant disposition was required, yet it had to be scruffy looking in keeping with Will Munney's poverty-stricken circumstances. Scott finally found the perfect horse on the Hobbema Indian Reserve, made the purchase, then trained it for a scene early in the film where Clint has difficulty mounting. This is an amusing sequence and, to me at least, the horse steals the show—much like Lee Marvin's drunken horse in *Cat Ballou*.

John Scott later told me that not only did the horse have to act, but it also had to endure being scrubbed down frequently. Clint's eyes water and his throat becomes constricted if his mount is not squeaky clean. Incredible as it may sound, given his decades of western movie experience, Clint Eastwood is allergic to horses!

Executive producer David Valdes was another Eastwood veteran, having made seventeen pictures with Clint. But even on his own, he has enjoyed great success, including the Oscar-nominated *The Green Mile*. David is a "details" man, on top of every situation. He is honest and direct, which are not common virtues in the business. He is also one of the nicest film executives it was my pleasure to work with. I was even given an unprecedented "thank you" credit on *Unforgiven*.

Unforgiven, released in 1992, became one of the most successful films—

PARKING IN EASTWOOD'S SPOT

Obtaining "drive-on" permission at a Hollywood studio is considered an honour. Finding a place to park on the lot is a nightmare. Empty spaces have name signs, reserved for VIP producers, directors, and actors.

Clint Eastwood's offices are in a building at the Burbank Studios. David Valdes told me during a visit one day that I could park in Clint's spot, since he was away.

I asked, "How far away?"

"Hawaii."

So I parked in the space marked "Clint Eastwood," well aware that he had once found a car parked in his spot and reputedly used a tire iron to smash the headlights of the offending vehicle.

financially and critically—to ever be produced in Alberta. In 1993, it was nominated for nine Academy Awards. It received four Oscars, the coveted Best Picture and Best Director awards, Best Editor for Joel Cox, and Best Supporting Actor for Gene Hackman.

Bummy Bumstead was nominated for his production design, and I received a letter from him: "I'm so happy for Jan Blackie-Goodine, Rick Roberts, and all the wonderful Albertans involved with the project. What a wonderful crew. They are the ones who made my nomination possible." These individuals and other craftspeople fill key positions during the production of foreign films in Alberta, positions that once employed only imported talent. Clint Eastwood, impressed by their work, commissioned Edmonton's Don Metz and his Aquila Productions to produce a video about the making of *Unforgiven*. Some of this footage is included in the DVD release of the film.

As for the fictional town of Big Whiskey, it experienced a strange aftermath following the departure of the film crews. The agreement with ranch owner John Cartwright called for removal of the town within thirty days of completion of filming and the site restored to its original condition. A Calgary promoter persuaded a local millionaire to purchase the town and relocate it as a haven for street kids. The town set was dismantled and moved to a location on the Bow River about thirty-two kilometres downstream from Calgary, but the responsible municipality would not rezone the land. Moving the town to yet another property caused more damage to construction elements, and zoning was once again refused.

Most of Big Whiskey, the setting for one of the most successful western movies ever, ended up in a large bonfire.

Intermission
—The Gamblers

Before and after my retirement from "show business," I always had a fascination and an ongoing interest in the history of Alberta filmmaking. Looking back, I feel the most significant factors in the development of a film industry in Alberta have been the ability and the commitment of individual artists and business people.

The first movie to be made in Alberta, a "one-reeler" called *An Unselfish Love*, was shot at Strathmore in 1910. It was made by the Edison Company of New York for the Canadian Pacific Railway (CPR). Many forgettable black and white American feature films were made in the province over the next several decades, including *Calgary Stampede* in 1925.

Alberta's first homegrown film studio was set up in Calgary in 1918, on the corner of 7 Avenue and 4 Street SW. The *Calgary Herald* called the Imperial Film Company of Canada, "a complete motion picture plant, the most progressive in Canada."

Imperial's first production, in 1918, was made for Calgary troops overseas. The movie opened with general views of Calgary, then a procession of seven hundred automobiles travelling four abreast down 7 Avenue, en route to St. George's Island for a family picnic and Victory Bond drive. The movie was advertised as "the first film to be made in Calgary with Calgary people as artists, and produced by a Calgary firm." The *Herald* printed the first hometown film review: "The picture was excellent and very well received."

In 1919, another film company was established in Calgary—Canadian Photoplay Ltd.—to produce theatrical motion pictures based on the novels of James Oliver Curwood. Businessmen in Calgary and Edmonton were investors —or gamblers, if you like. Their first film was made in northern Alberta on Lesser Slave Lake, in the dead of winter. It was called *Back to God's Country* and starred Nell Shipman.

Severe minus-forty-degree weather and other problems were encountered, and actor Ronald Byram ended up in an Edmonton hospital, where he died of pneumonia. Despite this setback, the film was a smash hit and made money. The company subsequently announced it would be building a "substantial studio in Calgary," but its second film, *The Yellowbacks*, was a failure, and it went into voluntary bankruptcy in 1920. The studio's investors had lost their gamble.

Hollywood made many silent black and white movies in Calgary, including the locally financed *His Destiny* in 1928, but no permanent studio facilities were established in the city at that time.

Early Alberta movie pioneers included Bill Oliver, a CPR cameraman based in Calgary, who filmed much of the province in thirty-five-millimetre black and white for newsreels in the 1920s and 1930s. The availability of sixteen-millimetre colour film in the 1940s inspired a few still photographers, including Calgary's Harry Pollard, Jr., and Edmonton's Alfred Blyth, to experiment with filmmaking. Their movie work was "MOS" (mit out sound), as they say in Hollywood.

Colour and sound sixteen-millimetre motion picture production in Alberta began with the government's Film and Photographic Branch in 1949. Some who learned the craft there later established private-sector film companies.

Those who leap into thirty-five-millimetre theatrical motion picture production are a special breed of risk takers and gamblers. Feature films made in Alberta provide employment for a large number of performers and craftspeople, but they have only a remote possibility of recouping their investment, since distribution is a Hollywood monopoly.

Alberta film pioneer Larry Matanski, who produced the features *Wings of Chance* in 1959 and *Naked Flame* in 1963, was a born gambler. Fil Fraser, following a successful career as a producer of educational films, became a gambler by entering the feature film "casino" in 1976 with *Why Shoot the Teacher?* His *Marie Ann* followed in 1977 and *Hounds of Notre Dame* in 1980. Fraser did not take a producer's fee up front, and violated another Hollywood principle by investing money of his own. He took a real beating and, like Matanski, became disillusioned with motion picture production—but that didn't stop him from creating some memorable films.

Mark Schoenberg, Jaron Summers, and those behind the scenes of the 1979 feature *Parallels* were also gamblers. This high school coming-of-age picture originated with Mark leaving the University of Alberta, where he taught drama, and teaming up with Jaron, who was a freelance writer. The producer of the film was a Grande Prairie anaesthetist, Dr. Jack Wynters, who had worked with Mark in live theatre. The movie was directed by Schoenberg, received mixed reviews, and did not recover costs. Nonetheless, it was a valuable experience for the participants, many of whom remain members of the Alberta film community. Jaron and Mark both moved on in the business. Jaron went on to a Hollywood writing career, which included penning episodes of *Miami Vice* and *Star Trek: The Next Generation*, as well as two feature films and five novels. Mark teaches and directs in Toronto.

The big screen continues to be a magnet, attracting another generation of Alberta film pioneers-cum-gamblers, perhaps because of the giant images, the captive audience, or the dream of big box-office returns. Participation by governments has made it easier.

Calgary's Bruce Harvey has produced twelve features with Alberta actors and other performers. Several of his movies have been international co-productions, including the award-winning Canada/Italy co-production of *Almost America*. David Winning of Calgary, a writer/director, made several films with Bruce, as well as producing two of his own.

Wendy Hill-Tout made *The Perfect Man*, with Phyllis Diller, and Wendy's company, Voice Pictures, recently brought the high-profile TV movie *Jackie Collins' Hollywood Wives: The New Generation* to film in Calgary, starring

Farrah Fawcett and Melissa Gilbert. Tofield's Francis Damberger, with his Damberger Film and Cattle Company Inc. (so named as "an ode to his rural Alberta roots"), is an auteur filmmaker, writer, producer, director, and actor, with several successful feature-film ventures under his belt, including his brilliant creations *Solitaire* and *Road to Saddle River.*

Television and video are the big markets of today, with their own share of gamblers. With the arrival of the five-hundred-channel universe, Canadian and international networks are seeking an almost endless supply of TV series, movies, and documentaries to fill their schedules. Videos and DVDs are also a large market.

The late Larry Shorter, after retiring as chief executive officer of ACCESS TV, produced a 1985 television series, *Bush Pilots*, in Edmonton, which was based on true flying adventures. Another series for a teenaged audience, a talk show entitled *Connections*, was made in Calgary in 1985 by Helene White and Garry Toth, with AMPDC (Alberta Motion Picture Development Corporation) assistance.

The Little Vampire, shot in Edmonton's Allarcom Studios in 1986, was a British/German/Canadian co-production, with Allarcom as the Canadian partner. It starred Gert Fröbe, who will be forever remembered as one of the great James Bond villains in *Goldfinger*, and Michael Gough, known to the youth of today as Alfred the butler in the *Batman* movies of the 1980s and 1990s. *The Ray Bradbury Theatre*, the science-fiction anthology TV series, subcontracted three years of production to Alberta companies, and in 1992, one of these companies, Alberta Filmworks, began shooting the drama *North of 60*, which continued for six years and ninety episodes.

Great North Productions started filming the adventure-drama *Destiny Ridge* in Jasper in 1992; Great North also produced a TV series adaptation of W. O. Mitchell's *Jake and the Kid* in Edmonton in 1995.

Mentors, a science-fiction series for youth created by Josh Miller and co-produced with Margaret Mardirossian, has been filming at Allarcom Studios since 1997. It is about the adventures of a young brother and sister who inherit a time machine that enables them to bring historical figures (like Einstein or Galileo) into their twenty-first-century lives to help solve problems. This show has been sold in sixty-eight countries so far, and 2004 is scheduled to be its final season, with sixty-five episodes completed.

Mardirossian's Anaid Productions, meanwhile, has produced thirty-nine episodes of a tongue-in-cheek travelogue called *The Tourist* and twenty-six episodes to date of *Taking it Off*, a reality series about weight loss. The latter show is currently in production for another season. *Caitlin's Way*, a teen drama series made in Calgary by Helene White, was picked up by the Nickelodeon cable network in the United States.

Alberta Filmworks produced twenty-six episodes of their original crime series *Tom Stone* in 2002. For once, Calgary actually played Calgary in this short-lived but well-received show, rather than doubling for New York, Los Angeles, or some other American centre. The series starred Chris Martin and Janet Kidder.

When they aren't producing TV series about troubled teens and police detectives, Albertans also continue to excel in the type of film that first put many regional filmmakers on the map decades ago—the documentary.

Edmonton's Albert Karvenon became one of the world's leading wildlife film producers in 1975, after leaving his position as a school principal to pursue professionally what had up until then been a hobby. Karvenon Films is now a multi-million-dollar operation, with substantial permanent staff, which also employs dozens of freelance cameramen worldwide. To date, the company has made 110 films, which are seen on television and sold as packaged videos in sixty-five countries.

Documentary production companies abound in Alberta. Pioneers in this area include Calgary's Bob Willis, now retired, with hundreds of credits over forty-five years. Edmonton's Denny Ranson, also retired, made dozens of industrial movies worldwide for a variety of clients over a forty-year period. Pioneer television producer Douglas Hutton is still very active. Over the past thirty years, he has accumulated 270 TV credits, producing music shows with world famous artists and television specials with international superstars. A dedicated naturalist, he donates distribution revenues from his high-definition TV production *This Living World* to a trust fund for environmental education.

Tom Radford and Dale Phillips are award-winning filmmakers with an impressive National Film Board of Canada background. Radford writes and directs subjects of international significance and has received many awards from the seventy-some documentaries he has made. Phillips, who has written and directed as well, works most frequently now as a producer of both documentaries and features. He is a pillar of the Alberta film community, devoting much of his time to industry causes.

Another multi-million-dollar operation is Calgary's White Iron, founded by Lance Mueller and Jean Merriman in 1990. It has four divisions, with a full-time staff in excess of thirty. They produce corporate videos, TV commercials, and television movies and series, including twenty-six episodes of *John Scott's World of Horses*. White Iron Digital is one of Canada's fastest-growing and most technically advanced post-production facilities. Meanwhile, Pyramid Productions in Calgary, with a twenty-year record of success in low-cost, high-quality production, was named Entrepreneur of the Year by Ernst & Young in 2003.

Resources that entice foreign companies to film in Alberta consist of more than our low dollar and alluring scenery. Well-qualified craftspeople and performers are also an attraction. Production managers like Edmonton's Doug Steeden and Calgary's Grace Gilroy, with proven big-budget reputations, are indispensable. Wendy Partridge is known internationally as an artist in wardrobe creation. Her Calgary-based Momentum Design Company is a multi-million-dollar operation, with extensive ready-to-wear wardrobe.

Renowned wrangler John Scott is also a provider of horses, wagons, and carriages. Combined with his Longview ranch and western town set, his operation is a very big business. Art director John Blackie has impressive credits, as does Rick Roberts in the same category.

Calgary photographer Chris Large, who specializes in motion picture stills, is much in demand. Once a film sound recordist, Chris was nominated for an Academy Award for his work on 1978's *Superman,* as well as for the British equivalent award, and he was nominated for an Emmy for 1980's *Amber Waves.*

Alberta is kept in the news by another of our assets, Calgarian Linda Kupecek, who writes for international motion picture publications like the *Hollywood Reporter* and *Screen International.* Linda is a noted actress, book author, script writer, and a director of AMPIA.

When selling the advantages of location filming in Alberta, we always stressed the capability of our craftspeople and performers. They never failed to live up to expectations.

The Alliance of Canadian Cinema Television and Radio Artists had seventy Alberta members in 1980. There were 659 active Alberta members in 2003.

The Alberta District Council of the Directors Guild of Canada provides directors, production managers, accountants, production designers, art department, location managers, and editors, including assistants and trainees. The Alberta District Council wasn't formed until 1982, and its active membership has increased from a very few to 220 in 2003. There are also about two hundred who work on permits.

The International Alliance of Theatrical and Stage Employees (IATSE) is the union representing the majority of film craftspeople, including electrical, grips, property, costume design, continuity, craft services, construction, makeup, hair styling, and special effects. Edmonton Local 210 and Calgary Local 212 have increased their combined Alberta membership from 249 in 1980 to 1,069 in 2003; not included are those who work on permits and camera crew who come under the jurisdiction of a Vancouver IATSE Local.

The many film industry professionals in Alberta continue to do this province proud in these major organizations.

The Alberta Motion Picture Industries Association (AMPIA) is *the* advocate for film in Alberta. It has garnered the attention and respect of governments, both federal and provincial. Many AMPIA members, although largely self-employed in a highly competitive business, have devoted much of their time to benefit the overall industry.

Some have received a coveted award named after a staunch supporter, the late *Edmonton Sun* entertainment columnist David Billington. To quote AMPIA: "This is an honour bestowed annually on individuals in recognition of outstanding dedication and contribution to the film and television industry in Alberta."

Many of my colleagues and friends have been honoured with the David Billington Award, including Fil Fraser, John Scott, and Les Kimber. In 1994, after my career in promoting Alberta filmmaking had drawn to a close, I was honoured to become part of this illustrious group.

DAVID BILLINGTON AWARD RECIPIENTS

1989: Thomas Peacocke, University of Alberta drama professor and award-winning actor

1990: Fil Fraser, pioneer feature filmmaker

1991: Albert Karvenon, wildlife film producer

1992: Dr. Charles Allard, investor and ITV founder

1993: Les Kimber, pioneer film production manager

1994: Bill Marsden, pioneer filmmaker, AMPIA past-president, yours truly

1995: Carrie Hunter, thirteen-year director of Banff Television Festival and industry supporter

1996: Jan Miller, founder of Local Heroes, now the Edmonton Film Festival

1997: Arvi Liimatainen, pioneer filmmaker and AMPIA past-president

1998: Bruce Nelson, CFCN-TV executive and champion of Alberta production

1999: Anne Wheeler, pioneer filmmaker and industry supporter

2000: Andy Thomson, pioneer filmmaker and AMPIA past-president

2001: John Scott, pioneer in several areas and staunch industry supporter

2002: Nick Zubko, pioneer and AMPIA's first president (posthumous)

2003: Fred Keating, producer, actor, writer, and for twenty-one years the host of the Alberta Film and Television Awards

John Scott, renowned Canadian stunt performer, supervisor, and production manager.

THE TWO-MILLION-DOLLAR COMMERCIAL

Television commercials are big business for Alberta. Commercial produc-ers can spend more money per minute of film production than Hollywood features.

Alberta's first six-figure, sixty-second TV commercial was made on Lake Kananaskis in 1987 for the French automobile maker Peugot.

The opening scene shows a red Peugot car, suspended beneath a parachute emblazoned with the car model identification, 205 GT1, descending into our Rocky Mountains. A sleek fighter jet screams into frame and fires a missile that explodes the parachute canopy. The car drops about thirty metres onto a frozen lake!

After the car lands, we see it is occupied by a tuxedo-wearing, James Bond type, who now drives the car at high speed across the ice. A huge four-engine aircraft, dead black in colour, flies into the scene, straight at the camera. It almost scrapes the roof of the car before dropping a clus-ter of parachute bombs in front of it. Explosions burst all around the Peugot as it weaves in and out, barely avoiding them, one after the other, before finally escaping onto a mountain road.

We cut to the interior of the Banff Springs Hotel where a lovely lady waits. The car skids to a snow-flying stop, and our debonair hero emerges.

The lady says, in French, "You're late, James." He replies, "The roads were treacherous."

Why did this mini-epic cost almost two million dollars? There was only one privately owned Hercules aircraft in Canada available to rent. It was flown to Calgary, stripped of all markings, and then painted flat black to give it a really villainous appearance.

Five identical Peugot cars were flown over from France for the shoot. Oil-bearing parts, including the engine, were removed from the automobile that was dropped on the frozen lake, to avoid polluting the lake.

Unfortunately, the parachute didn't open for the first drop, and that Peugot was a complete write-off. The second drop was successful, but that car was no longer usable.

Two other cars were damaged as they raced across the lake through bomb bursts, during the many takes. The final scene, at Banff Springs, was shot with the one remaining unscathed Peugot. *(continued on page 168)*

COMMERCIAL—CONT.

Filming took twelve days, with a crew of eighty. There were two helicopters employed, one with a special Tyler mount for the camera. In all, four camera crews were used to film the commercial. On completion of the aircraft scene, the Hercules was stripped and repainted in its original colour scheme.

The commercial is spectacular and was a big hit in France. John Scott was production manager for this extraordinary TV commercial. Sadly, no one in Alberta—or North America, for that matter—ever got to see it. Peugot vehicles were not sold on this continent, so the commercial was never broadcast on this side of the Atlantic.

Alberta's rugged terrain has hosted many utility vehicle and truck commercials, especially winter ones. Many car commercials have been filmed on our mountain roads for General Motors, Chrysler, Ford, Toyota, and Honda. Other big-budget commercials have been produced here for Wrigley's gum, Visa, Nestlé, Shell, Sony, Mobil Oil, Labatt Breweries, British Airways, Foster's Lager, Planters Peanuts, and the American Broadcasting Company (ABC), to name just a few.

This activity continues year-round, employing many Albertans and pumping tens of millions of dollars into the local economy.

North of 60, West of Calgary

North of 60, the CBC television series, was created in 1992 by the brilliant writing team of Barbara Samuels and Wayne Grigsby for Robert Lantos's Alliance Films. They formed a partnership with Calgary's Alberta Filmworks to produce the show, which would become the most ambitious drama series ever undertaken in Alberta, with an initial commitment by the CBC of $14.6 million for sixteen one-hour episodes.

The production needed a shooting location in a small town with a Northwest Territories look, preferably close to Calgary or Edmonton for crew availability. For a time, nothing suitable was found. This series had the potential to be as important to the growth of a film industry in Alberta as the long-running comedy-drama series *The Beachcombers* had been to British Columbia. It would provide a training ground for writers, directors, and craftspeople, and it would be able to film in all of our seasons, providing year-round employment for a cast and crew in excess of a hundred people. It was vital that we not let this production escape to British Columbia or Ontario; the stakes were too high. We had to find a location.

Murray Ord finally discovered the perfect place to build a town, a forty-hectare site on a picturesque bend of the Elbow River in Kananaskis Country. It was close to the village of Bragg Creek, in proximity to the mountains, and only a forty-five-minute drive from Calgary.

There were problems, however. First, building a town would be costly, and who knew how long the series might last. Second, Kananaskis is a provincial park, controlled by an authority representing seven departments of the Alberta government. The set for *North of 60* would require clearing a timbered area, constructing the town, and then cutting a road through the forest to the community. Previous proposals for development in the area, however minor, had been refused, and park wardens rigidly enforced a policy that wouldn't allow a twig to be cut, let alone a tree.

Lindsay Cherney, now Alberta's assistant film commissioner, dealt with the various departments of government, expressing our support for the project and detailing its importance to the province. She handled it very well; in fact, I doubt that anyone else could have achieved results so quickly. An agreement between Alberta Filmworks and the Kananaskis Authority was signed and work was underway within thirty days. The fictional town of Lynx River, NWT, would have an airstrip, about twenty buildings, a satellite dish, and its own postal code, displayed on the Post Office sign along with the town's Slavey name, *Noda Deh*.

In K-Country, the road to the site was being pushed through and the site cleared. Major components of the town were being constructed in the massive F&D Scene Changes shop in Calgary, to be moved onto the property when ready. Many of the buildings would house production facilities, offices, editing rooms, and hair, makeup, and wardrobe departments. Smaller log buildings were being erected on site, with Native craftsmen using trees that had been cleared. Nothing was wasted, and nothing would be allowed to pollute the site or the river. Garbage and sewage would be hauled away.

The RCMP, after reviewing scripts, was supportive of the show, allowing the producers to use its official crest and uniforms. Casting director Leslie Swann searched nationwide for the Native and non-Native cast. This series would provide extensive opportunities for Native performers.

Initially, *North of 60* was the story of a burned-out RCMP officer posted to a northern community and his difficulties in dealing with Native culture and the eccentric characters in an isolated outpost. Later, this character was dropped and the show focused on his partner—played by Tina Keeper in a ground-

SCOUTING LOCATIONS FOR HOLLYWOOD

Alberta government-owned aircraft, such as the twin-engine Bell 222 helicopter, played a big role in location scouting, especially when filmmakers expressed interest in shooting in remote locations.

Sylvester Stallone's producer, James Brubaker, looking for locations to double for Afghanistan in our badlands, proposed to have Stallone tour the sites as well, "if your helicopter is safe enough."

It was pointed out to him that Pope John Paul II, on his visit to Alberta, was flown around the province in this machine. Brubaker said, "Well, if it's good enough for the Pope, I guess its good enough for Mr. Stallone." But Stallone didn't make it to Alberta, and we didn't get that production. *Rambo III* was instead filmed in Israel and cost fifty-eight million dollars. I'm certain they would have saved at least ten or fifteen million shooting it in Alberta.

A few years later, we scouted another Stallone picture—the mountain-climbing epic *Cliffhanger*. Bruno Engler, Banff's "Old Man of the Mountains," and Murray Ord prepared awesome portfolios, but the film was ultimately shot in Europe, where mountaintops were easier to access as there were more lifts available for cast and crew. Italian funds also came into the project. You never know what the competition might be.

Our Rocky Mountains also appealed to Canadian director James Cameron as a potential location for the opening sequences of his 1994 Arnold Schwarzenegger spy blockbuster *True Lies*. We provided an extensive scout of the area, but they required a castle, and we don't have one, so the sequence was filmed elsewhere. Buildings of that type simply don't exist in Alberta, which accounts for much production ending up in older parts of Canada.

breaking TV role for a Native actress—and the challenges faced by the residents of the isolated town.

North of 60 began filming in late August 1992, with Stuart Margolin—an American actor/director best known for his recurring role on the James Garner TV series *The Rockford Files*—directing the first two shows. Doug MacLeod and Tom Dent-Cox were co-producers with Barbara Samuels and

Wayne Grigsby. Les Kimber was production manager and would train others in the job, including David MacLeod, who went on to become the producer of *Black Harbour*. The first-season cast included John Oliver as Mountie Eric Olsen, Tracey Cook as local nurse Sarah Birkett, and Tina Keeper as Mountie Michelle Kenidi, sister of band chief Peter Kenidi, played by Tom Jackson. Young actor Dakota House played Teevee.

On the first day of filming, I received an urgent phone call from Les Kimber. A Cessna 180 aircraft with cast members on board was circling the airstrip where the director and camera crew awaited to film their arrival. The pilot radioed that he could not land "because the strip is too short." The elevation was more than twelve hundred metres and the approaches were not clear. High trees were at both ends of the runway to preserve the provincial park's appearance.

An Alberta Highways crew was working in the vicinity, and by contacting their chief engineer I was able to get about two kilometers of Highway 68 closed, briefly. The Cessna landed and was then "walked" about half a kilometre down the trail to the Lynx River airstrip. This became a twice-annual event. Parked in front of the faux hangar, the Cessna was taxied, faking arrivals and departures and the loading and unloading of freight and passengers, but it was never able to actually land or take off from the Lynx River airstrip.

Ninety episodes of *North of 60* were made over a six-year period before CBC discontinued the series. Alberta Filmworks has since made five feature-length TV movies based on the show, filming not only at the Bragg Creek site, but in Calgary as well. The series and the movies, in many languages, continue to play in more than forty countries. Many believe this is the most "Canadian" TV series of all time, including me; the combination of the RCMP, the unique northern location, and the Native cast was something I found very refreshing, memorable, and above all *Canadian*.

Alberta Filmworks is now a multi-million-dollar operation, which continues to bring honour to Alberta. It makes distinctive feature films and recently had its own television series in production for the CBC, *Tom Stone*, filmed out of Calgary. It would likely take a full page to list all their nominations and awards. The *North of 60* fan Web site has received almost a million hits since its inception.

Legends of the Fall, a major American movie filmed at Morley in 1992, starred Anthony Hopkins, Julia Ormond, Brad Pitt, Tantoo Cardinal, and Gordon

Tootoosis, and it was directed by Edward Zwick. It shot in the worst weather I ever recall for filming in Alberta. Weeks of torrential rain created ankle-deep mud, in pools that surrounded every set. Despite these hardships, *Legends of the Fall* was nominated for three Academy Awards, receiving an Oscar for best cinematography. *Legends* became the third Oscar-winning film to be shot in Alberta, after *Days of Heaven* (for cinematography) and *Unforgiven*, which was nominated for nine Oscars and received four.

The early 1990s was an extremely exciting time for the Alberta film industry. By 1993, Andy Thomson was president of AMPIA, and at that year's AMPIA Awards, he summed up what a lot of us were feeling during those busy years.

"This particular year, 1993, I think will be without doubt the most successful year in the history of the film industry in Alberta," he said. "We have two major television series happening simultaneously in Alberta now. *North of 60* is happening in Bragg Creek, and *Destiny Ridge* is going to begin production in two weeks time in Jasper. These two series alone will maintain about 150 jobs and pump twenty-five million dollars into the Alberta economy, out of a predicted fifty million dollars in production over the next year.

"That represents a growth since 1987 of about 285 percent. We're now talking about fifty million dollars of production in the province as opposed to sixteen million dollars in 1987. . . . We're beginning to see opportunity for Alberta talent to grow and stay here."

Not bad for an industry that had such a modest beginning only forty or so years earlier.

The year 1993 was significant for me as well. After a film industry career dating back to the early 1950s, which saw me hanging out of helicopters, sharing spiritual thoughts with Burl Ives, and hobnobbing with the likes of Chuck Heston and Clint Eastwood, it would soon become time for me to hang up my spurs.

Coming Full Circle

In August 1993, I retired, but rather than disappearing to Palm Springs or some such place, I immediately found myself put under contract for two years to assist Lindsay Cherney, Alberta's newly appointed film commissioner, who was also still serving as president of AMPDC. After years of being involved in film production work, I found myself returning to my roots and one of my early passions—still photography.

Assigned to photograph potential movie locations for a new production manual, I covered the province in a one-year, all-seasons effort. It brought back memories of my days as a government photographer in the 1950s and was a wonderful way to close my career.

As I travelled the province, I marvelled at how much cities, towns, and villages—even in remote areas—had grown, substantially and gracefully, over the past forty years. A wonderful film could be, and should be, made for the one-hundredth birthday of the province in 2005. It would be a terrific opportunity to update the *West to the Mountains* concept, which had been such a success in the 1960s.

More Albertans should be made aware of what we have in this province; it's phenomenal.

American film and television industries continued to find Alberta an attractive filming location as the 1990s progressed.

The television series *Lonesome Dove,* a spin-off of a popular miniseries of the same name, moved into the Calgary area in 1994 and remained for several years, later adding the subtitle *The Outlaw Years.* Like *North of 60*, it employed many local technicians and actors and required the construction of a small town set. The five-hour miniseries *Children of the Dust* also shot in Calgary around this time, along with the TV movie *Convict Cowboy.* Meanwhile, the feature film *Last of the Dogmen* was made in Canmore.

Albertans continued to be involved in filmmaking milestones when the first dramatic movie in the IMAX format, *Wings of Courage,* was made near Saskatchewan Crossing, on the edge of Banff National Park. Prior to this, the huge format had been reserved for documentaries and concert films; this was the first time an actual drama would be enacted. The film starred Val Kilmer and Elizabeth McGovern.

Environmental activists, claiming that rare mountain grass and flowers would be damaged, created a problem for the production, which Lindsay Cherney effectively resolved, without interruption to the filming. In the film, our Rockies doubled for the Andes Mountains of South America.

My two-year "postscript" completed, I retired permanently in 1995, but continued to maintain an interest in Alberta's film industry.

In 1995, an interesting movie, originating in Alberta, was made for American television. *The Legend of the Ruby Silver* was filmed at Mount Yamnuska, near Canmore, and produced by Arvi Liimatainen. The script was written by Peter White, Arvi's original partner in Kicking Horse Productions.

This had been their dream project for almost twenty years, and a partnership with America's Green/Epstein Productions, for ABC Television, made it happen. Directed by Charles Wilkinson, who has directed many Alberta-made features over the years, the movie starred Rebecca Jenkins of *Bye Bye Blues*, John Schneider of *The Dukes of Hazzard*, and Bruce Weitz of *Hill Street Blues*. Calgary newscaster Larry Day played a significant role in the film.

Peter White's script, based in part on his own experiences, tells the tale of a promoter from Spokane who, along with a young widow, her teenaged son, and a grizzled old miner, sets out to search for a fabled lode of silver. ABC allowed it to be filmed as a Canadian story, which was (and is) most unusual for

The Legend of the Ruby Silver, a story about four people who head off into the mountains to find the long dead Ruby Silver mine, won the Top Ten Award from the Writers Guild of Canada. Photo: Myrl Coulter

an American network. The mountainside sets by production designer Rick Roberts were outstanding, exuding character rarely seen in a television movie. *Ruby Silver* received excellent ratings.

Arvi Liimatainen has been a stalwart of the Alberta film community for many years, donating a great deal of his time to industry causes. He has ability in both production management and the creative side, having worked as a writer, story editor, and director, as well as production manager, producer, and production supervisor. He is a past president of AMPIA, a Billington Award winner, and former chairman and now lifetime appointed director of the Banff Television Festival, among his other awards and honours. Arvi produced the Anne Wheeler films *Cowboys Don't Cry*, *Bye Bye Blues*, *Angel Square*, and, more recently, *Marine Life*. Anne and Arvi are remarkable individually; as a team, they are unequalled. To our great loss, neither is a resident of Alberta today. We were

Angel Square(1990), directed by Ann Wheeler and filmed in Edmonton and Quebec, is a mystery comedy caper, set in 1948, in which a fourteen-year-old turns detective, inspired by his comic book and radio heroes. Photo: Myrl Coulter

fortunate to have them here as long as we did, to influence and inspire young Albertans.

The film industry was doing well in the mid-1990s. According to the Alberta Film Review Committee, the value of film production in Alberta at that time was $150 million, and Alberta-owned or -controlled companies accounted for a full third of this amount. But Alberta is known as a boom-bust province and, like the oil industry in the early 1980s, the bubble had to burst on the film business sometime.

You may recall Sir Humphrey's statement from *Yes, Minister*: "The system has the engine of a lawn mower, and the brakes of a Rolls-Royce." Film industry development in Alberta came to a screeching halt in March 1996, when Dr. Steve West, the minister of Economic Development, terminated

AMPDC. Shortly after, hitting the brakes again, he eliminated the position of film commissioner and Lindsay Cherney was let go (as were about twenty others in Economic Development, including an assistant deputy minister).

The effect on the province's film industry was devastating. As the Alberta Film Review Committee later stated, by summer 1998, Alberta had lost "so many skilled workers . . . it was difficult to field two major productions at the same time."

The industry agonized over the loss of many good people. AMPIA past-president Andy Thomson told *Playback* magazine in 1997 that it no longer made sense for his company, Great North, to restrict its operation to Alberta, so it moved to Toronto. Arvi Liimatainen moved to Vancouver and went on to produce the acclaimed CBC crime drama *Da Vinci's Inquest* out there. His departure was greeted with the *Edmonton Journal* headline: "Adieu Arvi. Frustrated by provincial policies, Edmonton's last best filmmaker turns off the lights."

Politicians leave Alberta, too, often for a warmer climate—but I have rarely heard anyone bemoan the loss of a politician.

The Alberta film industry was down, but not out. A privatized Alberta Film Commission was established in Calgary, with Murray Ord engaged as film commissioner. Murray was very well qualified, with good connections to the Hollywood industry. Some financial support was also provided by the Alberta government. The board of directors was active with fundraising, and craft unions asked their membership to assist. Nonetheless, the operation was still underfunded.

Another problem facing the reorganizing film industry was the lack of available government aircraft, and there were no funds available to charter such equipment when required. Needless to say, competing film commissions were delighted.

Ord became discouraged and eventually returned to film production. Well-qualified and respected Paul Rayman replaced him as film commissioner. He was soon dealing with the same problems and observed that it was difficult for an outside agency to obtain instant co-operation at the provincial level, which was often required. Film commissions in the United States, working out of the state governor's office, can slash red tape anywhere in the state, instantly. Not so up here; the Alberta Film Commission simply wasn't working.

What was working, and very hard, was a committee headed by dynamic Airdrie–Rockyview MLA Carol Haley. It was comprised of heavyweights from the film industry and government, including: Dale Phillips of Edmonton's Black Spring Pictures; Doug MacLeod of Calgary's Alberta Filmworks; Bruce Green of the Alberta Film Commission; Rick Sloan, assistant deputy minister of Alberta Economic Development; Dr. Clive Padfield, executive director of the Alberta Arts Development Branch; and Jane Bisbee, Arts Development officer. Their *Film Review Study Committee Report* of 1998 stated: "If the film industry is to be a meaningful part of the Alberta economy, before we can expect growth we must stabilize what is left of the industry."

Rejuvenation of the film industry may have been moving at "lawn mower speed," to quote Sir Humphrey again, but the Carol Haley machine certainly cut a wide swath. Within months, a fifteen-million-dollar, three-year pilot program was underway in Alberta Community Development. It provided grants to Alberta film producers to cover ten percent of the production costs spent in Alberta, to a maximum of a half-million dollars.

An immediate impact was a surge in production between 1998 and 2001. This inspired a permanent Film Development Program in Alberta Community Development, which now has ten million dollars annually to assist Alberta filmmakers.

Grants are based on twenty percent of the production costs spent in the province, to a maximum of $750,000 for films and $1.5 million for a television series. Financial support is also provided to film and video co-operatives, AMPIA, the Edmonton and Calgary Film festivals, the National Screen Institute, and the Banff Television Festival. As well, funds are available for the development and training of emerging filmmakers, screenwriters, and other creative contributors. Alberta producers say it is the best program in Canada.

Comparing this to the original Alberta Motion Picture Development Corporation, the total cost to government for AMPDC was sixteen million dollars, six million dollars of which was for operating expenses. The fund, for loans and investments (slow grants), was only ten million dollars in total during its fourteen-year lifespan.

The mission of AMPDC, however, was to develop a film industry in Alberta. In this, it succeeded. It was the right program at the right time, and it was adequately funded, well managed, and eventually copied by every province in Canada. There was even an unexpected benefit: the proliferation of provincial film agencies made it necessary for federal funds to be apportioned, which resulted in regional production, something that was unique in North America, perhaps in the world. Local artists more effectively portray the beauty and sensitivities of their home turf, as in Alberta's *Bye Bye Blues*, Nova Scotia's *Black Harbour* TV series, Saskatchewan's popular comedy series *Corner Gas*, and Vancouver's *Da Vinci's Inquest*. Regional production provides some of Canada's best film and television. Regional production in English began in Alberta; AMPDC debunked the myth that Canadian culture could only be depicted by filmmakers from Toronto or Montreal.

Film production in Alberta went through some difficult years after the termination of AMPDC and the office of film commissioner but, as in football, if you fumble, it's the recovery that counts. The Film Development Fund, under the management of Jane Bisbee, is now providing substantial support. Jane is a protégé of Ruth Bertelsen, who contributed significantly to the film industry during her years with Alberta Culture.

In August 2002, Dan Chugg, who had built Alberta's Vicom into the largest corporate video production company in Canada, was appointed film commissioner. He is vigorously promoting the province as a location for foreign film production. Alberta's indigenous industry should soon rebound. *Bisbee & Chugg* would be a good title for an action film, complete with heroes saving the day against all odds.

The Alberta Film Development Fund, I'm told, has become inadequate to support both our indigenous production and "guest" productions with Alberta co-producers, despite a boost of one million dollars in 2004, which raised the fund to eleven million dollars. Alberta was once second only to Ontario with indigenous film production in English. I believe our main goal should be to recapture, or even exceed, that distinction.

We have auteur artists like Francis Damberger, who has written, produced, and directed wonderful Alberta feature films like *Solitaire* and *Road to Saddle River*, following the tradition established by Fil Fraser and Anne Wheeler in telling our own Alberta stories. In my opinion, this type of production is far more important than partnering up to produce American made-for-TV movies.

OPEN RANGE

In 2002, a big American western, *Open Range*, came to shoot in Alberta, with Kevin Costner. He is a filmmaker who looks for unique stories and has an affinity for westerns.

This project appealed to him as it represented part of an era that has not been recognized: a time before fences, when cowboys with all their possessions behind the saddle, or in the chuckwagon, moved herds to the market while they fed on open ranges. Having previously worked with David Valdes on *A Perfect World*, Costner enlisted him as the producer for *Open Range*. With his knowledge of Alberta, its crews, and the rangelands where he produced Clint Eastwood's *Unforgiven* a decade earlier, Valdes recommended this new western be based in Calgary.

Location scouting began in March 2002, mainly by helicopter since there was still snow on the ground. The Turner Ranch, west of Calgary, was chosen for some scenes, as was the Nicoll Ranch. The Hughes spread at Longview was picked, and picturesque Fireguard Coulee on the Kinnear Ranch also appealed to the production team. A perfect site for the fictional town of Harmonville was finally found on the Stoney Nakoda First Nation Reserve, near Seebe. Unfortunately, when the snow melted, it was discovered there was no access to that site for vehicles, so three kilometres of road had to be built before construction of the town could begin.

Harmonville was built in seven weeks, to the specifications of production designer Gae Buckley and under the supervision of construction coordinator Alf Arndt. The lumber was specially milled, then weathered, for the building exteriors. Floors were laid with lumber cupped and buckled for realism. The window glass was hand-blown and imported. Details like oiled-paper window shades, ornate kerosene lamps, and flocked wallpaper added authenticity.

The town was designed and built for a stormy washout. Kevin Costner would not make a typical western "duster." A dugout twenty metres long, ten metres wide, and five metres deep was filled with more than a million litres of water pumped from the Bow River. It was dressed to look like a pond on the outskirts of town, but its real purpose was to provide the water for a spectacular flood sequence.

(continued on page 182)

OPEN RANGE—CONT.

Filming began on 17 June 2002. In addition to Costner, the movie co-starred Robert Duvall, Annette Bening (a.k.a. Mrs. Warren Beatty), and Irish-born actor Sir Michael Gambon. Rounding out the cast were Michael Jeter, Diego Luna, and Abraham Benrubi. Since he doubled as both director and leading actor, Costner often had to direct scenes while dressed for the role he played. It must have been intimidating to work for a director who wore a gun. (I'm sure any director would appreciate the opportunity.)

The flood took place at night, with dramatic lighting and 950,000 litres of water rushing down the main street of Harmonville. Huge pumps moved the water and recycled it to the pond. Torrential rain came down at 2,200 litres a minute from a rain trestle on a twenty-three-metre-high crane and a smaller second unit, both fed from large tanker trucks. During the flood, removal of a wedge allowed part of a building to float down the main street for added realism.

The climax of the film is a downtown shootout, likely the greatest gunfight ever seen in a motion picture. It took three days to film. Thousands of rounds of fake ammunition were expended under the supervision of property master Dean Goodine.

The Alberta crew numbered 90, and there were 105 Alberta extras in the town scenes. The film finished on time and within budget, despite some stormy weather that David Valdes said "provided opportunities for some unusual filming." The stormy scenes in the movie are beautiful and were captured by director of photography James Muro.

The critics called *Open Range* one of Kevin Costner's best films and a worthy follow-up to his multiple-Oscar-winning *Dances with Wolves*, which won seven Academy Awards, including Best Picture and Best Director. Surprisingly, *Open Range* failed to receive a single nomination for the 2003 Oscars.

Epilogue

I was diagnosed as diabetic in 1985, which ended my flying as a "pilot in command." I am still a licenced pilot who can fly as a co-pilot, and sometimes I do, with friends who own aircraft.

I took up sailing as an alternative and built a sailboat that looked somewhat like a Chinese junk. I had the sails made in Hong Kong in the customary tan bark colour and named the boat *Mai Toi* (*My Toy*). I have to say, it created considerable interest on the waters of Lake Wabamun, where we have a summer cottage.

I gave up sailing in 2000; advancing years cause many a change in adventurous activities. I have never been one to be idle for too long, although I do read a lot. I hope to do more writing.

Is there an unmade film I wish I had been able to produce? Yes—*All the World's Religions as I See Them,* which was the dream project of my friend Burl Ives. The theme, as he saw it, was: "There are many different Faiths. There is only one God." Sadly, Burl left us in 1995.

Sally and I have been married for fifty-five years. Our three children attended university and they are all quite successful. None is in the film business. Our five grandchildren are also not involved with film, at least not yet. The eldest granddaughter has an honours degree in English and is currently taking three more years of university in Australia. Both she and her brother, who is an aspiring composer (playing piano and guitar), display considerable ability as writers. This comes naturally since their paternal grandfather is the noted Alberta author Cliff Faulknor. Our youngest grandson, who sings with two choirs, is experimenting with video and says he's going to become a professional. His two sisters are more interested in business than art, although both are accomplished horsewomen in dressage, riding, and jumping.

When American President Woodrow Wilson first saw D. W. Griffiths's 1915 masterpiece *Birth of a Nation,* he said, "Film is like writing history with lightning!" Computer-age miracles have made filmmaking even more spectacular, but potential problems still exist, from weather to human frailties. As a prominent Alberta producer has said, "The real world of television and motion picture production is not a business for cowards." Although the product can't be manufactured in the same orderly manner as packaged goods, it is a renewable resource that lends itself to globalization like no other.

The mechanics of production have been simplified by technology, but nothing will replace creativity. That most essential element can only be provided by artists. They will always be in demand and in control. It is a wonderful way to be employed, and over the years, I've learned that when you do something you love, you'll never do a day's work in your life.

Arvi Liimatainen once told a film class: "When you embrace the dream of making films, it's a full-content intoxication, and I'm not talking about making it rich, although that's a potential fringe benefit. I am talking about the opportunity to charm, to change, expose, engage, to inform, to inspire. To make a difference." I encourage our youth to "embrace the dream."

I wrote this book for three reasons: to recognize Alberta's film pioneers, to inform readers about an important industry, and to tell young people about career opportunities. When I was making movies, Alberta filmmakers were competing with each other for a limited amount of work on sponsored films. When we formed AMPIA and sought assistance from government to expand into speculative filmmaking, we were told that making movies was "about as important to the economy as fur trapping." At the time, it was true. But we argued there was potential and asked for help to prove it. Government commissioned a study, and the rest is history.

More recently, on 26 March 2004, the minister of Community Development, Gene Zwozdesky, who is responsible for the relatively new Alberta Film Development Program, told the *Edmonton Journal*: "We are going to grow the film industry, I hope, into a billion dollar industry in this province. It has a huge impact, not only on the arts and cultural and the social side of the agenda but also on the economic side. It helps to attract tourism to this province in a major way."

Alberta-made productions now appear on motion picture and television screens around the world. We are far beyond the formative years of film industry development, and I'm fortunate to have participated in it. My life in the movies was wonderful, and it was joyously spent in Alberta—Big Screen Country!

Afterword

Introducing "The Team"

Every movie or TV production—whether it's a large Hollywood blockbuster or a one-minute commercial—involves the work of dozens, sometimes hundreds, of professionals, each with specific jobs. In this book, I have often referred to some of these individuals. Here is a more detailed look at what some of them do to help create movie magic.

The *director* is responsible for the overall quality of a film. His (or her) main concern is working with actors and developing the story. He has absolute control when shooting is underway. One prominent director, on his first day on the set, fired a crew member for some minor reason, simply to demonstrate his authority. Fortunately, few of them are that nasty or egotistical. The director works closely with the director of photography, whom he usually handpicks.

The *first assistant director* has responsibilities that enable the director to worry only about the art. He (or she) organizes all departments, preparing their schedules from his breakdown of the script, and ensures that performers are made up and on the set when the director is ready to roll. If there are difficult stars to organize, he must deal with them. The *second* and *third assistant directors* help him with lesser problems. Under his supervision, they arrange everything in front of the camera.

The *second unit director* specializes in directing action sequences and other scenes that don't involve the principal performers. In many cases, it is the second unit that travels around the world, filming breathtaking scenery, while the main crew stays behind in the comfort of the studio.

The *director of photography* (DOP) deals with camera, lighting, and exposure. Working with the film director, the DOP establishes camera positions and then instructs his crew, or crews. The DOP seldom touches a camera, leaving that to the *camera operator,* who expertly composes within the frame and follows action smoothly.

Once, when working as a camera operator, I was shooting a pick-up scene where the leading man exited to the left and the leading lady to the right. The director was not present. I didn't know whether to follow the male or female actor with the camera. The DOP told me, "Always follow the money." In other words, follow the higher-paid performer.

During a production where I was a camera assistant, the Hollywood star, although in his sixties at the time, was playing the part of a much-younger leading man. On the set, makeup would take an hour—and, even so, we had to use a diffusion filter on the camera for his close-ups. He was quite nasty on occasion and made the mistake of verbally abusing the DOP. On the last day of shooting, in a critical close-up scene, the DOP quietly told me to "pull the diffusion!" The result was a scene in the movie in which the audience saw the actor as he really was! It is always advisable for actors to treat the DOP with respect.

An *assistant cameraman* is responsible for many facets of filming. He (or she) threads film from the magazine around rollers and through the gate to an exact number of sprocket holes. When shooting is underway, he stands or sits alongside the camera, opening it to check the film gate before and after every shot, ensuring it is unobstructed and clean. He is responsible for focus. (On an English camera crew, the assistant is called a *focus puller.*) He measures and controls the camera focus, sets the f-stop for the exposure, with a light reading provided by the DOP, and keeps a written report of footage used and at what exposure.

There is often a *second assistant cameraman,* who assembles and dissembles the camera, unloads the exposed film, packs it for shipment, and then reloads the magazines.

The *rushes* are the developed and printed film of the various takes that have been shot during filming. They are usually back from the lab and screened within a few days. If there are faults with focus, exposure, or almost anything else, the assistant cameraman will likely take the rap.

Grips are important members of a film crew, as they have a variety of expertise. They set up and tear down sets, stands, and dolly tracks and perform specialized labour functions like rigging. The head of the department is a *key grip.* The second-in-command is called the *best boy*. A *dolly grip* is a specialist who supervises the laying of tracks for the camera dolly, then manually provides a smooth push for the dolly, with crew and camera on board, as it moves into a scene or follows the action. A good dolly grip is highly respected by the camera crew.

A handy item in the grip's bag of tricks is the *apple box*; built with strong plywood, a "full apple" measures 18 by 24 by 12 inches high. A "half apple" is 6 inches high and a "quarter apple" is 3 inches. (They are an American film industry standard and you will never see them measured in centimetres.) Apple boxes are used to elevate stands, a camera, or even actors. A "vertically challenged" Hollywood star of the 1950s who filmed in Alberta required a "half apple" to stand on during close-up scenes with his more statuesque leading lady.

There are dozens of different jobs on a film set. The next time you see a movie, pay attention to the closing credits and you might be amazed. Here are just a few more.

The *location manager* is responsible for negotiating and securing, by contract with property owners, the chosen filming locations. He is responsible for the care of locations and for ensuring that all is returned to normal when filming is completed.

The *production designer* and his crew, consisting of *art director*, *assistant art director*, and *draftsmen*, are responsible for the design of anything built as a set or on a set.

The *set decorator* and *set dressers* obtain and place everything required to dress a set, whether it is furniture, carpets, lamps, chinaware, paintings, or cushions, you name it.

The *construction coordinator* employs a *head carpenter* and *carpenters* to build whatever is needed to make the production designer's vision a reality—even entire towns.

The *head painter* supervises painters who will paint the set, or town, or anything else. He also has *sign painters* to call upon if needed, which they usually are if a town or city is being created on a set.

On big pictures, or period shows, the *costume designer* will design the cast costumes. Key staff in the costume department are the *wardrobe head,* the *cutter,* and the *seamstresses.* They ensure that all costumes are a tailored fit, are duplicated or triplicated when necessary, and are properly stored for easy access.

The *sound mixer* is head of the sound crew and entirely responsible for the quality of what you hear. His staff includes a *boom operator*—the one who holds the long pole with the microphone on the end.

The *greensperson* is responsible for all living "green" things, be they grass, trees, flower beds, or anything else growing on a set.

The *hair stylist* has a staff of *assistant stylists*, who are kept busy making sure both male and female actors don't have a bad hair day on the set—unless the script calls for it.

The people in *craft services* are arguably the most popular people on a movie set. They are responsible for food and drink at all hours of work, and they can also provide first aid.

The *projectionist* screens the rushes.

Movies Made in Alberta 1946 to 2003

The following list covers the majority, if not all, of the film productions made in Alberta from 1946 to 2003. They are primarily feature-length films made for theatrical and television distribution; short films and documentaries are not listed. Some productions never obtained a theatrical or television release, so there is no complete record of their cast and crew. Others were made in Alberta under one title and then released with a different title, while some were not released until several years after production was completed. We apologize for errors or omissions. This list was compiled by Brock Silversides of the University of Toronto Library and the author. Augmented by Alex Frazer-Harrison.

1946

THE EMPEROR WALTZ 106 min.
(United States)
Paramount Pictures
Producer: Charles Brackett
Director: Billy Wilder
Cast: Bing Crosby, Joan Fontaine, Roland Culver, Richard Haydn, Lucile Wilson, Sig Ruman, Harold Vermilyea
Filmed in: Jasper National Park

This film was released in 1948 and nominated for two Academy Awards—costume design and music. Wilder had twenty thousand dollars worth of pine trees imported from California to augment those on location.

1948

NORTHWEST STAMPEDE 79 min.
(United States)
Eagle-Lion Films Inc.
Producers: David Hersh, Albert S. Rogell
Director: Albert S. Rogell
Cast: Joan Leslie, James Craig, Jack Oakie, Chill Wills, Victor Kilian, Stanley Andrews, Ray Bennett, Lane Chandler, Lane Bradford, Harry Cheshire, Kermit Maynard, Harry Shannon
Filmed in: Calgary and Banff

Jack Oakie co-starred with Charlie Chaplin in The Great Dictator. Chill Wills appeared in more than a hundred films—many of them westerns—in a career that spanned from the 1930s to the 1970s.

189

1949

CANADIAN PACIFIC 93 min. (United States)
Twentieth Century-Fox
Producer: Nat Holt
Director: Edwin Marin
Cast: Randolph Scott, Jane Wyatt, Victor Jory, Robert Barrat, Don Haggerty, John Hamilton, Mary Kent, J. Carrol Naish, Howard Negley, Nancy Olson, John Parrish, Grandon Rhodes, Walter Sande
Filmed in: Banff National Park

Canadian TV pioneer and filmmaker Norman Jewison had a small role in this film.

1953

SASKATCHEWAN 87 min. (United States)
Universal International
Producer: Aaron Rosenberg
Director: Raoul Walsh
Cast: Alan Ladd, Shelley Winters, Jonas Applegarth, Anthony Caruso, Frank Chase, Robert Douglas, Bob Herron, Lowell Gilmore, Richard Long, Antonio Moreno, J. Carrol Naish, Hugh O'Brian, Jay Silverheels, Henry Wills
Filmed in: Banff National Park

Native Canadian actor Jay Silverheels is best known as Tonto in the Lone Ranger *films.*

RIVER OF NO RETURN 97 min. (United States)
Twentieth Century-Fox
Producer: Stanley Rubin
Director: Otto Preminger
Cast: Marilyn Monroe, Robert Mitchum, Claire Andre, Hal Baylor, Don Beddoe, Rory Calhoun, Edmund Cobb, John Doucette, Ed Hinton, Jarma Lewis, Tommy Rettig, Douglas Spencer, Murvyn Vye, Will Wright
Filmed in: Banff and Jasper National Parks

Marilyn Monroe and Robert Mitchum narrowly escaped disaster during filming when a raft they were using during a scene nearly overturned.

1954

THE FAR COUNTRY 97 min. (United States)
Universal International
Producer: Aaron Rosenberg
Director: Anthony Mann
Cast: Jimmy Stewart, Ruth Roman, Walter Brennan, Steve Brodie, Corrine Calvet, Royal Dano, Jack Elam, Kathleen Freeman, Connie Gilchrist, Chubby Johnson, John McIntyre, Harry Morgan, Connie Van, Robert J. Wilke
Filmed in: Jasper National Park

Harry Morgan later became a TV legend as Col. Potter on the long-running TV series M★A★S★H.

1959

WINGS OF CHANCE 76 min. (Alberta)
Producers: Larry Matanski, Tony Mokry
Director: Edward Dew
Cast: James Brown, Frances Rafferty, Brian Burke, Len Crowther, Larry Trahan, Richard Tretter, Patrick Whyte
Filmed in: Edmonton and Jasper

1960

NIKKI, WILD DOG OF THE NORTH 72 min. (United States)
Walt Disney Productions
Producers: Walt Disney, Winston Hibler
Directors: Don Haldane, Jack Couffer
Cast: Jean Coutu, Émile Genest, Uriel Luft, Robert Rivard, Don Haldane
Filmed in: Kananaskis Country

1963

NAKED FLAME 88 min. (Alberta)
a.k.a. *Deadline for Murder*
Corona Productions

Producers: Larry Matanski, Tony Mokry
Director: Larry Matanski
Cast: Dennis O'Keefe, Kasey Rogers, Al Ruscio, Mort Van Ostrand, Linda Bennett, Bruce McInnes, Jack Goth, Kay Grieve, Les Kimber, John Bruce, Robert Gibb, Barton Heyman, Bob Howay, Colin Hamilton, Tony Mokry
Filmed in: Calgary and Canmore

Lead actor Dennis O'Keefe wrote the screenplay under the pseudonym Everett Dennis.

1969

LITTLE BIG MAN
147 min. (United States)
Cinema Centre 100 Productions
Producers: Stuart Millar, Gene Lasko
Director: Arthur Penn
Cast: Dustin Hoffman, Faye Dunaway, Chief Dan George, James Anderson, Carole Androsky, Dessie Bad Bear, Martin Balsam, Jack Bannon, Cal Bellini, Emily Cho, Bert Conway, Jeff Corey, Lou Cutell, Thayer David, Ray Dimas, Linda Dyer, Aimée Eccles, Len George, William Hickey, Alan Howard, Philip Kenneally, Cecelia Kootenay, Robert Little Star, Ken Mayer, Steve Miranda, Ruben Moreno, Jack Mullaney, Richard Mulligan, Alan Oppenheimer, Kelly Jean Peters, Steve Shemayne, Helen Verbit, Jesse Vint, M. Emmet Walsh, Les Kimber
Filmed in: Morley

Chief Dan George was nominated as Best Supporting Actor for both the Academy Awards and the Golden Globe Awards.

1970

KING OF THE GRIZZLIES 72 min. (United States)
Walt Disney Productions
Producer: Winston Hibler
Director: Ron Kelly
Cast: Chris Wiggins, Hugh Webster,

Jack Van Evera, John Yesno, and Wahb the Bear
Filmed in: Kananaskis Country, Morley, and Banff National Park

1971

HACKSAW 120 min. (United States)
a.k.a. *Ol' Hacksaw*
Walt Disney Productions
Producer: Larry Lansburgh
Director: Larry Lansburgh
Cast: Tab Hunter, Susan Bracken, Albert Cooper, Victor Millan
Filmed in: Kananaskis Country and Calgary

I'M GOING TO GET YOU . . . ELLIOT BOY 92 min. (Alberta)
a.k.a. *Caged Men Plus One Woman*
Cinepro Productions
Producer: J. M. Slutker
Director: Edward J. Forsythe
Cast: Ross Stephenson, Maureen McGill, Richard Gishler, Jeremy Hart, Bob McCord, Don Cook, John Fraser, Abdullah, Cliff Betty, Edward Blessington, Bob Harvey, Doug Hepburn, Paul Kellman, Don MacQuarrie, Anthony Weaver
Filmed in: Edmonton

PRIME CUT 91 min. (United States)
Cinema Centre 100 Productions
Producers: Joe Wizan, Mickey Borofsky, Kenneth L. Evans
Director: Michael Ritchie
Cast: Lee Marvin, Gene Hackman, Sissy Spacek, Janet Baldwin, Craig Chapman, Eddie Egan, Clint Ellison, Hugh Gillin, Jr., Les Lannom, E. Lund, William Morey, Howard Platt, Therese Reinsch, David Savage, Gordon Signer, Jim Taksas, Angel Tomkins, Gregory Walcott, Gladys Watson, Bob Wilson
Filmed in: Calgary and Rockyford

SKRÄCKEN HAR 1000 ÖGON 99 min. (Sweden)

a.k.a. *Fear Has 1,000 Eyes*
Swedish Film Production
Producer: Inge Ivarson
Director: Torgny Wickman
Cast: Hans Wahlgren, Anita Sanders, Solveig Andersson, Barboro Hiort af Ornäs, Willy Peters, Gösta Prüzelius
Filmed in: Dinosaur Provincial Park and Sweden

Cast: Pia Shandel, Eric Peterson, Hetty Clews, Georgie Collins, Amy Doolittle, Joyce Doolittle, Joseph Gollard, John Heywood, Scott Hylands, Walter Mills, V. F. Mitchell, Alan Robertson, Patricia Vickers
Filmed in: Calgary

Film debut of Saskatchewan-born Eric Peterson, who became an acclaimed actor with his stage play Billy Bishop Goes to War *and his long-running* TV *series* Street Legal. *In 2004, he co-starred in the popular sitcom* Corner Gas.

1973

PIONEER WOMAN 100 min. (United States)
Filmways Pictures
Producers: Richard Rosenbloom, Edward Feldman
Director: Buzz Kulik
Cast: David Janssen, William Shatner, Joanna Pettet, Helen Hunt, John Scott, Linda Kupecek, Les Kimber, Lloyd Berry, Russell Baer, Frank Edge, Robert Koons, Lance LeGault, Agatha Mercer, John Murrell, Una Pulson
Filmed in: Waterton National Park and at the Palmer Ranch

This was the film debut of Emmy and Academy Award-winning actress Helen Hunt. David Janssen was best known for his long-running series The Fugitive. *William Shatner was reprising his famous role of Capt. James T. Kirk for an animated version of* Star Trek *around this time.*

SLIPSTREAM 93 min. (Canada)
Pacific Rim Films
Producer: James Margellos
Director: David Acomba
Cast: Scott Hylands, Debbie Rottenberg, Allan Anderson, Luke Askew, Danny Friedman, Patti Oatman, Debbie Peck, Eli Rill
Filmed in: Spring Coulee

This won the Etrog Award for Best Feature Film.

THE VISITOR 96 min. (Canada)
Producers: Margaret Dallin, John Wright
Director: John Wright

1974

LOCUSTS 100 min. (United States)
Paramount Television, Carson Productions
Producers: Herbert Wright, Michael Donohew, Judith Coppage
Director: Richard T. Heffron
Cast: Ron Howard, Ben Johnson, Les Kimber, Jack Goth, William Speerstra, Belinda Balaski, Bill Berry, Robert Cruse, Richard Dayton, Jacqueline Dunckel, Nancy Dunckel, Lisa Gerritsen, Trevor Hayden, Katherine Helmond, Bob W. Hoffman, Rance Howard, Michael James, Robert Koons, Michael Zawadski
Filmed in: Spring Coulee

Carson Productions was owned by talk-show-host Johnny Carson. Ron Howard's next job was the TV *series* Happy Days.

THE BOY WHO TALKED TO BADGERS 100 min. (United States)
Walt Disney Productions
Producer: Jim Alger
Director: Gary Nelson
Cast: Denver Pyle, Georgie Collins, Jim Roberts, Bill Berry, Robert Cruse, Chief Rufis Goodstriker, Robert Donner, Salome Jens, Stewart Lee, Carl Betz
Filmed in: Kananaskis Country, Drumheller, and Okotoks

Denver Pyle is best known as Uncle Jesse on the 1979–85 TV *series* The Dukes of Hazzard. *Salome Jens had a recurring role on* Star Trek: Deep Space Nine *in the 1990s.*

WHEN THE NORTH WIND BLOWS
95 min. (United States)
a.k.a. *Snow Tiger*
Producers: Joseph Raffill, Stewart Raffill
Director: Stewart Raffill
Cast: Dan Haggerty, Jan Smithers, Henry Brandon, Fernando Celis, Rex Holman, Dale Ishimoto, Sander Johnson, Herbert Nelson, Henry Olek, Jack Ong
Filmed in: Banff National Park

Dan Haggerty is best known for his TV portrayal of Grizzly Adams. Jan Smithers went on to co-star in the TV sitcom WKRP in Cincinatti.

1975

GOLDENROD 99 min. (Canada)
August Productions
Producers: Gerry Arbeid, Lionel Chetwynd
Director: Harvey Hart
Cast: Donald Pleasance, Ed McNamara, Barry Merrells, Hagan Beggs, Gloria Carlin, Patricia Hamilton, Tony Lo Bianco, Andrew Ian McMillan, Don Nablo, Donnelly Rhodes, Patrick Sinclair, Norman Edge, Duane Howard
Filmed in: Calgary and High River

MUSTANG COUNTRY 79 min. (United States)
Universal Pictures
Producer: John C. Champion
Director: John C. Champion
Cast: Joel McCrea, Patrick Wayne, Nika Mina, Robert Fuller
Filmed in: Banff National Park

Patrick Wayne is the son of movie legend John Wayne. Robert Fuller was co-starring in the TV medical drama Emergency! at this time.

BUFFALO BILL AND THE INDIANS, OR SITTING BULL'S HISTORY LESSON 120 min. (United States)
United Artists
Producers: Robert Altman, David Susskind, Scott Bushnell, Jac Cashin, Robert Eggenweiler, Executive Producer: Dino de

Laurentis
Director: Robert Altman
Cast: Paul Newman, Joel Grey, Burt Lancaster, Geraldine Chaplin, Frank Kaquitts, John Considine, Dennis Corrie, Robert DoQui, Shelley Duvall, Humphrey Gratz, Mike E. Kaplan, Harvey Keitel, Ken Krossa, Fred N. Larsen, Bonnie Leaders, Evelyn Lear, Kevin McCarthy, Pat McCormick, Alan F. Nicholls, Denver Pyle, Bert Remsen, Noelle Rogers, Will Sampson
Filmed in: Morley

1976

WHY SHOOT THE TEACHER? 99 min. (Alberta)
Lancer Productions
Producers: Fil Fraser, Lawrence Hertzog, Mike Cheda
Director: Silvio Narizzano
Cast: Bud Cort, Samantha Eggar, Chris Wiggins, Kenneth Griffith, Michael J. Reynolds, Karen Bernstein, Doug Blake, Rick Bremness, Dale Crowle, Richard Daviso, Jim Devereaux, Phyllis Ellis, David Figenshaw, John Friesen, Merrilyn Gann, George Gwin, Jennifer Hill, Margery Hill, Cynthia MacDonald, Larissa MacLean, Vernis McCuaig, Murray McCune, Dale McGowan, Joanne McNeal, Andrea Paulson, Curtis Peterson, Gary Reineke, Michael Ross, Jody Gaye Scott, Alan Stebbings, Warren Sulatycky, Scott Swan, Ronald Urban, Cathy Lynn Viste, Norma West, Joe Yasinsky, Michael Zwiers
Filmed in: Hanna

This film won the 1976 Golden Reel Award.

DAYS OF HEAVEN 95 min. (United States)
Paramount Productions
Producers: Bert Schneider, Harold Schneider, Jacob Brackman
Director: Terrence Malick
Cast: Richard Gere, Stuart Margolin, Sam Shepard, Brooke Adams, Gene Bell, King Cole, Muriel Jolliffe, Doug Kershaw, Frenchie

Lemond, Richard Libertini, Linda Manz, Sahbra Markus, Tim Scott, Jackie Shultis, Robert J. Wilkie, Bob Wilson
Filmed in: Waterton and Calgary

Nominated for three Academy Awards, it won for Best Cinematography.

SILVER STREAK 114 min. (United States)
Twentieth Century-Fox
Producers: Edward K. Milkis, Thomas L. Miller, Martin Ransohoff, Frank Yablans
Director: Arthur Hiller
Cast: Gene Wilder, Jill Clayburgh, Richard Pryor, Patrick McGoohan, Ned Beatty, Clifton James, Ray Walston, Stefan Gierasch, Len Birman, Valerie Curtin, Lucille Benson, Scatman Crothers, Richard Kiel, Fred Willard, Henry Beckman, Steve Weston, Harvey Atkin, Ed McNamara
Filmed in: Calgary, Drumheller, and other Alberta locations, and Ontario, Chicago, and Los Angeles

This film was nominated for an Oscar for Best Sound. It was the first of several popular films that would team up comics Gene Wilder and Richard Pryor. Patrick McGoohan is best known for his TV work on Danger Man *(a.k.a.* Secret Agent*) and* The Prisoner. *Valerie Curtin was starring in* Saturday Night Live *at the time.*

1977

MARIE ANN 90 min. (Alberta)
a.k.a. *Marie-Anne; Mari-Anne*
Motion Picture Corporation of Alberta
Producer: Fil Fraser
Director: Martin Walters
Cast: John Juliani, Andrée Pelletier, Linda Kupecek, Gordon Tootoosis, Bill Meilen, Tantoo Cardinal, Claire Caplan, Jim Dougall, Bill Dowson, Patrick Hughes, Paul Jolicoeur, Sam Motrich, David Schurmann, Maurice Wolfe
Filmed in: Edmonton

SUPERMAN and **SUPERMAN II** 143 and 127 min. (United States)

a.k.a. *Superman: The Movie* (first film only)
Warner Brothers
Producers: Ilya Salkind, Alexander Salkind (*Superman* only), Pierre Spengler, Charles F. Greenlaw (*Superman* only)
Directors: Richard Donner/Richard Lester (*Superman II* only)
Cast: (both films combined): Christopher Reeve, Marlon Brando, Glenn Ford, Gene Hackman, Margot Kidder, Jackie Cooper, Sarah Douglas, Ned Beatty, Larry Hagman, Jeff East, Valerie Perrine, Jeff Atcheson, Clifton James, E. G. Marshall, Paul Avery, Bill Bailey, David Baxt, Phil Brown, Brad Flock, Weston Gavin, George Harris II, Robert Henderson, Trevor Howard, Jill Ingham, Marc McClure, Graham McPherson, Billy J. Mitchell, David Petrou, Lee Quigley, Rex Reed, Bo Rucker, William Russell, Matt Russo, Maria Schell, Dianne Sherry, Colin Skeaping, Chief Tug Smith, Aaron Smolinski, Terrence Stamp, Roy Stevens, Phyllis Thaxter, Paul Tuerpe, Susannah York, John Ratzenberger
Filmed in: Calgary, Drumheller, High River, Barons, and Kananaskis Country

Although originally scheduled to be filmed simultaneously, only some scenes for Superman II *were filmed at the same time as the first film. Richard Lester replaced Richard Donner as director for most of the second film, which was released in 1980. Later, the two films were combined to form a miniseries for TV broadcast.* Superman *was nominated for three Oscars and received a Special Achievement Award;* Superman II *won the 1982 Saturn Award for Best Science Fiction Film.*

SKI LIFT TO DEATH 100 min. (United States)
a.k.a. *Snowblind*
Paramount Television
Producers: Gerald W. Abrams, Richard Bridges, Bruce J. Sallan
Director: William Wiard
Cast: Howard Duff, Don Johnson, Deborah Raffin, Murray Ord, Charles Frank, Don Galloway, Clu Gulager, Veronica Hamel, Trevor Hayden, Kendal Hunter, Pierre Jalbert, Jim Love, Don MacKay, Bruce MacLeod, Walter Marsh, Graham

McPherson, Jack Olsen, Steve Orchin, Leni Pear, Lisa Reeves, Jim Roberts, Gail Strickland, Jackie Verner, Kathy Wetherell, Tony White
Filmed in: Banff

Many of this film's actors went on to TV stardom: Howard Duff (Dallas), Veronica Hamel (Hill Street Blues), and Don Johnson (Miami Vice), to name three.

JUST A LITTLE INCONVENIENCE
100 min. (United States)
Universal Pictures, NBC
Producers: Lee Majors, Allan Balter
Director: Theodore J. Flicker
Cast: Lee Majors, James Stacy, Barbara Hershey, Lane Bradbury, Jim Davis, Charles Cioffi, John Furey, Bob Hastings, Robert Burgios, Stephen Burleigh, Tim Haldeman, Anthony Mannino, Frank Parker, Christopher Woods, Robert S. Woods
Filmed in: Banff National Park

It was nominated for two Emmys, including one for James Stacy's performance. Star/executive producer Lee Majors was starring as The Six Million Dollar Man *at the time.*

1978

WILD HORSE HANK 96 min. (Canada)
Canadian Film Consortium
Producers: Les Kimber, William Marshall
Director: Eric Till
Cast: Richard Crenna, Linda Blair, Kay Grieve, Al Waxman, Cy Berry, Lloyd Berry, Norris Bick, James C. Bryant, Les Carlson, Richard Fitzpatrick, Barbara Gordon, Helen Hughes, Hardee Lineham, Stephen E. Miller, W. O. Mitchell, James D. Morris, Gary Reinecke, Michael J. Reynolds, Gordie Tapp, Dale Wilson, Michael Wincott, Dennis Cory, Robert Koons, Graham McPherson, Jefferson Mappin
Filmed in: Waterton and Dinosaur Provincial Park

This film received five Genie Award nominations, including a Supporting Actress nomination for Barbara Gordon.

FAST COMPANY 91 min. (Canada)
Canadian Film Development Corporation, Quadrant Films
Producer: Michael Lebowitz
Director: David Cronenberg
Cast: Don Francks, John Saxon, Douglas Man, Judy Foster, Michael Bell, George Buza, Nicholas Campbell, Chuck Chandler, L. Peter Feldman, Patricia Goodwin, David Graham, Robert Haley, Cheri Hilsabeck, Claudia Jennings, Graham Light, David Petersen, Sonia Ratke, Cedric Smith, William Smith
Filmed in: Edmonton, International Speedway

Some video releases of this film erroneously indicate that Jodie Foster is in the cast. Canadian director David Cronenberg became a cult figure a few years later with successful films such as Scanners, Videodrome, *and* The Dead Zone.

LOST AND FOUND 108 min. (United States)
Columbia Pictures Corporation
Producers: Arnold Kopelson, Melvin Frank
Director: Melvin Frank
Cast: George Segal, Glenda Jackson, John Candy, Paul Sorvino, Martin Short, Maureen Stapleton, Cec Linder, Barbara Hamilton, Lois Maxwell, Bruno Engler
Filmed in: Banff and Lake Louise

Bruno Engler, one of Ken Hutchinson's "men of the mountains" from the early 1950s, had a small role as a ski patroller. John Candy and Martin Short would soon achieve international stardom as movie and TV comics. Canadian Lois Maxwell played Miss Moneypenny in the James Bond films for nearly twenty-five years when she wasn't moonlighting as a Toronto Sun *newspaper columnist.*

1979

PARALLELS 90 min (Alberta)
Group 3 Films
Producers: Jack Wynters, Mark Schoenberg
Director: Mark Schoenberg

Cast: Walter Kaasa, Judith Mahbey, Colin MacLean, David Ferry, David Fox, Drew Borland, Howard Dallin, Olive Finland, Kyra Harper, Gerald Lepage, Gord Marriot, Jennifer Riach, Bob Spence, Stephen Walsh, Chris Jack, Tyler Schmidt, Tom Starko
Filmed in: Edmonton

AMBER WAVES 100 min. (United States)
Time-Life Productions
Producers: Stuart Kallis, Philip Mandelker
Director: Joseph Sargent
Cast: Dennis Weaver, Kurt Russell, Fran Brill, Mare Winningham, Jack Goth, Les Kimber, Murray Ord, Eloy Casados, Wilfred Brimley, Ted Dykstra, Penny Fuller, Rossie Harris, Grainger Hines, Cathryn Johnston, Don MacKay, Bill Morey, Ted Stidder, Michael Talbott, Robby Weaver, Tony Whibley, Ted Wilson, Jon York
Filmed in: Calgary

Dennis Weaver was best known as the star of the TV series McCloud. *Kurt Russell, a veteran of Disney teen comedies, would soon become a movie superstar with* Escape from New York. *This film was nominated for six Emmy Awards, winning for Best Supporting Actress (Mare Winningham).*

1980

SILENCE OF THE NORTH 94 min. (Canada/United States)
Universal Pictures
Producers: Murray Shostak, Robert Baylis
Director: Allan King
Cast: Gordon Pinsent, Ellen Burstyn, Tom Skerritt, Frank Adamson, Ken Babb, Jeff Banks, Robert Clothier, Donna Dobrijevic, Richard W. Farrell, Colin Fox, David Fox, Bryan Fustukian, Lydia Mason Green, Tom Harvey, Thomas Hauff, Kay Hawtrey, Chapelle Jaffe, Jennifer McKinney, Graham McPherson, Ken Pogue, Larry Reynolds, Chet Robertson, Dennis Robinson, Booth Savage, Sean Sullivan, Frank C. Turner, Paul Verden, Murray Westgate
Filmed in: Fort McMurray, Lesser Slave Lake, and Edmonton

Although nominated for nine Genie Awards, including acting nominations for Pinsent, Burstyn, and Skerritt and a Best Original Song nomination for Neil Young, it won only a single award, for cinematography.

TOUCHED BY LOVE 95 min. (United States)
a.k.a. *To Elvis, With Love*
Producer: Michael Viner
Director: Gus Trikonis
Cast: Deborah Raffin, Michael Learned, John Amos, Clu Gulager, Diane Lane, Cristina Raines, Clive Shalom, Twyla Volkins, Mary Wickes, Jason Bates, Joseph Bondok, Beverly Chapman, Jennifer Collins, Cathy Corns, Rhonda De Jong, Robbie Olisoff, Melissa Quigg, Darren Taylor, Sharlene Taylor, Darren Wall, Carla Wildeman, Gordon Bullivant, Darrel Beingessner, May Brackenbury, Patti Gunther, Ruth Harwig, Margaret Kuyt, Dorothy Shalom
Filmed in: Banff

This was Diane Lane's second film appearance. Michael Learned was playing Olivia in The Waltons *at the time. Deborah Raffin won both a Golden Globe Award and a Razzie Award (for worst performance) for her work on this film.*

HOUNDS OF NOTRE DAME 95 min. (Alberta)
Pere Film Productions
Producer: Fil Fraser
Director: Zale Dalen
Cast: Thomas Peacocke, Barry Morse, Frances Hyland, David Ferry, Bill Ashley, Ginny Bast, Mike Bova, Jim Brock, Doug Brown, Paul Bougie, J. Vernon Buller, Frank Germann, Dale Heibein, Greg Heibein, Chris Kambeitz, Matt Keegan, Herb Lahann, Ed Maclag, Rob MacLean, Larry Reese, Phil Ridley, Bob Scheibel, John Sexsmith, Bill Sorensen, John Weishaar, Lenore Zann
Filmed in: Saskatchewan by an Alberta producer

It was nominated for nine Genie Awards, winning for Thomas Peacocke's performance. Barry Morse is best known for his role as Lt. Philip Gerard in The Fugitive.

FIREBIRD 2015 AD 97 min. (United States)
Mara Film Productions
Producers: Glenn Ludlow, Harold Sobel
Director: David M. Robertson
Cast: Doug McClure, Darren McGavin, Bill Berry, Lee Broker, Alex Diakun, Graham Paller, Frank Pellegrino, Mary Beth Rubens, Tony Sharpe, George Touliatos, Barbara Williams, Robert Wisden
Filmed in: Drumheller

Both this film and the Ontario-filmed The Last Chase, *starring Lee Majors, were released in 1981. Both take place in a future where automobiles have been forbidden.*

GHOSTKEEPER 89 min. (Alberta)
a.k.a. *Ghost Keeper*
Badland Pictures Ltd.
Producers: Harold J. Cole, Jim Makichuk
Director: Jim Makichuk
Cast: Georgie Collins, Les Kimber, Riva Spier, Murray Ord, Bill Grove, James Hutchinson, John MacMillan, Sheri McFadden
Filmed in: Calgary and Lake Louise

HARRY TRACY, DESPERADO 107 min. (Canada/United States)
Producers: Ronald I. Cohen, Albert J. Tenzer, Sid and Marty Krofft
Director: William A. Graham
Cast: Bruce Dern, James DeFelice, Helen Shaver, Joe Dodds, Jack Ackroyd, Marty Corsberg, Fred Diehl, Conrad Fitzgerald, Daphne Goldrick, Michael C. Gwynne, Ed Hong-Louie, Jacques Hubert, Jak King, Lynne Kolber, Gordon Lightfoot, Richard MacBride, Peter Manning, Harvey M. Miller, Christopher Moss, Lou Patterson, Suzie Payne, Jim Roberts, Dennis Robertson, Kerry Salisbury, Walter Scott, Charles Siegel, Jim Sparkman, Frank C. Turner, Mike Tyree, Alex Willows
Filmed in: Canmore and Jasper

This film was nominated for seven Genie Awards, including Best Picture. Executive producers Sid and Marty Krofft were best known for their American family TV programs such as H. R. Pufnstuf *and* Donny and Marie. *Canadian folk*

music legend Gordon Lightfoot made his acting debut.

THE HIGH COUNTRY 98 min. (Canada/United States)
a.k.a. *The First Hello*
Saguenay Films
Producers: Bruce Mallen, Ken Gord, Gene Slott
Director: Harvey Hart
Cast: Timothy Bottoms, Linda Purl, Jack Ackroyd, Paul Coeur, Murray Ord, Jon Andersen, Bill Berry, Richard E. Butler, Barry Graham, James C. Lawrence, Grant Lowe, Walter Mills, George Sims, Marsha Stonehouse
Filmed in: Banff, Canmore, and British Columbia

LATITUDE 55° 102 min. (Alberta)
Savage God One Film Productions
Producers: Fil Fraser, Donna Wong-Juliani, Harold Tichenor
Director: John Juliani
Cast: Andrée Pelletier, August Schellenberg
Filmed in: Sherwood Park

It was nominated for six Genie Awards, including Best Picture.

KELLY 94 min. (Canada)
a.k.a. *Like Father, Like Daughter*
Canadian Film Development Corporation, Famous Players Film Corporation
Producer: Samuel V. Freeman
Director: Christopher Chapman
Cast: George Clutesi, Mona Cozart, Dan Graniret, Jack Leaf, Doug Lennox, Robert Logan, Elaine Nalee, Twyla-Dawn Vokins, Alec Willows
Filmed in: Calgary, Canmore, and Field, BC

1981

DEATH HUNT 97 min. (United States)
Golden Harvest Productions
Producers: Murray Shostak, Albert S. Ruddy, André E. Morgan, Raymond Chow,

Robert Baylis
Director: Peter Hunt
Cast: Lee Marvin, Angie Dickinson, Charles
Bronson, Andrew Stevens, Tantoo Cardinal,
Carl Weathers, Rayford Barnes, Henry
Beckman, Jon Cedar, Maury Chaykin,
Richard Davalos, Steve O. S. Finkel, Amy
Marie George, Scott Hylands, Maurice
Kowaleski, Denis Lacroix, Ed Lauter, Len
Lesser, Sean McCann, James McIntire, James
O'Connell, William Sanderson, August
Schellenberg, Dennis Wallace
Filmed in: near Canmore, Kananaskis
Country

*Based upon a true story, it was heavily criticized
for taking dramatic licence with the events.*

THE WARS 120 min. (Canada)
Neilsen-Ferns
Producers: Richard Neilsen, Robert Verrall
Director: Robin Phillips
Cast: Brent Carver, Jackie Burroughs, Shirley
Douglas, Alan Scarfe, Richard Austin, Rodger
Barton, Paul Batten, Rod Beattie, Kirsten
Bishop, Tom Bishop, Richard Blackburn,
Domini Blythe, Fred Booker, Dwayne
Brenna, Barbara Budd, Shirley Cassidy, Clare
Coulter, Richard Curnock, David Dunbar,
Rupert Frazer, Graeme Gibson, Maurice
Good, Bob Hannah, Martha Henry, Paul
Hubbard, William Hutt, Jeff Hyslop, Eleanor
Kane, James Kidnie, Jean LeClerc, Leo
Leyden, Hardee T. Lineham, Ann-Marie
MacDonald, David Main, William Merton
Malmo, Jefferson Mappin, Marti Maraden,
Robin McKenzie, Richard McMillan, David
Robb, Abigail Seaton, Heather Summerhayes,
Margaret Tyzack, Timothy Webber, Susan
Wright
Filmed in: Longview

*This won three Genie Awards, including acting
awards for Martha Henry and Jackie Burroughs.*

QUEST FOR FIRE 100 min.
(Canada/France/United States)
a.k.a. *La Guerre du feu*
Belstar Productions, Ciné Trail, Famous
Players, Stephan Films
Producers: Véra Belmont, Jacques
Dorfmann, Michael Gruskoff, Denis Héroux,

Claude Nedjar, Garth Thomas
Director: Jean-Jacques Annaud
Cast: Everett McGill, Ron Perlman,
Nicholas Kadi, Rae Dawn Chong, Gary
Schwartz
Filmed in: the Alberta Badlands, Ontario,
British Columbia, Kenya, and Iceland

*This film won the 1983 Oscar for Best Make-Up.
It was the film debut of Ron Perlman, who has
specialized in roles that require heavy makeup in
TV series such as* Beauty and the Beast *and
films like* Hellboy.

1982

RUNNING BRAVE 106 min.
(Canada/United States)
Englander Productions for Disney
Producers: Ira Englander, Maurice Wolfe
Directors: Donald Shebib, D. S. Everett
Cast: Robby Benson, Pat Hingle, Graham
Greene, Tantoo Cardinal, Tommy Banks,
Bonar Bain, Thomas Peacocke, Francis
Damberger, Maurice Wolfe, Jack Ackroyd,
Albert Angus, Barbara Blackhorse, Derek
Campbell, George Clutesi, Claudia Cron,
Merrill Dendorff, Donna Devore, Seymour
Eaglespeaker, Paul Hubbard, Chris Judge,
Margo Kane, Denis Lacroix, John Littlechild,
Douglas Marquardt, Jeff McCracken, Graham
McPherson, Gail Omeasoo, Barbara Reese,
Michael J. Reynolds, Rob Roy, Billy
Runsabove, August Schellenberg, Kendall
Smith, Wendell Smith
Filmed in: Edmonton, Drumheller, and
Wayne

*This was the film debut of Canadian Native actor
Graham Greene, who would receive an Oscar
nomination for his performance in 1990's* Dances
with Wolves.

THE WILD PONY 97 min. (Alberta)
Sullivan Entertainment
Producer: Eda Lishman
Director: Kevin Sullivan
Cast: Art Hindle, Marilyn Lightstone,
Tommy Banks, Josh Byrne, Kelsey McLeod,

Murray Ord
Filmed in: Calgary and Pincher Creek

Kevin Sullivan is best known for his television adaptation of Anne of Green Gables *and the subsequent series* Road to Avonlea.

SUPERMAN III 125 min. (United States)
Dovemead Productions
Producers: Pierre Spengler, Ilya Salkind
Director: Richard Lester
Cast: Christopher Reeve, Annette O'Toole, Richard Pryor, Pamela Stephenson, Robert Vaughn, Margot Kidder, Marc McClure, Gavan O'Herlihy, Robert Beatty, R. J. Bell, Justin Case, Jackie Cooper, Lou Hirsch, Helen Horton, Pamela Mandell, Al Matthews, Nancy Roberts, Annie Ross, Gordon Signer, Graham Stark, Peter Wear, Henry Woolf, Les Kimber, Sandra Dickinson
Filmed in: Calgary and High River and at the Columbia Icefields

Annette O'Toole later played Superman's adopted mother in the TV series Smallville. *An early title for this film was* Superman vs. Superman. *Some sequences in this film were originally shot for* Superman II. *It was nominated for two Razzie Awards for Worst Musical Score and Worst Supporting Actor (Richard Pryor).*

1983

FINDERS KEEPERS 96 min. (United States)
Soundcross Films
Producers: Sandra Marsh, Terence Marsh
Director: Richard Lester
Cast: Michael O'Keefe, Pamela Stephenson, Ed Lauter, Timothy Blake, Jim Carrey, John Schuck, David Wayne, Robert Clothier, Beverly D'Angelo, Paul Coeur, Brian Dennehy, Jayne Eastwood, Frances Flanagan, Louis Gossett, Jr., Margaret Hertlein, Alf Humphreys, Barbara Kermode, Campbell Lane, Judy Leigh-Johnson, Bill Mankuma, Margaret Martin, Richard Newman, Jack Riley, Wayne Robson
Filmed in: Calgary and Vulcan

This was one of Jim Carrey's first films; he would go on to become a comedy superstar in the 1990s.

DRAW! 98 min. (Canada/United States)
Astral Films
Producers: Ronald I. Cohen, Harold Greenberg, Stuart B. Rekant
Director: Steven Hilliard Stern
Cast: Kirk Douglas, James Coburn, Bonar Bain, James DeFelice, Frank Adamson, Victor Bain, Alexandra Bastedo, Jason Michas, Maurice Brand, Tom Dasko, Richard Donat, James Forsythe, Bryan Fustukian, Brian George, Stuart Gillard, Graham Jarvis, Sherill DeMarco, Derek McGrath, Graham McPherson, Wedge McWhorter, Gerard Parkes, Wilf Rowe, Linda Sorenson, Bob Supeene, Charlie Turner, Frank C. Turner, Vladimir Valenta, Miles Vasey
Filmed in: Drumheller and Fort Edmonton

Nominated for five Genie Awards, it won for Linda Sorenson's supporting performance.

SENTIMENTAL REASONS 90 min.
(Alberta)
a.k.a. *Death Target, Order to Assassinate*
Cinetel Film Productions
Producer: Peter Haynes
Director: Jorge Montesi
Cast: Jorge Montesi, Elaine Lakeman, Joseph Patrick Finn, Peter Haynes, Arvi Liimatainen
Filmed in: Edmonton

Director/star Jorge Montesi is a prolific director of fantasy, adventure, and science fiction TV shows.

ISAAC LITTLEFEATHERS 100 min.
(Alberta)
Lauron Productions, King Motion Pictures
Producers: William Johnston, Ronald Lillie, Doug Hutton, Arvi Liimatainen, Barry Pearson, Gerald Soloway
Director: Les Rose
Cast: Lou Jacobi, Scott Hylands, Michelle Thrush, Lynda Mason Green, William Korbut, Fred Keating, Mark Schoenberg, Brent Allan, Robert Astle, Lorraine Behnan, Steve Blackman, Geoff Brumlik, George Clutesi, Christine Daniels, Glenn Davidson, Tommy Fletcher, Marek Forysinski, Bryan Fustukian, Vincent Gale, Darren Heaps, Tom

Heaton, Robert Koons, Larry Musser, Eido Waida
Filmed in: Edmonton

This film was nominated for five Gemini Awards. Lynda Mason Green went on to become a regular on the Canadian-made TV series Night Heat *and* War of the Worlds.

1984

THE JOURNEY OF NATTY GANN
105 min. (United States)
Walt Disney Productions
Producers: Michael Lobell, Les Kimber, Jeanne Rosenberg
Director: Jeremy Kagan
Cast: Meredith Salenger, Ray Wise, John Cusack, Zachary Ansley, Verna Bloom, Scatman Crothers, Matthew Faison, John Finnegan, Bruce M. Fischer, Lainie Kazan, Campbell Lane, Barry Miller, Jordan Pratt, Robert Clothier
Filmed in: the Crowsnest Pass and British Columbia

The film was nominated for an Academy Award for Costume Design. It was the first major acting role for Meredith Salenger, who became a popular teen star in the late 1980s.

BIRDS OF PREY 80 min. (Alberta)
Trapped Productions
Producers: Peter Haynes, Jorge Montesi
Director: Jorge Montesi
Cast: Peter Haynes, Jorge Montesi, Arvi Liimatainen, Maurice Bland, Mike Douglas, Linda Elder, Joseph Patrick Finn, Jennifer Keene, Sam Motrich, Suzanne Tessier
Filmed in: Edmonton

1985

STRIKER'S MOUNTAIN 99 min. (Alberta)
Wacko Productions
Producer: Wendy Wacko

Director: Alan Simmonds
Cast: Leslie Nielsen, Jessica Steen, Bruce Greenwood, Mimi Kuzyk, Thomas Peacocke, August Schellenberg, Steve Atkinson, Caroline Barclay, Darlene Bradley, Ernst Buehler, Francis Damberger, Frances Flanagan, Robin Gammell, Stephen E. Miller, Don Nordgren, Pat Peck, Heiner Piler, Booth Savage, Lawrence Schaffeur, Brian Skehill, Chris St. Pierre, Dwain Wacko
Filmed in: Jasper

LOYALTIES 98 min. (Alberta)
Dumbarton Films
Producers: Ronald Lillie, William Johnston
Director: Anne Wheeler
Cast: Kenneth Welsh, Susan Wooldridge, Tom Jackson, Tantoo Cardinal, Christopher Barrington-Leigh, Yolanda Cardinal, Diane Debassige, Vera Marin, Don MacKay, Meredith Rimmer, Wesley Semenovitch, Jeffrey Smith, Paul Whitney, Dale Willier, Janet Wright
Filmed in: Lac La Biche

This was the film debut of singer Tom Jackson, who would later become the star of North of 60 *and the originator of the* Huron Carole *charity concerts.*

RAD 91 min. (United States)
Taliafilms
Producers: Robert L. Levy, Sam Bernard, Mary Eilts, Jack Schwartzman
Director: Hal Needham
Cast: Talia Shire, Jack Weston, Lori Loughlin, Ray Walston, Jack Goth, Maureen Thomas, Bill Allen, Bill Berry, Darlene Bradley, Shawna Burnett, Jamie Clarke, Georgie Collins, Bart Conner, Norman Edwards, H. B. Haggerty, Carey Hayes, Chad Hayes, Beverley Hendry, Laura Jacoby, Marta Kober, Jeff Kress, Kellie McQuiggin, Alfie Wise
Filmed in: Calgary

Ray Walston will forever be remembered as Uncle Martin in the 1960s comedy series My Favorite Martian.

HYPER SAPIEN 106 min. (United States)
Taliafilms
Producers: Jack Schwartzman, Talia Shire, Ariel Levy, Christopher Adcock

Director: Peter Hunt
Cast: Keenan Wynn, Talia Shire, Jack Goth, Army Archerd, Patricia Brookson, Robert Christie, Jamie Clarke, Linda Elder, Ricky Paull, Jim Gray, Gina Hecht, Dennis Holahan, Peter Jason, Rosie Marcel, Clarice McCord, Barry Onody, Hersha Parady, Sydney Penny, Chuck Shamata, David Silverston, Gladys Taylor, Jeremy Wilkins
Filmed in: Calgary

Army Archerd is a well-known columnist for Variety *and has been a fixture at Oscar red-carpet ceremonies for decades. Director Peter Hunt is a long-time veteran of the James Bond movies.*

FOO GWAI LIT CHE 96 min. (Hong Kong)
a.k.a. *Shanghai Express, Millionaire's Express, Nobles' Express*
Golden Harvest
Producer: Raymond Chow
Director: Sammo Hung Kam-Bo
Cast: Kenny Bee, Lung Chan, Olivia Cheng, Kar Lok Chin, Fat Chung, Mei Sheng Fan, Sammo Hung Kam-Bo, Jan Lee Hwang, Shek Kin, Phillip Ko, Yasuaki Kurata, Rosamund Kwan, Ching-Ying Lam, Randy Mang, Richard Ng, Richard Norton, Cynthia Rothrock, Po Tai, James Tier, Eric Tsang, Yu Wang, Dick Wei, Ma Wu, Bolo Yeung, Biao Yuen, Wah Yuen, Yukan Oshima
Filmed in: Jasper and Hong Kong

Director Sammo Hung Kam-Bo, a colleague of Jackie Chan's, is one of Hong Kong's top action filmmakers, and in the 1990s he enjoyed moderate success in America as star of the TV series Martial Law. *Cynthia Rothrock, one of only three Western actors in this film, later became an action film star in her own right.*

THE CLIMB 99 min. (Alberta)
Wacko Productions
Producer: Wendy Wacko
Director: Don Shebib
Cast: Bruce Greenwood, James Hurdle, Kenneth Welsh, Jeremy Wilkin, David Elliott, Denis Forest, Ken Pogue, Thomas Hauff, Tom Butler
Filmed in: Jasper and Pakistan

The Climb was nominated for two Genie Awards.

1986

DUNG FONG TUK YING 93 min. (Hong Kong)
a.k.a. *Eastern Condors*
Producer: Leonard Ho
Director: Sammo Hung Kam-Bo
Cast: Lung Chan, Haing S. Ngor, Kwok Keung, Cheun-Lam Chin, Kar Lok Chin, Joyce Godenzi, Chi Jan Ha, Sammo Hung Kam-Bo, Phillip Ko, Ching-Ying Lam, Angela Mao, James Tien, Dick Wei, Ma Wu, Biao Yuen, Cory Yuen, Wah Yuen, Woo-Ping Yuen
Filmed in: Jasper National Park

Dr. Haing S. Ngor won the 1985 Best Supporting Actor Oscar for his role in 1984's The Killing Fields; *he was murdered in 1996.*

VANISHING ACT 95 min. (United States)
Robert Cooper Productions
Producer: Robert M. Cooper
Director: David Greene
Cast: Elliott Gould, Margot Kidder, Mike Farrell, Fred Gwynne, Graham Jarvis, Wally MacSween, Heather Ward Siegel, Paul Coeur
Filmed in: Banff

This film was written by William Link and Richard Levinson, the creators of TV detective Columbo.

AMERICAN HARVEST 93 min. (United States)
Roth-Stratton Productions
Producers: Bill Finnegan, E. Darrell Hallenbeck, Ron Roth
Director: Dick Lowry
Cast: Wayne Rogers, Kelly McQuiggin, Jill Carroll, John Anderson, Ancel Cook, Mariclare Costello, Terrence Evans, John Ferguson, Courtney Gains, Earl Holliman, Jay Kerr, Robert Koons, Fredric Lehne, Robb Madrid, Matt McCoy, Graham McPherson, Murray McRae, Randal Patrick, Casey Siemaszko

Filmed in: Calgary

*Wayne Rogers is best known as Trapper John on the TV series M*A*S*H.*

STONE FOX 96 min. (Canada/United States)
Allarcom Productions
Producers: Tony Allard, Peter J. Thompson
Director: Harvey Hart
Cast: Buddy Ebsen, Gordon Tootoosis, Larry Musser, Joey Cramer, Belinda J. Montgomery, Jason Michas, Joel Dacks, Nikky Jansen, Franklin Johnson, J. C. Roberts, Gordon McIntosh, Dale Wilson, Jerry Wasserman, Frank C. Turner, Sherry Wells
Filmed in: Kananaskis Country

This was the final lead-actor role for Buddy Ebsen, who gained fame as a song-and-dance man in 1930s' Hollywood musicals before gaining TV immorality on The Beverly Hillbillies. He would make only two more film appearances in minor roles before passing away in 2003.

HELLO MARY LOU: PROM NIGHT II 97 min. (Canada)
a.k.a. *The Haunting of Hamilton High*
Producers: Peter R. Simpson, Ray Sager, Peter Haley, Ilana Frank
Director: Bruce Pittman
Cast: Michael Ironside, Judith Mahbey, Larry Musser, Steve Atkinson, Lorretta Bailey, Laura Derwentwater, Michael Evans, John Ferguson, Marek Forysinski, Vincent Gale, Beth Gondek, Kirk Grayson, Glen Gretzky, Terri Hawkes, Deryck Hazel, Beverly Hendry, Howard Kruschke, Robert Lewis, Justin Louis, Wendy Lyon, Paul McGaffey, Richard Monette, David Robertson, Dennis Robinson, Lisa Schrage, Brock Simpson, Jay Smith, Wendell Smith
Filmed in: Edmonton

Many of the characters in this film are named after popular horror film writers and directors.

GUO BU XIN LANG 94 min. (Hong Kong)
a.k.a. *Paper Marriage*
Producer: Sammo Hung Kam-Bo
Director: Alfred Cheung

Cast: Sammo Hung Kam-Bo, Alfred Cheung, Maggie Cheung, Billy Chow, Joyce Godenzi, Phillip Ko
Filmed in: Edmonton, Jasper, and Hong Kong

At this time, Maggie Cheung, one of Hong Kong's most popular actresses, was best known for her recurring role in Jackie Chan's Police Story film series.

1987

STORM 107 min. (Alberta)
Groundstar Entertainment
Producer: David Winning
Director: David Winning
Cast: David Palffy, Stacy Christensen, Derek Coulthard, Stan Edmonds, Lawrence Elion, Harry Freedman, James Hutchison, Stan Kane, Michael Kevis, Sean O'Byrne, Thom Schioler, Tibi, Vic Trickett, David Winning
Filmed in: Calgary and Bragg Creek

Storm won five AMPIA Awards: Best Actor, Best Feature Drama, Best Original Score, Best Sound, and Best of Festival. Production began in 1983, with an additional twenty-three minutes of footage shot in early 1987.

BETRAYED 128 min. (United States)
United Artists
Producers: Joe Eszterhas, Hal W. Polaire, Irwin Winkler
Director: Costa-Gavras
Cast: Tom Berenger, Debra Winger, Fred Keating, Betsy Blair, Brian Bosak, David Clennon, Joel Daly, Jeffrey DeMunn, Ralph Foody, Albert Hall, John Heard, Bob Herron, Leroy R. Horn, Ted Levine, Richard Libertini, John Mahoney, Stephen E. Miller, Terry David Mulligan, Suzie Payne, Clifford A. Pellow, Howard Siegel, Leslie Stolzenberger, Robert Swan, Maria Valdez, Alan Wilder, Timothy Hutton
Filmed in: Carmangay and Lethbridge

Debra Winger, a three-time Oscar nominee, is best known for her roles in Terms of Endearment and An Officer and a Gentlemen.

THE GUNFIGHTERS 99 min. (Canada)
Alliance Entertainment
Producers: Sonny Grosso, Larry Jacobson, Stephen J. Roth, Allan Stein
Director: Clay Borris
Cast: Art Hindle, George Kennedy, Anthony Addabbo, Lori Hallier, Michael Kane, Reiner Schoene
Filmed in: Edmonton

George Kennedy is a prolific character actor best known for his roles in the Airport *and* Naked Gun *movie series; he won an Oscar for his performance in 1967's* Cool Hand Luke.

THE VIRGIN QUEEN OF ST. FRANCIS HIGH 87 min. (Alberta)
Producer: Lawrence G. Ryckman
Director: Francesco Lucente
Cast: Terrance Ballinger, Lee Barringer, Stacy Christensen, Ron Grondin, Anna Lisa Iapaolo, John Michaud, Barry Allan Onody, Ian Schmaltz, Joseph R. Straface, Tara Wilder, J. T. Wotton.
Filmed in: Calgary and Lake Louise

This film was produced by Larry Ryckman, who owned the Calgary Stampeders football club for several years.

FRIENDS 90 min. (Japan/Sweden)
Tiger Films, Shinchosh Co.
Producer: Börje Hansson
Director: Kjell-Åke Andersson
Cast: Lars-Erik Berenett, Edita Brychta, Dennis Christopher, Heinz Hopf, Anki Lidén, Lena Olin, Ann Petrén, Stefan Sauk, Stellan Skarsgård, Aino Taube, Anita Wall, Sven Wollter
Filmed in: Calgary

Co-star Lena Olin rose to international stardom around this time with her film The Unbearable Lightness of Being. *Years later, she would co-star on the popular American TV series* Alias.

COWBOYS DON'T CRY 97 min. (Canada)
Atlantis Films
Producers: Arvi Liimatainen, Anne Wheeler
Director: Anne Wheeler
Cast: Rebecca Jenkins, Ron White, Janet-Laine Green, Francis Damberger, Michael Hogan, Thomas Peacocke, Valerie Pearson, James DeFelice, Orest Kinasewich, Brian Aebly, Joshua Ansley, Zachary Ansley, Adria Budd, Ryan Byrne, Darrell Cholach, Robert Clinton, Georgie Collins, Ivan Daines, Pat Darbassie, Jim Finkbeiner, Susan Gilmour, Thomas Hauff, Jeffrey Hirschfield, Bill Kehler, William Korbut, Byron Leffler, Mae Leffler, Dave Malek, Ernie Marshall, Graham McPherson, Barney O'Sullivan, Allan Ord, Murray Ord, Candace Ratcliffe, Larry Reese, Dennis Robinson, Wendell Smith, Susan Sneath, Ruby Swekla, Frank Totino, Allison Wells, Ron White, Jason Wolff, Janet Wright
Filmed in: Pincher Creek

Nominated for five Genie Awards, it won for Best Original Song.

BODY OF EVIDENCE 96 min. (United States)
Producer: CBS Entertainment
Director: Roy Campanella II
Cast: Margot Kidder, Paul Coeur, Barry Bostwick, Jennifer Barbour, Peter Bibby, Debbie Carr, Robert Clinton, Georgie Collins, Bill Croft, Don S. Davis, Michelle Fansett, Lee Gilchrist, David Hayward, Stan Kane, Caroline Kava, Elizabeth Keefe, Tony Lo Bianco, Don MacKay, Blu Mankuma, Jane McDougal, Karen McMillan, Tyler Pearson, Donna Peerless, Kerrie Pennie, Freda Perry, Betty Phillips, Garwin Sandford, Maureen Thomas, Karen Tilly, Caroline Woodside
Filmed in: Calgary

A few years later, actor Don S. Davis co-starred in Twin Peaks *and in the late 1990s he became a regular on the long-running TV series* Stargate SG-1.

GUNSMOKE: RETURN TO DODGE 96 min. (United States)
CBS Television
Producers: John Mantley, Stan Hough
Director: Vincent McEveety
Cast: James Arness, Amanda Blake, Tantoo Cardinal, Denny Arnold, Patrice Martinez, Robert Clinton, Georgie Collins, Louie Elias, Tony Epper, Steve Forrest, Alex Green, Earl Holliman, Frank Huish, Mickey Jones, Walter Kaasa, Ken Kirzinger, Robert Koons,

Larry Musser, Ken Olandt, Jacob Rupp, Fran Ryan, W. Morgan Sheppard, Buck Taylor, Frank Totino, Mary Jane Wildman, Paul Daniel Wood
Filmed in: near Seebe

The first of a series of made-for-TV films reuniting the cast of the 1955–75 CBS series, it was the only one to be shot in Canada.

1988

BYE BYE BLUES 117 min. (Alberta)
Allarcom Productions
Producers: Arvi Liimatainen, Tony Allard, Anne Wheeler
Director: Anne Wheeler
Cast: Rebecca Jenkins, Michael Ontkean, Stuart Margolin, Kate Reid, Margaret Bard, Kaye Grieve, Francis Damberger, Tom Alter, Laurie Bardsley, Hamish Boyd, Ross Campbell, Ron Carothers, Jyoti Dhembre, Kirk Duffee, Beverly Elliott, John Ferguson, Blayne Fowler, Vincent Gale, Aaron Goettel, Gary Koliger, Chad Krowchuck, Aline Levasseur, Frank Manfredi, Sumant Mastaher, Murray McCune, Sheila Moore, Leon Pownall, Luke Reilly, Wayne Robson, Susan Sneath, Robyn Stevan, John Walters, Susan Wooldridge, Leslie Yeo
Filmed in: Rowley, Wabamun, Edmonton, and India

It was nominated for thirteen Genie Awards, winning for Lead Actress (Rebecca Jenkins), Supporting Actress (Robyn Stevan), and Original Song.

PRIMO BABY 110 min. (Alberta)
Producer and director: Eda Lishman
Cast: Janet-Laine Green, Art Hindle, Jackson Cole, Linda Kupecek, Margaret Bard, Tim Battle, Esther Purves-Smith, Daniel Libman, Valerie Pearson, Duncan Regehr
Filmed in: Millarville and Pincher Creek

Alberta-born Duncan Regehr starred in the TV series Zorro from 1990 to 1993 and was also a regular on the science-fiction series V.

DEAD-BANG 102 min. (United States)
Lorimar Productions
Producers: Stephen J. Roth, Robert L. Rosen
Director: John Frankenheimer
Cast: Don Johnson, Penelope Ann Miller, William Forsythe, Christine Cable, Ricardo Ascencio, Hy Anzell, Bob Balaban, Jerome Beck, Ron Campbell, Tate Donovan, James B. Douglas, Evans Evans, Phyllis Guerrini, Tiger Haynes, Michael Higgins, Ron Jeremy, Michael Jeter, Mickey Jones, Frank Military, Daniel Quinn, Tim Reid, Mic Rogers, Sam Scarber, Justin Stillwell, Antoni Stutz, Brad Sullivan, Darwyn Swalve, William Traylor, David "Dutch" Van Dalsem
Filmed in: Calgary, Drumheller, and Kananaskis Country

Don Johnson co-starred in the popular TV crime series Miami Vice from 1984 to 1989. Tim Reid is best known for playing Venus Flytrap on WKRP in Cincinatti in the early 1980s.

GETTING MARRIED IN BUFFALO JUMP 97 min. (Canada)
Canadian Broadcasting Corporation
Producers: Peter Kelly, Flora Macdonald
Director: Eric Till
Cast: Paul Gross, Victoria Snow, Eva Bad Eagle, Alexander Brown, Wendy Crewson, Murray Crutchley, Ewan Ferrier, Kirk Grayson, Marion Gilsenan, Diane Gordon, Kyra Harper, Ivan Horsky, Harry Lynch-Staunton, Andy Maton, Kent McNeill, Florence Patterson, J. C. Roberts, Lesley Schatz
Filmed in: near Pincher Creek

Paul Gross is best known as RCMP Const. Benton Fraser on the TV series Due South.

PERSONAL EXEMPTIONS 97 min. (Alberta)
West Sky Productions
Producer: Madeline Hombert
Director: Peter Rowe
Cast: Nanette Fabray, John Cotton
Filmed in: the Calgary area

Nanette Fabray's movie career dates back to the 1930s. Her best-known movie role was in The

Band Wagon *opposite Fred Astaire.*

THE RANCH 97 min. (Alberta)
a.k.a. *Wild Rose Ranch*
West Sky Productions
Producer: Madeline Hombert
Director: Stella Stevens
Cast: Andrew Stevens, Elizabeth Keefe, Gary Fjellgaard
Filmed in: the Calgary area

Andrew Stevens is director Stella Stevens's son.

1989

SMALL SACRIFICES 205 min. (United States/Canada)
Louis Rudolph Films
Producer: S. Bryan Hickox
Director: David Greene
Cast: Farrah Fawcett, Ryan O'Neal, Tommy Banks, Elan Ross Gibson, Julie Bond, Tom Butler, Gary Chalk, Ken James, Sean McCann, Maxine Miller, Emily Perkins, Bob Roitblat, John Shea, Alana Stewart
Filmed in: Edmonton and Allarcom Studios

Former Charlie's Angels *star Farrah Fawcett received Emmy and Golden Globe nominations for her performance.*

SYLVAN LAKE SUMMER 96 min.
(Alberta)
Kitch in Sync Productions
Producers: Tom Dent-Cox, Peter Campbell, Arvi Liimatainen, Doug MacLeod, Allan Stein
Director: Peter Campbell
Cast: Shaun Clements, Allan Grant, Wes Henderson, Christianne Hirt, Christine McInnes, Robyn Stevan, Johannah Newmarch, Andrew Rhodes, Spencer Rochfort, Henry Woolf
Filmed in: at Sylvan Lake

THE REFLECTING SKIN 95 min.
(United Kingdom)
BBC, Fugitive Features
Producers: Di Roberts, Dominic Anciano, Jim Beach, Ray Burdis

Director: Philip Ridley
Cast: Viggo Mortensen, Lindsay Duncan, Jeremy Cooper, Duncan Fraser, Sherry Bie, David Bloom, Linda Duncan, Evan Hall, Walt Healy, Robert Koons, David Longsworth, Sheila Moore, Joyce and Jacqueline Robbins, Jeff Walker, Codie Lucas Wilbee, Jason Wolfe
Filmed in: near Calgary

This film won awards at the Catalonian International, Locarno International, and Stockholm Film Festivals. More than a decade later, Viggo Mortensen would play Aragorn in Peter Jackson's The Lord of the Rings *trilogy.*

TEN TO CHI TO 104 min. (Japan)
a.k.a. *Heaven and Earth*
Producer: Yutaka Okada
Director: Haruki Kadokawa
Cast: Atsuko Asano, Takaaki Enoki, Hideo Mirota, Masahiko Tsugawa, Tsunechiko Watase, Naomi Zaizen, and thousands of Alberta extras
Filmed in: Morley

Filming began with Ken Watanabe in the role of Kagetora, but he had to pull out due to illness and was replaced by Takaaki Enoki. It was nominated in five categories at the 1991 Awards of the Japanese Academy.

THE FOURTH WAR 91 min. (United States)
Kodiak Films
Producers: Robert L. Rosen, Sam Perlmutter, Wolf Schmidt, William Stuart
Director: John Frankenheimer
Cast: Roy Scheider, Jürgen Prochnow, Harry Dean Stanton, Guy Buller, Ron Campbell, John Dodds, Richard Durven, Dale Dye, Gregory A. Gale, Neil Grahn, Lara Harris, Harold Hecht, Jr., Ernie Jackson, Henry Kope, Bill MacDonald, David Palffy, Tim Reid
Filmed in: near Bragg Creek

TOM ALONE 95 min. (Alberta)
a.k.a. *Last Train Home*
Atlantis Films and Great North Productions
Producers: Andy Thomson, Michael MacMillan, Seaton McLean, Tom Radford, Peter Sussman

MOVIES MADE IN ALBERTA

Director: Randy Bradshaw
Cast: Ned Beatty, Paul Coeur, Nick Mancuso, Bill Meilen, Glenn Beck, Robert Clinton, Georgie Collins, Joel Dacks, Trevor Devall, Floyd Favel, Jean-Pierre Fournier, Gordon Tootoosis, Vincent Gale, Elan Ross Gibson, Donna Goodhand, Dee Jay Jackson, Walter Kaasa, James Kidnie, Robert Koons, Ed Hong-Louie, Arne MacPherson, Paul McGaffey, Katie Murray, Johannah Newmarch, Aileen O'Shea, Rino Pace, Tim Sell, Kevin S. Smith, C. K. Tan, Timothy Webber, Ron White, Donovan Workun, Lenore Zann, Noam Zylberman
Filmed in: Banff National Park

Ned Beatty was nominated for an Emmy Award for his performance.

LIFE AFTER HOCKEY 90 min. (Alberta)
Great North Productions Inc.
Producers: Andy Thomson, Dale Phillips
Director: Tom Radford
Cast: Kurt Browning, Patricia Phillips, Glen Sather, Elizabeth Brown, Kenneth Brown, Maurice "Rocket" Richard
Filmed in: Edmonton

This film received six AMPIA awards, including Best of Festival.

1990

BLOOD RIVER 96 min. (United States)
CBS Entertainment
Producers: Merrill H. Karpf, Mel Damski, Andrew Gottlieb
Director: Mel Damski
Cast: Wilford Brimley, Rick Schroder, Adrienne Barbeau, Lori Anderson, Henry Beckman, James Bell, Jay Brazeau, Don S. Davis, Stephen Hair, Brian Jensen, Dwight McFee, David McNally, J. C. Roberts, John P. Ryan, Venus Terzo, Maureen Thomas, Jordi Thompson, Gordon Tootoosis, Mills Watson
Filmed in: Calgary

This film was originally written for John Wayne in the 1970s. Screenwriter John Carpenter is best known for creating the Halloween *movie series.*

KILLER IMAGE 94 min. (Alberta)

Producers: Bruce Harvey, Rudy Barichello, André Lauzon, Jim Murphy, David Winning
Director: David Winning
Cast: Michael Ironside, Chantelle Jenkins, M. Emmett Walsh, Jack Ackroyd, Paul Austin, Kristie Baker, Krista Errickson, Barbara Gajewskia, John Pyper-Ferguson, Joel Stewart, Al Duerr
Filmed in: Calgary and Bragg Creek

It includes a cameo appearance by Calgary's thenmayor Al Duerr.

LANDSLIDE 95 min. (Norway/United Kingdom)
Producers: Stein Monn-Iverson, Peter Cotton, Conny Lernhag
Director: Jean-Claude Lord
Cast: Anthony Edwards, Lloyd Bochner, John F. Dodds, John Scott, Joan Bendon, Pat Benedict, Guy Buller, Tom Burlinson, Joanna Cassidy, William Colgate, Ken James, Ronald Lacey, Franco Lasic, Grant Lowe, John Tench, Melody Anderson
Filmed in: Blairmore and at the Oldman Dam

Two years later, Anthony Edwards joined the cast of the long-running TV medical drama ER.

ANGEL SQUARE 106 min. (Alberta)
Western International Communications
Producers: Arvi Liimatainen, Tony Allard
Director: Anne Wheeler
Cast: Ned Beatty, Julie Bond, Damien Atkins, Michel Barrette, Wes Borg, Leona Brausen, Jay Brazeau, Kurtis Brown, Nicola Cavendish, Robert Clinton, Robert Corness, Paul Despins, Brian Dooley, Marie-Stéphane Gaudry, Guillaume Lemay-Thivierge, Sarah Meyette, Leon Pownall, Jeremy Radick, Vlasta Vrana
Filmed in: Edmonton and Quebec

Angel Square was nominated for four Genie Awards, winning three.

JESUIT JOE 100 min. (France)
Duckster Productions
Producers: Jean-Jacques Grimblat, Joe H. Jaizz, Aziz Ojjeh
Director: Olivier Austen
Cast: Geoffrey Carey, Chantal DesRoches, Valerio Popesco, Peter Tarter, Lawrence Treil,

John Walsh
Filmed in: Kananaskis Country

BLOOD CLAN 87 min. (Alberta)
Whiting Communications Ltd.
Producers: Glynis Whiting, Thomas
Lightburn
Director: Charles Wilkinson
Cast: Gordon Pinsent, Len Crowther, Shaun
Johnston, Ross Campbell, Jacqueline
Dandeneau, Jamie Ann Haiden, Blair Haynes,
Michele Little, Anne Mansfield, Caolaidhe
Wharton, Robert Wisden, John Wright
Filmed in: Edmonton

*Gordon Pinsent is one of Canada's most prolific
actors, with a career in film and TV dating back to
the early 1960s.*

QUEST FOR THE LOST CITY
(Canada)
a.k.a. *The Final Sacrifice*
Flying Dutchman Productions Ltd.
Director: Tjardus Greidanus
Cast: Shane J. Mitchell, Shane Marceau, Ron
Anderson, Bharbara Egan, Randy Vasseur, Bryan
C. Knight, Catherine O'Connel, Felice Wills
Filmed in: location unknown

DE ZOMER VAN '45 Miniseries
(Netherlands)
NCRV Television
Producers: Fred Koster, Joe Thornton
Director: Bram van Erkel
Cast: Dian Dobbelman, Tom Jansen, Renée
Fokker, Lotje Lohr, Christianne Hirt, John
Hartnett, Rod Padmos
Filmed in: Calgary, Pincher Creek, Ottawa,
Halifax, the Netherlands, and Belgium

1991

SHOWDOWN AT WILLIAMS CREEK
94 min. (Canada)
a.k.a. *The Legend of Kootenai Brown*
Crescent Entertainment
Producer: Harold Tichenor
Director: Allan Kroeker
Cast: Tom Burlinson, Raymond Burr, John

Grey, John Pyper-Ferguson, Donnelly
Rhodes, Brent Stait, Michelle Thrush, Frank
C. Turner
Filmed in: Waterton National Park

*This film was nominated for two Genie Awards.
At the time, Canadian-born actor Raymond Burr
was starring in a series of TV movies based upon
his old* Perry Mason *TV series; he died in 1993.*

UNFORGIVEN 131 min. (United States)
Warner Brothers/Malpaso Productions
Producers: Clint Eastwood, David Valdes,
Julian Ludwig
Director: Clint Eastwood
Cast: Clint Eastwood, Gene Hackman,
Morgan Freeman, Richard Harris, Rob
Campbell, Beverley Elliot, Frances Fisher,
Tara Dawn Frederick, Anthony James, Anna
Levine, David Mucci, Liisa Repo-Martell,
Saul Rubinek, Josie Smith, Anna Thompson,
Jaimz Woolvett
Filmed in: near High River, Brooks, and
Drumheller

The most successful film shot in Alberta to date,
Unforgiven *was nominated for nine Oscars, win-
ning four, including Best Picture and Best Director
(Clint Eastwood), and Best Supporting Actor for
Gene Hackman, and Best Editor for Joel Cox.*

COOL RUNNINGS 97 min. (United
States)
Disney Productions
Producer: Dawn Steel
Director: John Turtletaub
Cast: John Candy, Paul Coeur, Malik Yoba,
Raymond J. Barry, Jay Brazeau, Kristoffer
Cooper, Doug E. Doug, Larry Gilman, Jack
Goth, Charles Hyatt, Campbell Lane, Leon,
Rawle D. Lewis, Bertina Macauley, Pauline
Stone Myrie, Peter Outerbridge, Teddy Price,
Winston Stona, Fritz Weir
Filmed in: Calgary

Cool Runnings *is loosely based on the real-life
exploits of the Jamaican bobsled team at the 1988
Calgary Winter Olympics.*

SOLITAIRE 105 min. (Alberta)
Highway One Motion Pictures
Producers: Lars Lehmann, Lorne W.

MacPherson
Director: Francis Damberger
Cast: Paul Coeur, Michael Hogan, Valerie Pearson, Larry Lievre, Lee Royce, Kevin S. Smith, Ashley Wright
Filmed in: Edmonton

It was nominated for four Genie Awards; Michael Hogan won for his performance.

1992

SAMURAI COWBOY 101 min.
(Alberta/Japan)
Samurai Cowboy Productions
Producers: Bruce Harvey, Robert Vince, J. Max Kirishima
Director: Michael Keusch
Cast: Robert Conrad, Catherine Mary Stewart, Tom Glass, Ian Tyson, Mark Acheson, Tom Bonny, Duncan Callander, Enid Elman, Conchata Ferrell, Hiromi Gô, Rick Harvey, J. Max Kirishima, Harold Ludwig, Matt McCoy, Byron Chief-Moon, Bradley M. Rapier, Owen Smith
Filmed in: Waterton National Park

Star Hiromi Gô was a popular singer in his native Japan. Robert Conrad is a long-time American leading man best known for his TV series The Wild Wild West *and* Baa Baa Black Sheep.

MEDICINE RIVER 96 min. (Alberta)
CBC Production
Producers: Arvi Liimatainen, Barbara J. Allinson, John Danylkiw
Director: Stuart Margolin
Cast: Graham Greene, Tom Jackson, Sheila Tousey, Maggie Blackkettle, Byron Chief-Moon, Janet-Laine Green, Jimmie Herman, Thomas King, Raoul Trujillo, Dakota House
Filmed in: High River

The director, American character actor Stuart Margolin, was a regular on TV's The Rockford Files *for many years.*

ROAD TO SADDLE RIVER 90 min.
(Alberta)
Damberger Film & Cattle Co.

Producers: Arvi Liimatainen, Dale Phillips, Francis Damberger, Dale Phillips
Director: Francis Damberger
Cast: Michael Hogan, Paul Coeur, Ben Cardinal, Bryan Fustukian, Thomas Peacocke, Brick Bard, Sam Bob, Norma Campbell, Tom Charlton, Robert Clinton, Francis Damberger, Mark Gibbon, Jim Gray, Andrea House, Paul Jarrett, Keith Jones, Eric Allan Kramer, Robert Larmont, Larry Musser, Vern Peterson, Larry Reese, Lenna Tost
Filmed in: the Red Deer Valley, Drumheller, and Edmonton

Road to Saddle River *was nominated for two Genie Awards.*

ORDEAL IN THE ARCTIC 94 min.
(Canada/United States)
Provocative Productions
Producers: Ronald I. Cohen, R. B. Carney, David R. Ginsburg, Jeff King, Robert Lantos, Wayne Stuart
Director: Mark Sobel
Cast: Richard Chamberlain, Catherine Mary Stewart, Scott Hylands, Francis Damberger, Per Aabel, Cecily Adams, Steve Adams, Christopher Bolton, Tom Butler, David Cameron, Gary Chalk, Robert Clinton, Nathan Fillion, Page Fletcher, Mark Gibbon, Blair Haynes, Brian Jensen, Francis Keating, Mike Kobayashi, Melanie Mayron, David McNally, Larry Musser, Dave Nichols, Dodd Rougeau, Roger Shank, Daryl Shuttleworth, Wendell Smith, Stephen Sparks, Brian Taylor, Paul Whitney, Larry Yachimec
Filmed in: Edmonton and at the Namao Airbase

Richard Chamberlain, "the king of the miniseries," is best known for his roles in Shogun *and* The Thorn Birds; *he became a TV star in the 1960s with* Dr. Kildare.

TWO BROTHERS, A GIRL, AND A GUN 93 min. (Canada)
Black Market Motion Pictures, Katydid Productions
Producer and director: William E. Hornecker
Cast: Kim Hogan, Paul Herbert, Shaun Johnston, Terry Orletsky, David Everhart, William E. Hornecker, Kate Holowach, Peter

LaCroix, Scott Silva, William MacDonald, Colleen Wheeler, Craig Marsden, Darren McBride, Tyler Stuart, Stacy Lahr
Filmed in: Edmonton and Brooks

1993

LEGENDS OF THE FALL 134 min. (United States)
Bedford Falls Films
Producers: Edward Zwick, William D. Wittliff, Marshall Herskovitz, Patrick Crowley, Sarah Caplan, Jane Bartelme
Director: Edward Zwick
Cast: Anthony Hopkins, Brad Pitt, Julia Ormond, Gordon Tootoosis, Tantoo Cardinal, Paul Desmond, Bill Dow, Karina Lombard, John Novak, Christina Pickles, Aiden Quinn, Sam Sarker, Henry Thomas, Kenneth Welsh, Robert Wisden, Nigel Bennett
Filmed in: Calgary and Morley

Legends of the Fall was nominated for three Academy Awards, winning for Best Cinematography. It was also nominated for four Golden Globe Awards, including Best Motion Picture–Drama, Best Director, and Best Actor in a Motion Picture–Drama (Brad Pitt).

THE PERFECT MAN 90 min. (Alberta)
Midnite Café Productions
Producer: Wendy Hill-Tout
Director: Wendy Hill-Tout
Cast: Phyllis Diller, Brian Jensen, Michelle Little, Garwin Sanford
Filmed in: Calgary

Phyllis Diller is a veteran American comic actress who rose to fame in the 1960s starring opposite the likes of Bob Hope and Jack Benny.

STRANGE AND RICH 97 min. (Alberta)
Kicking Horse Productions, WDC Entertainment Inc.
Producer: Glynis Whiting
Director: Arvi Liimatainen
Cast: Ron White, Melissa Beltan, Amy Christie, Georgie Collins, Len Croater, Patricia Darbash, William Davidson, Nathan

Fillion, Jim Finkbeiner, Michele Goodger, Neil Grahn, James Iwasiuk, Nikky Jansen, Shaun Johnston, Mark Kerr, Eugene Lipinski, Christine MacInnes, Larry Musser, Glen Nelson, Alison Petroff, Fiona Ragan, David St. Pierre, David Sivertsen, Brian Taylor, Heidi Thomas, Murray Utas, Jan Wood, Marline Wurfel
Filmed in: Leduc

ONE MORE MOUNTAIN 90 min. (United States)
Producer: John A. Kuri
Director: Dick Lowry
Cast: Meredith Baxter, Chris Cooper, Byron Lucas, Frances Conroy, Bill Croft, Don S. Davis, Larry Drake, Grace Johnston, Pat Johnston, Jean Louisa Kelly, Bryce Krentz, Aline Levasseur, Walter Marsh, Kathe E. Mazur, Robert Duncan McNeill, James MacDonald, Lachlan Murdoch, Laurie O'Brien, Molly Parker, Joshua Silberg, Jean Simmons, Marie Stillin, Matthew Walker
Filmed in: near Calgary

Robert Duncan McNeill next joined the cast of Star Trek: Voyager. *Meredith Baxter is best known for her long-running TV sitcom* Family Ties. *Jean Simmons's film career dates back to the 1940s, and she became a Hollywood star with films like* Guys and Dolls *and* The Egyptian. *Molly Parker has gone on to become one of Canada's most prolific actresses.*

WINGS OF COURAGE IMAX 50 min. (United States)
Sony Pictures
Producers: Richard Briggs, Jean-Jacques Annaud, Antoine Compin, Charis Horton
Director: Jean-Jacques Annaud
Cast: Elizabeth McGovern, Tom Hulce, Val Kilmer, Molly Parker, Ken Pogue, Ron Sauvé, Craig Sheffer
Filmed in: near Lake Abrahams and the Kootenay Plains

This is the first dramatic film to be made in the IMAX format.

SAVAGE LAND 98 min. (United States)
Savage Land Productions/Motion Picture Village

Producers: Ermanno Barone, Dean Hamilton, Donald Borza II, Mark Daniel Jones, Eric Parkinson, Jim Townsend, Randolf Turrow
Director: Dean Hamilton
Cast: Corbin Bernsen, Vivian Schilling, Graham Greene, Bo Svenson, Brion James, Nathaniel Arcand, Roger Balm, Collin Bernsen, Aaron Bornstein, Donald Borza II, Helen Calahasen, Corey Carrier, Page Fletcher, Dean Hamilton, Maxine James, Martin Kove, Sonny Landham, Mercedes McNab, Charles Napier, Vincent Rain, Charlotte Ross, Leslie Ryan, Sam Scarber, Jack Schneider, Jim Townsend
Filmed in: Millarville

This film was nominated for a Genie Award for Best Original Song. Star Corbin Bernsen is best known for his role on the long-running TV series LA Law.

PROBABLE CAUSE 90 min. (Alberta)
Allarcom Pay Television Ltd.
Producers: Bruce Harvey, Richard Davis, Michael Ironside, Philip Swift
Director: Paul Ziller
Cast: Kate Vernon, James Downing, Michael Ironside, Brooke Adams, Rick Ash, Nola Auguston, Kirk Baltz, Marshall Bell, Paul Coeur, David Neale, Candice Elzinga, Tim Erickson, John Hudson, Shaun Johnston, Greg Lawson, Lisa McIntosh, David McNally, Michelle Miller, Craig T. Nelson, Larry Reese, David Silverston, Michelle Thorn, Wes Tritter, M. Emmett Walsh
Filmed in: Edmonton

Craig T. Nelson was midway through production of his long-running TV sitcom Coach. *M. Emmett Walsh is a prolific character actor with more than 140 film credits since the late 1960s.*

1994

CONVICT COWBOY 106 min. (United States)
Producers: Norman S. Powell, Jim Rowe, Diane Schneier, Frederick Schneier

Director: Rod Holcomb
Cast: Jon Voight, Ben Gazzara, Marcia Gay Harden, Mark Acheson, Jim Blake, Tyrone Benskin, Kyle Chandler, Bill Croft, Nathaniel DeVeaux, Tom Heaton, Truman Hoszouski, Deejay Jackson, Zook Matthews, Stephen McHattie, Chris Nannarone, Fred Perron, Glen Plummer, Dave Poulsen, Jeremy Ratchford, Stefan Stasiuk, Dean Wray
Filmed in: Calgary

Star Jon Voight was nominated for an Oscar for his role in the similarly titled Midnight Cowboy *in 1970. His daughter, Angelina Jolie, became a movie superstar in the late 1990s.*

LAST OF THE DOGMEN 118 min. (United States)
Carolco Pictures
Producers: Donald Heitzer, Thomas Hedman, Hannah Hempstead, Mario Kassar, Joel B. Michaels
Director: Tab Murphy
Cast: Tom Berenger, Molly Parker, Kurtwood Smith, Barbara Hershey, Parley Baer, Eugene Blackbear, Hunter Bodine, Mark Boone, Jr., Helen Calahasen, Gregory Scott Cummins, Robert Donley, Anthony Holland, Mitchell LaPlante, Dawn Lavand, Andrew Miller, Sherwood Price, Steve Reevis, Sidel Standing Elk, Brian Stollery
Filmed in: Canmore

Kurtwood Smith went from playing villains in movies like Robocop *to TV stardom on* That '70s Show *in the late 1990s.*

HOW THE WEST WAS FUN 96 min. (Canada/United States)
Producers: Mark Bacino, Arvi Liimatainen, Jim Green, Adria Later
Director: Stuart Margolin
Cast: Mary-Kate Olsen, Ashley Olsen, Martin Mull, Michelle Greene, Bartley Bard, Ben Cardinal, Patrick Cassidy, Georgie Collins, Shaun Johnston, Bryce Krentz, Dan Libman, Heather Lea MacCallum, Elizabeth Olsen, Peg Phillips, Leon Pownall, Jacqueline Robbins, Wes Tritter
Filmed in: Calgary and Kananaskis Country and at the Rafter 6 Ranch

This was one of the first films to feature the Olsen twins, who rose to TV stardom on Full House. *They would soon become two of the richest teens on earth. During filming, the producers convinced Calgary City Hall to allow a horse to board a C-Train light rail transit vehicle for a scene.*

CHILDREN OF THE DUST 175 min.
Miniseries (United States)
a.k.a. *A Good Day to Die*
Vidmark Entertainment/CBS Television
Producers: Harold Tichenor, Frank Konigsberg, Joyce Eliason
Director: David Greene
Cast: Sidney Poitier, Farrah Fawcett, Michael Moriarty, Robert Guillaume, Hart Bochner, Jack Ackroyd, Charles Andre, Donna Belleville, James Caviezell, Lindsey Campbell, Byron Chief-Moon, Michael Elias, Joanna Going, Katherine Isobel, Brian Jensen, Eric Keenleyside, Shirley Knight, Mitchell LaPlante, Jesse Lipscomb, Kevin McNulty, Joshua Myers, Wilma Pelly, John Pyper-Ferguson, Edward C. K. Richardson III, Zachary Savard, Tom Schanley, Brent Stait, Regina Taylor, Michelle Thrush, Crystal Verge, Basil Wallace, Dale Wilson, Billy Wirth, Grace Zabriskie
Filmed in: near Calgary

This film was nominated for three Emmy Awards. Michael Moriarty had just left the TV series Law & Order *and would soon settle in Canada, where he would later talk about starting his own political party. In 2002, Sidney Poitier received a lifetime achievement honour at the Academy Awards.*

BLACK FOX, **BLACK FOX: THE PRICE OF PEACE**, and **BLACK FOX: GOOD MEN AND BAD** 92, 96, and 90 min. (Canada/United States)
Producers: Les Kimber, Tony Allard, Robert Halmi, Jr., Norman S. Powell
Director: Steven Hilliard Stern
Cast: Christopher Reeve, Raoul Trujillo, Tony Todd, Janet Bailey, Nancy Sorel, Chris Wiggins, Lawrence Dane, Cynthia Preston, Dale Wilson, Leon Goodstrike, Morningstar Mecredi, Joel Phage-Wright, Don S. Davis, Byron Chief-Moon, Buffalo Child, Denis Lacroix, Lorette Clow, Bryce Krentz, David

Lereaney, Chris Benson, Kim Coates
Filmed in: at the CL Ranch near Calgary and other locations

These three made-for-TV movies were shot back-to-back. During production, Christopher Reeve served as Grand Marshall of the 1994 Calgary Stampede Parade. The next year, he was paralyzed from the neck down in a riding accident and became an advocate for the disabled.

WHILE JUSTICE SLEEPS 84 min.
(United States)
Blue André Productions
Producer: Blue André
Director: "Alan Smithee"
Cast: Cybill Shepherd, Tim Matheson, Karis Paige Bryant, Dion Anderson, Henry Beckman, Anna Ferguson, Kurtwood Smith, Robyn Stevan, Elan Ross Gibson, Crystal Verge, Chelsey G. Marshall, Gabrielle Rose, Paul Coeur, Valerie Pearson, Alf Humphreys, Barbara Pollard, Brenda Shuttleworth, David Lereaney
Filmed in: Calgary, Red Deer, and Vancouver

This film carries an "Alan Smithee" directing credit. It is a Hollywood tradition that the fictitious name "Alan Smithee" be applied whenever a film director requests to be uncredited (usually indicating a dispute over the handling of the movie by other parties).

THE SUBURBANATORS 87 min.
(Alberta)
Burns Film Ltd., Red Devil Films Ltd.
Producer: John Hazlett
Director: Gary Burns
Cast: Joel McNichol, Stephen Spender, Stewart Burdett, Jacob Banigan, Jihad Traya, Ahmad Taha, Rogy Masri, Peter Strand Rumpel, Jon Raitt, Andy Curtis, Curt McKinstry, Lyle St. Goddard, Aramis Padmos, Tim Andrews, Jim Travis, Jason Scott Arsonau, Jeff Adler, Carrie Schiffler
Filmed in: Calgary

1995

THE LEGEND OF THE RUBY SILVER
96 min. (Alberta/United States)
Silver Productions, Allarcom
Producers: Arvi Liimatainen, Pete White, Jim Green, Allen S. Epstein
Director: Charles Wilkinson
Cast: Rebecca Jenkins, John Schneider, Larry Day, David Everhart, Stephen Hair, Jonathan Jackson, Stephen Eric McIntyre, Chris Nannarone, Bruce Wells
Filmed in: near Canmore

This film won the Top Ten Award from the Writers Guild of Canada. John Schneider was best known at the time as the co-star of TV's The Dukes of Hazzard *and more recently as Jonathan Kent on* Smallville. *Larry Day was best known as a Calgary newscaster.*

ANGEL FLIGHT DOWN 90 min.
(United States)
Producers: Carla Singer, Norton Wright, Joan Carson, Bob Banner, Richard C. Berman, Myra Model, Deborah Morris, Norvell Rose
Director: Charles Wilkinson
Cast: Christopher Atkins, Gary Graham, Donna Belleville, Judith Buchan, Daniel Busheiken, Ron Carothers, David Charvet, Paul Coeur, Dennis Corrie, Michael Fansett, Christopher Hunt, Patricia Kalember, Duval Lang, Donna Larson, Terry Lawrence, Daniel Libman, Paige Magnusson, Andy Maton, Stephen E. Miller, Deanna Milligan, Jesse Moss, Nirmala Naidoo-Hill, Rod Padmos, Larry Reese, Garwin Sanford, Brenda Shuttleworth, Maureen Thomas, Ed Washington
Filmed in: Calgary and Kananaskis Country

Gary Graham starred in the TV series Alien Nation *and later had a recurring role on* Star Trek: Enterprise. *Nirmala Naidoo-Hill is a Calgary TV newscaster.*

PORTRAITS OF A KILLER 93 min.
(Alberta/United States)
a.k.a. *Portraits of Innocence*

Illusion Entertainment, Allarcom
Producers: Stefano Dammicco, Bruce Harvey, David A. Jackson, Shauna Shapiro Jackson
Director: Bill Corcoran
Cast: Jennifer Grey, Michael Ironside, Mark Anderako, Meaghan Ball, Patricia Charbonneau, Paul Coeur, Brian Dooley, Danielle Evans, Aisha Freeman, Currie Graham, Stephen Hair, Tracy Hemeyer, Mary Hennigan, Stephen Holgate, Roxane Kraemer, David Lereaney, Costas Mandylor, Andy Maton, David McNally, Val Planche, Esther Purves-Smith, Carrie Schiffler, Daryl Shuttleworth, Sherry Sonnleitner, M. Emmett Walsh, Kenneth Welsh.
Filmed in: Calgary

Jennifer Grey is best known for her roles in the 1980s' films Ferris Bueller's Day Off *and* Dirty Dancing.

1996

GONE IN A HEARTBEAT 90 min.
(United States)
a.k.a. *Taken Away*
Producers: Carla Singer, Joan Carson, Lizzy Shaw
Director: Jerry Jameson
Cast: Michael Tucker, Jill Eikenberry, James Marsden, Enid-Raye Adams, Colin A. Campbell, Paul Cowling, David Everhart, Christian Goutisis, Mark Holden, Stephen Holgate, Linda Kupcock, Donna Larson, Greg Lawson, Nancy MacDonald, Doug MacLeod, Michael MacRae, Brian Martel, Shane Meier, Stephanie Mills, Anthony Santiago, Jerry Wasserman, Robert Wisden, Gordon Michael Woolvett, Izabella Zalewski
Filmed in: Calgary

Michael Tucker and Jill Eikenberry are a husband-and-wife acting team who worked together on the TV series LA Law.

ROSE HILL 90 min. (United States)
Hallmark Productions
Producer: Andrew Gottleib

Director: Christopher Cain
Cast: Jennifer Garner, Peggy Ann Adams, David Aaron Baker, Addison Bell, Jim Brooks, Justin Chambers, Courtney Chase, Vera Farmiga, Kristin Griffith, Michael Alexander Jackson, David Klein, James MacDonald, Carmen Moore, David Newsom, Zak Orth, Vanya Rose, Jeffrey D. Sams, Casey Siemaszko, Blair Slater, Tristan Tait, Stewart Wilson, Donovan Workun, Kevin Zegers
Filmed in: Longview and Calgary

Jennifer Garner would achieve stardom in 2001 as the star of the ABC TV series Alias.

IN COLD BLOOD 200 min. Miniseries (United States/Canada)
Pacific Motion Picture Corporation
Producers: Tom Rowe, Robert Halmi, Sr., George Horie, David W. Rose
Director: Jonathan Kaplan
Cast: Anthony Edwards, Eric Roberts, Sam Neill, Kevin Tighe, Stella Stevens, Gwen Verdon, Mark Anderako, Gillian Barber, Chuck Bennett, Randy Birch, Robbie Bowen, Wolfgang Brunner, Lindsey Campbell, Paul Coeur, Georgie Collins, Don S. Davis, Pamela Diaz, Troy Evans, Margot Finley, John Gibbs, Christian Anthony Goutsis, Brad Greenquist, Stephen Hair, Mark Herring, Susan Hogan, Frank Holt, L. Q. Jones, Chezlene Kocian, Campbell Lane, Louise Latham, Greg Lawson, Matthew Lerigny, Bethel Leslie, Jesse Lipscomb, Tom McBeath, Liese McDonald, John McDonough, Johnny Ray McGhee, Stephanie Mills, Renae Morriseau, Harry Northup, Bruce Parkhouse, Emily Perkins, Valerie Planche, Francisco Puig, Esther Purves-Smith, Larry Reese, Ryan Reynolds, Leo Rossi, Tom Rowe, Joe Norman Shaw, Brenda Shuttleworth, Isobel Smith, Veronica Sztopa, Patricia M. Tkachuk, Frank C. Turner, Rhys Williams
Filmed in: Calgary

In Cold Blood was nominated for two Emmy Awards, including Outstanding Miniseries. It was based on the Truman Capote novel, which had been filmed in 1967. Gwen Verdon was a Broadway musical legend and one of the original

stars of the musicals Chicago, Damn Yankees, Can-Can, *and others.*

THE EDGE 117 min. (United States)
Fox Film Corporation
Producers: Art Linson, Lloyd Phillips
Director: Lee Tamahori
Cast: Anthony Hopkins, Alec Baldwin, Elle Macpherson, Brian Arnold, Bob Boyd, L. Q. Jones, Mark Kiely, Kelsa Kinsly, David Lindsiedt, Larry Musser, Harold Parrineau, Jr., Gordon Tootoosis, Kathleen Wilhoite, and Bart the Bear
Filmed in: Kananaskis Country and Edmonton

Lee Tamahori later directed the James Bond film Die Another Day. *By 1998, Anthony Hopkins had been nominated for four Academy Awards, winning Best Actor for 1991's* Silence of the Lambs. *Bart the Bear had also appeared in* Legends of the Fall.

OUT OF NOWHERE 120 min. (United States)
Producers: Mark Bacino, Joseph Nasser
Director: Charles Wilkinson
Cast: Lisa Hartman, Brian McNamara, Tam Ang, Rick Ash, Eva La Rue, Lorne Cardinal, Lisa Chapman, Babs Chula, Lorette Clow, Wally Dalton, Rhonda Fisekci, Fred Keating, Darren Lucas, Colleen Rennison, J. C. Roberts, Brian Rutledge, Michael David Simms, Brian Stollery, Frank Takacs, Rebecca Toolan
Filmed in: location unknown

Lisa Hartman is best known for co-starring in the TV soap opera Knot's Landing *in the 1980s, as well as in the 1970s' sitcom* Tabitha, *an obscure spin-off of* Bewitched.

WILD AMERICA 106 min. (United States)
Morgan Creek Productions
Producers: Gary Barber, James G. Robinson, Kearie Peak, Irby Smith, Mark Stouffer, Steve Tisch, Bill Todman, Jr.
Director: William Dear
Cast: Jonathan Taylor Thomas, Scott Bairstow, Danny Glover, Maggie Blackkettle, Amy Lee Douglas, Frances Fisher, Rachel Fowler, Larry Reese, Devon Sawa, Jamey

Wild America: Stunt moose from the movie about the real-life Stouffer brothers' childhood adventures. Photo: Chris Large

Sheridan, Sonny Shroyer, Claudia Stedelin, Anastasia Spivey, Don Stroud, Norman Taber, Leighanne Wallace, Tracey Walter, Zack Ward
Filmed in: Calgary, Bragg Creek, Canmore, and Drumheller

Danny Glover's appearance is uncredited; he is best known as Mel Gibson's partner in the Lethal Weapon *movies. Jonathan Taylor Thomas was a teen actor then starring in the sitcom* Home Improvement.

HARVEST OF LIES 115 min. (United States)
a.k.a. *Seduction of a Small Town*
Green/Epstein Productions
Producers: Mark Bacino, Allen S. Epstein, Jim Green, Diane Jeanné, Ned Welsh
Director: Charles Wilkinson
Cast: G. W. Bailey, Melissa Gilbert, Joely Fisher, Dennis Weaver, Bartley Bard, Judith Buchan, Shawna Lori Burnett, Lindsay Burns, Babs Chula, Ashley Doty, Stephen Hair, Hal Kerbes, Donna Larson, Christine MacInnis, Liese McDonald, Brian McNamara, Stephanie Mills, Joel Palmer, Thomas Peacocke, Valerie Ann Pearson, Valerie Planche, Maureen Thomas
Filmed in: Calgary

Character actor G. W. Bailey played Capt. Harris in the Canadian-made Police Academy *movie series and also had a recurring role on* M★A★S★H. *Melissa Gilbert grew up on TV in the series* Little House on the Prairie.

HEART FULL OF RAIN 100 min. (United States)
Producers: Bruce Margolis, Karen Moore, Dori Weiss
Director: Roger Young
Cast: Rick Schroder, Carroll Baker, Tom Bews, Richard Crenna, Kim Dickens, Paul Dunphy, Judith Mahbey, Gabriel Mann, Tyler Niles, Wendell Smith
Filmed in: Fort Macleod

Carroll Baker became a film legend as the star of the controversial 1956 film Baby Doll.

SURVIVAL ON THE MOUNTAIN 120 min. (United States)
Jaffe/Braunstein Films Ltd.
Director: John Patterson
Cast: Markie Post, Dennis Boutsikaris, Ian Tracey, Anthony Holland, Hiromoto Ida, Jan D'Arcy, Hiro Kanagawa, Kameron Louangxay, Manoj Sood, Katie Stuart, Chris Lovick, Shauna Nep, Kelsa Kinsly, Claire Riley, Michael Sunczyk, Jessica Van der Veen, Scott Heindl
Filmed in: location unknown

Markie Post co-starred in the long-running TV sitcom Night Court.

A SIMPLE WISH 89 min. (United States)
a.k.a. *The Fairy Godmother*
Universal Pictures, The Bubble Factory
Producers: Michael S. Glick, Jeff Rothberg, Bill Sheinberg, Jonathan Sheinberg, Sid Sheinberg
Director: Michael Ritchie
Cast: Martin Short, Mara Wilson, Robert Pastorelli, Amanda Plummer, Francis Capra, Ruby Dee, Teri Garr, Alan Campbell, Jonathan Hadary, Deborah Odell, Lanny Flaherty, Kathleen Turner
Filmed in: Brooks and New York, Oklahoma, and Ontario

Co-star Mara Wilson won honours from the Young Artist Awards and YoungStar Awards for her performance.

THE SECRET LIFE OF ALGERNON 105 min. (United Kingdom/Canada)
Marano Productions Inc., Phare-Est Productions

Producers: Jeff Hänni, Nancy Marano
Director: Charles Jarrott
Cast: John Cullum, Carrie-Anne Moss, Charles Durning, Harant Alianak, Kay Hawtrey, Ivan VanHecke, Malcolm Wilson, Dawn McKelvie Cyr, Adèle Bourque, John F. O'Halloran, Wally McKinnon, Kathleen Barr, Adam S. Bristol
Filmed in: St. Albert

Canadian actress Carrie-Anne Moss is best known for her work in the Matrix *trilogy (as well as an unrelated TV series of the same name).*

EXCESS BAGGAGE 101 min. (United States)
Columbia Pictures Corporation, First Kiss Productions
Producers: Bill Borden, Casey Grant, Carolyn Kessler, Alicia Silverstone
Director: Marco Brambilla
Cast: Alicia Silverstone, Benicio Del Toro, Christopher Walken, Jack Thompson, Nicholas Turturro, Sally Kirkland, Michael Bowen, Leland Orser, Robert Wisden, Harry Connick, Jr., Hiro Kanagawa, Brendan Beiser, Jorge Vargas
Filmed in: Waterton, Victoria, and Vancouver

Benicio Del Toro was nominated for an ALMA Award for his performance. Alicia Silverstone, best known for her comedy film Clueless, *was an uncredited producer on this film.*

AMERICAN BEER 85 min. (Canada)
Producers: Grant Harvey, Brent Kawchuk, Jordan Kawchuk
Director: Grant Harvey
Cast: Scott Urquhart, C. Adam Leigh, Jordan Kawchuk, Jason Thompson, Myles Clayton, Jon Raitt, Arayan Starre, Tyson Eichenlaub, Churqui, A. J. Cotton, Michael Lozinski, Brent Kawchuk, Lindsay Burns, Jesse Ed Azure
Filmed in: Calgary

1997

EBENEZER 94 min. (Alberta)
Nomadic Pictures

Producers: Doug Berquist, Michael Frislev, Cindy Lamb, Barbara Ligeti, Chad Oakes
Director: Ken Jubenvill
Cast: Jack Palance, Rick Schroder, Amy Locane, Albert Schultz, Linden Banks, Morris Chapdelaine, Kyle Collings, Richard Comar, Susan Coyne, James Dugan, Darcy Dunlap, Karina Frislev, Richard Halliday, Zoe Rose Hesse, Des Jardine, Hal Kerbes, Alex Kutchycki, Thomas F. Legg, Daniel Libman, Jocelyn Loewen, Heather Lea MacCallum, Billy Morton, John R. Nelson, Aaron Pearl, J. C. Roberts, Brenda Shuttleworth, Daryl Shuttleworth, Joshua Silberg, Michelle Thrush
Filmed in: Calgary

This was one of the first film productions supported by the A-Channel Drama Fund.

SILENT CRADLE 95 min. (Canada)
Illusions Entertainment
Producers: Bruce Harvey, Ciro Dammicco, Nancy Laing
Director: Paul Ziller
Cast: Lorraine Bracco, John Heard, Margot Kidder, R. H. Thomson
Filmed in: Edmonton

In 1999, Lorraine Bracco joined the cast of the HBO series The Sopranos.

THINGS TO DO ON A SATURDAY NIGHT 95 min. (Alberta)
Producer: Kate Holowach
Director: Norm Fassbender
Cast: Ken Brown, Chris Fassbender, Jean-Paul Fournier, Mark Gibbon, Christine MacInnis, David McNally, Kate Ryan, Tim Ryan
Filmed in: Edmonton

ONE OF OUR OWN 95 min. (Alberta)
Illusion Entertainment
Producers: Richard Davis, Michael Ironside, David A. Jackson
Director: David Winning
Cast: Michael Ironside, Frederic Forrest, Currie Graham, Peta Wilson, Marshall Bell, Robbie Bowen, Paul Coeur, David Ferry, Richard Riehle, Jacqueline Samuda, Joe Norman Shaw, Jorge Vargas

Filmed in: Calgary

This film won the Gold Award for Best Feature Film—Thriller at the 1997 WorldFest Charleston. Australian-born actress Peta Wilson was about to become an international TV star with her role in the Canadian-filmed spy drama Nikita.

HEART OF THE SUN 96 min. (Alberta)
Dancing Stones Film Production, Ennerdale Productions, Makara Pictures
Producers: Kim Hogan, Sydney Banks, John Danylkiw, Shaun Johnston, Brenda Liles
Director: Francis Damberger
Cast: Christianne Hirt, Shaun Johnston, Michael Riley, Merrilyn Gann, Eric Johnson, Graham Greene
Filmed in: Medicine Hat and Edmonton

Heart of the Sun *won the 2000 Genie Award for Best Screenplay, Adapted.*

FARGOT TV Pilot
Director: Cathy Bates
Filmed in: Edmonton and at Hubbles Lake
No other information available.

SUMMER OF THE MONKEYS 101 min. (Canada)
The Edge Productions Corporation
Producers: David Doerksen, Ellen Freyer, Chris Harding, Michael J. LeGresley, Torin Stefanson
Director: Michael Anderson
Cast: Michael Ontkean, Leslie Hope, Wilford Brimley, Corey Sevier, Katie Stuart, Don Francks, André Thérien, B. J. McLellan, Danny Mulvihill, Kim Schraner, Melissa Thompson, Wayne Best, Beverly Cooper, Blaine Hart, Russell Badger, Cody Kurz
Filmed in: Calgary and Saskatoon

This film won awards at the Breckinridge Festival of Film, Heartland Film Festival, and Marco Island Film Festival.

OKLAHOMA CITY: A SURVIVOR'S STORY (United States)
ABC Pictures Corporation, Lifetime Television
Producer: Andrea Baynes
Director: John Korty
Cast: Kathy Baker, Roy Baker, Eric Johnson,

Kyla Anderson, Patrick Cassidy, Dennis Corrie, John Hawkes, David Lereaney
Filmed in: Calgary

Calgary doubled for Oklahoma City in this made-for-cable-TV recreation of the 1995 terrorist bombing.

ATOMIC DOG 95 min. (United States)
Producers: Ted Bauman, Mark H. Ovitz
Director: Brian Trenchard-Smith
Cast: Daniel Hugh Kelly, Isabella Hofmann, Cindy Pickett, Micah Gardener, Katie Stuart, Deryl Hayes, Scott Olynek, Ryan Northcott, Matt Clarke, Hal Kerbes, J. C. Roberts, Andy Curtis, Carrie Schiffler, Paul Cowling, Tara Howie
Filmed in: Calgary

Cindy Pickett's TV roles include St. Elsewhere *and* The Guiding Light.

1998

NOAH 120 min. (United States)
Noah Productions, Walt Disney Television
Producers: Stephen North, Karen Tangorra
Director: Ken Kwapis
Cast: Tony Danza, Wallace Shawn, Kyla Anderson, Lloyd Berry, Randy Birch, Nicola Cavendish, Matt Clarke, Paul Coeur, Georgie Collins, Dennis Corrie, Paul Dunphy, Bharbara Egan, Bunny Harris, Tara Howie, Karen Johnston-Diamond, John Marshall Jones, Larry Lefebvre, Chris Marquette, Anita Matthys, Jane McGregor, Don McManus, Kevin McNulty, Melanie Merkosky, Jesse Moss, Scott Olynek, Aaron Pearl, Valerie Planche, Hazel Proctor, Ed Richardson, Joe Norman Shaw, Daryl Shuttleworth, Jane Sibbett, Michal Suchánek, Maureen Thomas
Filmed in: Calgary

Tony Danza is best known for his long-running TV sitcoms Taxi *and* Who's the Boss?

NAKED FRAILTIES 91 min. (Canada/Alberta)
Producers: Arvi Liimatainen, Harold Tichenor, Don Armstrong, Harley Hay, Jayme Pfahl, Larry Reese

Director: Larry Reese
Cast: Travis Woloshyn, Reagan Dale Neis, Terry Ladd, Paul Boultbee, Terrence Cross, Myron Deardon, Fiona O'Brien, John Treleaven, Jeremy A. Weddell
Filmed in: Red Deer

During the 2002–03 TV season, Manitoba-born Reagan Dale Neis made several guest appearances on the popular Fox sitcom Malcolm in the Middle.

WHEN TRUMPETS FADE 95 min.

(United States)
a.k.a. *Hamburger Hill 2*
Citadel Entertainment, Home Box Office
Producers: John Kemeny, David R. Ginsburg, Judy Hofflund, Gavin Polone
Director: John Irvin
Cast: Dylan Bruno, Bobby Cannavale, Matthew Rutson Cooney, Jeffrey Donovan, Martin Donovan, Ron Eldard, Dan Futterman, Devon Gummersall, Frank Köbe, Timothy Olyphant, Zak Orth, Steven Petrarca, András Stohl, Frank Whaley, Dwight Yoakam
Filmed in: Calgary

Dwight Yoakam is best known as a popular country singer, but he has dabbled in acting since the early 1990s.

IN THE BLUE GROUND 97 min.

(Alberta)
Alberta Filmworks
Producers: Tom Dent-Cox, Doug MacLeod
Director: Alan Simmonds
Cast: Tina Keeper, Tracey Cook, Robert Bockstael, Peter Kelly Gaudreault, Dakota House, Lorne Cardinal, Paul Kuster
Filmed in: Bragg Creek

First of several made-for-TV movies based on the CBC series North of 60. *Peter Kelly Gaudreault received an Emmy nomination for his performance. Paul Kuster is a TV news reporter for a Calgary station. Lorne Cardinal later co-starred in the comedy series* Blackfly *and* Corner Gas.

I'LL BE HOME FOR CHRISTMAS 86

min. (United States)
Walt Disney Productions
Producers: Robin French, Justis Greene,

David Hoberman, Tracey Trench
Director: Arlene Sanford
Cast: Jonathan Taylor Thomas, Jessica Biel, Gary Cole, Mark Acheson, Awaovieyi Agie, Bart Anderson, Natalie Barish, Mike Battie, Brendan Beiser, J. B. Bivens, Lesley Boone, Dmitry Chepovetsky, Mark de la Cruz, Dolores Drake, Annette Dreeshen, Kathleen Freeman, Eve Gordon, Kevin Hansen, Manami Hara, Tom Heaton, Ernie Jackson, Peter Kelamis, Jack Kenny, Graeme Kingston, Celia Kushner, Andrew Lauer, Adam LaVorgna, Betty Linde, Lauren Maltby, Sarah May, Alexander Milani, Nick Misura, Alexandria Mitchell, David Neale, Paul Norman, Michael P. Northey, Sean O'Bryan, Nicole Oliver, Eileen Pedde, Eric Pospisil, P. J. Prinsloo, Ian Robison, Kurt Max Runte, Melissa Barker Sauer, James Sherry, Tasha Simms, Blair Slater, Amzie Strickland, Ron Timms, Cathy Weseluck, Chris Willis
Filmed in: Canmore

Teen actress Jessica Biel was co-starring in the popular TV series 7th Heaven *at the time this film was made.*

THE JACK BULL 120 min. (United States)

River One Productions, Home Box Office
Producers: John Cusack, Cammie Crier, D. V. DeVincentis, Doug Dearth, William E. Githens, Thomas J. Mangan IV, John C. McGinley, Daniel C. Mitchell, Steve Pink, Kevin Reidy
Director: John Badham
Cast: John Cusack, John Goodman, Miranda Otto, Drake Bell, Ned Bellamy, Nick Gillie, Brent Briscoe, Bill Cusack, Dick Cusack, Nathaniel DeVeaux, Bruce Flewelling, Duncan Fraser, Kurt Fuller, Raoul Ganeev, Nick Gillie, Corry Glass, Rodney A. Grant, Tom Heaton, Jimmy Herman, Ken Hurlburt, L. Q. Jones, Campbell Lane, Madeleine Lefebvre, Robert Lewis, Rex Linn, John C. McGinley, Glenn Morshower, Chad Nobert, John Payne, Byrne Piven, Valerie Planche, Ken Pogue, Rick Poltaruk, Esther Purves-Smith, Patrick Richards, J. C. Roberts, Jay O. Sanders, John Savage, Gina Williams, Scott Wilson
Filmed in: Calgary

John Goodman rose to fame as co-star of the long-running TV sitcom Roseanne. *Australian actress Miranda Otto later joined the massive cast of the* Lord of the Rings *movie trilogy.*

MYSTERY, ALASKA 129 min. (United States)
Hollywood Pictures, Rocking Chair Productions
Producers: David E. Kelley, Howard Baldwin, Karen Elise Baldwin, Jack Gilardi, Jr., Dan Kolsrud, Shauna Robertson
Director: Jay Roach
Cast: Hank Azaria, Russell Crowe, Colm Meaney, Mike Myers, Mary McCormack, Burt Reynolds, Maury Chaykin, Lolita Davidovich, Cameron Bancroft, Adam Beach, Michael Buie, Ross Drew, Kevin Durand, Ron Eldard, Jason Gray-Stanford, Scott Grimes, Stephen Hair, Zoe Rose Hesse, Tara Howie, Linda Jarvis, Rod Jarvis, Beth Littleford, George Maniotakis, Ryan Northcott, Leroy Peltier, Megyn Price, Brent Stait, Rachel Wilson, Terry David Mulligan, Michael McKean
Filmed in: Canmore and Banff

Writer-producer David E. Kelley has created many popular and award-winning TV series, including Picket Fences, Ally McBeal, Chicago Hope, *and* The Practice. *The next year, Russell Crowe starred in* Gladiator, *which won him a Best Actor Oscar and superstardom. Director Jay Roach directed the three* Austin Powers *films, starring Canadian comic Mike Myers, who also appears in this film.*

NIGHTMARE IN BIG SKY COUNTRY 119 min. (United States)
ABC Pictures Corp.
Producers: Andrea Baynes, Greg Gugliotta
Director: Alan Metzger
Cast: Patricia Wettig, M. Emmett Walsh, Matt McCoy, Stephen Hair, Tara Howie
Filmed in: location unknown

Patricia Wettig is best known for her role in the 1980s' TV comedy-drama series thirtysomething; *in 2004, she had a recurring role on the spy drama* Alias.

The Jack Bull: According to producer/star John Cusack, Clint Eastwood recommended Alberta as a shooting location after the success he had had with *Unforgiven*. Photo: Chris Large

QUESTION OF PRIVILEGE 94 min. (Alberta)
Illusion Entertainment
Producer: Bruce Harvey
Director: Rick Stevenson
Cast: Jessica Steen, David Keith, Wendy Crewson, Nick Mancuso, Michael Ironside, Tom Butler, Coralie Cairns, Christopher Lee Fassbinder, Myles Ferguson, Jessica Harvey, Jessica Hopper, Eric Johnson, David McNally, Andrew Misle, Paul Punti, Benjamin Ratner, Larry Reese, Victoria Rutwind, Jan Alexandra Smith, Wendell Smith
Filmed in: Edmonton

In the mid-1980s, Nick Mancuso starred in the Calgary-filmed TV series Stingray.

YOU KNOW MY NAME 94 min. (United States)
a.k.a. *Bill Tilghman*
Turner Network Television
Producers: Sam Elliott, Amy Adelson, Andrew Gottleib, Brandon Stoddard
Director: John Kent Harrison
Cast: Sam Elliott, Carolyn McCormick, Sheila McCarthy, Perla Batalla, Mel Crumb, R. Lee Ermey, James Gammon, Stephen Hair, Arliss Howard, James Parks, Natalia Rey, Jonathan Young

You Know My Name: A fact-based biography of early film director-producer Bill Tilghman (Sam Elliott) who was also a real life cowboy with connections to the Earps. Photo: Chris Large

Filmed in: at the Copithorne Ranch, west of Calgary

This film won the Bronze Wrangler Award at the 2000 Western Heritage Awards. Sheila McCarthy is an award-winning Canadian actress who rose to notoriety with her role in I've Heard the Mermaids Singing *(1987); she also co-starred with Bruce Willis in* Die Hard 2: Die Harder.

BAD MONEY 95 min. (Alberta)
Red Devil Films Ltd.
Producers: James Gottselig, John Hazlett
Director: John Hazlett
Cast: Graham Greene, Karen Sillas, Stephen Spender, Alisen Down, Denis Gagnon, Walt Healy, John Heywood, Rainer Kahl, Brent Kawchuk, Jordan Kawchuk, Tamsin Kelsey, Terry King, Daniel Libman, Valerie Planche, Jon Turvey, Josh Williams
Filmed in: Calgary

TAIL LIGHTS FADE 87 min. (Canada)
Telefilm Canada, British Columbia Film Commission, CITY-TV, Highwire Entertainment, CTV
Producers: Christine Haebler, Doug Hardwick, Scott Kennedy, Karen Powell, Shawn Williamson, Daegan Fryklind, Jennifer

Moore, Kevin Smith
Director: Malcolm Ingram
Cast: Jaimz Woolvett, Breckin Meyer, Jake Busey, Elizabeth Berkley, Tanya Allen, Ben Derrick, Doug Hardwick, Denise Richards, Marcus Hondro, Tristin Leffler, Tyler Labine, Matthew Gissing, Darryl Quon, Gordie Giroux, Lisa Marie, Sean Campbell, John Dryden, Chris Hagel, Max Martini
Filmed in: Calgary, British Columbia, Toronto, and New Jersey

Executive producer Kevin Smith went from writing comic books to directing cult-classic films such as Clerks *and* Chasing Amy. *Denise Richards went on to co-star in the James Bond film* The World is Not Enough.

HEARTBEAT: CHANGING PLACES
(United Kingdom)
Yorkshire Television
Producer and director: Bob Mahoney
Cast: Nick Berry, Randy Birch, Adrian Hough, Alice Jones, Terry Lawrence
Filmed in: Cochrane, Lake Louise, and Kananaskis Country

This British made-for-TV movie followed on from the long-running series Heartbeat.

CHEERFUL TEARFUL 99 min. (Canada)
Director: Donna Brunsdale
Cast: Susan Bristow, Jarvis Hall, Douglas MacLeod, Curt McKinstry, Stephen Spender
Filmed in: Calgary

1999

THE SHELDON KENNEDY STORY
(Canada)
CTV
Producers: Pierre Sarrazin, Doug MacLeod
Director: Norma Bailey
Cast: Jonathan Scarfe, Polly Shannon, Jack Ackroyd, Ryan Addams, Shannon Anderson, Edanna Andrews, Marty Antonini, Lynda Boyd, Christy Bruce, Ben Campbell, David Chapman, Paul Coeur, Rob Daprocida, Larry Day, Paul Dunphy, Chris Enright, Noel Fisher, Stephen Hair, Kiel Harvey, David

Hayson, Gary Hetherington, Rod Jarvis, Terry King, Bryce Kulak, Sandra Laratta, Terry Lawrence, Jonathan Love, Darren Lucas, Brian Martell, Anita Matthys, Shawn McCann, Stephen Eric McIntyre, Doug McKeag, David McNally, Melanie Merkosky, Ty Olsson, Valerie Planche, Will Reeb, Larry Reese, Kathy Shane, Gillian Skupa, Brent Stait, Jodi Stecyk, Justin Stillwell, Maureen Thomas, Brad Turner, Dan Willmott, Robert Wisden
Filmed in: Calgary

Nominated for two Gemini Awards, this film won Best Actor in a Leading Role for Jonathan Scarfe's performance.

TEXAS RANGERS 90 min. (United States)
Producers: David S. Cass, Sr., Mary Church, Jessica Cunningham, Frank Q. Dobbs, Cary Granat, Alan Greisman, Greg Krutilek, Larry Levinson, Doug Metzger, Frank Price, Bob Weinstein, Harvey Weinstein
Director: Steve Miner
Cast: James Van Der Beek, Rachael Leigh Cook, Ashton Kushter, Dylan McDermott, Oded Fehr, Alfred Molina, Tom Skerritt, Robert Patrick, Stephen Bridgewater, Marco Leonardi, Usher Raymond, Randy Travis, Leonor Varela, James Coburn
Filmed in: Brooks

*Not released until 2001, many of its young stars were popular on TV and in movies, such as James Van Der Beek (*Dawson's Creek*), Rachael Leigh Cook (*Josie and the Pussycats*), and Ashton Kushter (*That '70s Show and Punk'd*).*

THE VIRGINIAN (United States)
Producers: Daniel H. Blatt, Ruth Fainberg, Grace Gilroy, Gary M. Goodman, Bill Pullman, Lynn Raynor
Director: Bill Pullman
Cast: Bill Pullman, Diane Lane, John Savage, Dennis Weaver, Harris Yulin, Mark Anderako, Larry Austin, Jessica Blatt, Farron Deardon, Gary Farmer, Colm Feore, Arnold Lawson, Maureen Rooney, Brent Stait, Dillinger Steele
Filmed in: Longview and at the Scott

Ranch and western town

Winner of the Bronze Wrangler Award at the 2001 Western Heritage Awards, this film was based on the novel by Owen Wister, which has been adapted for the screen many times since 1914.

SHANGHAI NOON 110 min. (United States)
Touchstone Pictures
Producers: Jackie Chan, Gary Barber, Roger Birnbaum, Willie Chan, Jules Daly, Ned Dowd, Jonathan Glickman, Bruce Moriarty, Solon So
Director: Tom Dey
Cast: Jackie Chan, Owen Wilson, Lucy Liu, Jason Connery, Curtis Armstrong, Xander Berkeley, Eric Chen, Adrien Dorval, Walt Goggins, Tong Lung, Brandon Merrill, Jody Thompson, Roger Yuan
Filmed in: Calgary and Drumheller

It was a major box-office success and spawned a 2003 sequel, Shanghai Knights. *Lucy Liu made this film at about the same time she made* Charlie's Angels. *Jason Connery, who has a small role, is the son of Sean Connery.*

SNOW DAY 95 min. (United States)
Paramount Pictures
Producers: Raymond Wagner, Grace Gilroy, Albie Hecht, David Kerwin, Will McRobb, Julia Pistor, Chris Viscardi
Director: Chris Koch
Cast: Chris Elliot, Chevy Chase, Mark Webber, Jean Smart, Schuyler Fisk, Iggy Pop, Pam Grier, Kyle Alisharan, J. Adam Brown, Emmanuelle Chriqui, Zena Grey, David Paetkau, John Schneider, Rozonda "Chilli" Thomas, Jade Yorker, Damian Young
Filmed in: Calgary and Edmonton

This film was nominated for two Young Artist Awards (Best Family Feature Film–Comedy and Best Performance by an Actor Age Ten or Under). Some of the winter scenes were shot in Calgary at the height of summer, requiring tons of snow to be shipped into the prestigious Mount Royal neighbourhood. Chevy Chase is best known for his work on Saturday Night Live *and the* Vacation *movie series.*

KILLING MOON 94 min. (Alberta)
a.k.a. *Framed*
Trinity Pictures
Producers: Stefano Dammicco, John
Gillespie, Tony Johnston
Director: John Bradshaw
Cast: Kim Coates, Daniel Baldwin, Penelope
Ann Miller, Dennis Akayama, William B.
Davis, Matthew Godfrey, Tracey Cook,
Daniel Kash, Miranda Kwok, Audrey Lupke,
Peter Outerbridge
Filmed in: Edmonton

Daniel Baldwin was regular on TV's Homicide:
Life on the Street *from 1993 to 1995.*

TRIAL BY FIRE 90 min. (Alberta)
CBC, Alberta Filmworks
Producer: Tom Dent-Cox, Doug MacLeod
Director: Francis Damberger
Cast: Tina Keeper, Tom Jackson, Peter Kelly
Gaudreault, Tracey Cook, Graham Greene,
Brian Dooley, Jimmy Herman, Dakota
House, Erroll Kinistino, Peter LaCroix,
Douglas MacLeod, Kevin McNulty, Lubomir
Mykytiuk, Michael Obey, Wilma Pelly, Yvan
Ponton, Joe Norman Shaw, Michelle Thrush,
Timothy Webber, Lori Ravensborg
Filmed in: Bragg Creek

This was the second of the North of 60 *made-
for-TV movies.*

A FATHER'S CHOICE 86 min. (United
States)
a.k.a. *Cowboy Dad*
Nasser Entertainment Group
Producers: Eda Lishman, Jack Nasser, Joseph
Nasser, Bernard Sofronski
Director: Christopher Cain
Cast: Peter Strauss, Mary McDonnell,
Michelle Trachtenberg, Susan Hogan, Judith
Bachan, Karen Barker, Ryan Barron, J. Winston
Carroll, Georgie Collins, Roger R. Cross,
Barbara Duncan, Reg Glass, Stephen Hair,
David H. Leader, Judith Maxie, Rod Padmos,
Joe Norman Shaw, Jim Shield, Susan L. Smith,
Brian Stollery, Frank Takacs, Monte Timmons,
Eddie Velez, Dan Willmott, Yvonne Zima
Filmed in: Calgary and Airdrie

Michelle Trachtenberg went on to become a teen

The Claim: Based on Thomas Hardy's *The
Mayor of Casterbridge*, this movie tells the tale of
a man who sells his wife and daughter for the
claim to a gold mine. Photo: Chris Large

idol with her role as Dawn on TV's Buffy the
Vampire Slayer. *Mary McDonnell rose to movie
stardom in 1990's* Dances with Wolves.

THE CLAIM 98 min. (Alberta/United
Kingdom/France)
a.k.a. *Kingdom Come*
DB Entertainment, Revolution Films
Producers: Andrew Eaton, Douglas
Berquist, Andrea Calderwood, Martin Katz,
Alexis Lloyd, Anita Overland, Mark Shivas,
David M. Thompson
Director: Michael Winterbottom
Cast: Peter Mullan, Milla Jovovich, Nastassja
Kinski, Sarah Polley, Roy Anderson, Marty
Antonini, Wes Bentley, Gil Rivera Blas, Marie
Brassard, Artur Ciastkowski, Fernando
Davalos, Shirley Henderson, Kate Hennig,
Jimmy Herman, Marc Hollogne, Christopher
Hunt, Tim Koetting, Lydia Lau, David
Lereaney, Tom McCamus, Sean McGinley,
Billy Morton, Karolina Muller, Phillipa Peak,
Julian Richings, Royal Sproule, Barry Ward,
Frank Zotter
Filmed in: Calgary and Kananaskis Country

*Based on a novel by Thomas Hardy, this film was
nominated for three Genie Awards, including a
supporting actor nod for Julian Richings; it was*

also nominated for the Golden Berlin Bear at the 2001 Berlin International Film Festival. Co-star Nastassja Kinski rose to stardom in the lead role of another Hardy adaptation, 1979's Tess.

BAD FAITH 97 min. (Alberta)
A-Channel
Bradshaw MacLeod and Associates
Producers: Doug MacLeod, Phil Alberstat, Tom Dent-Cox, Randy Bradshaw
Director: Randy Bradshaw
Cast: Tony Nardi, John Kapelos, Kenneth Welsh, Brian Markinson, Michael Moriarty, Gloria Reuben, Billy Morton, Jim Baker, David Chapman, Paul Coeur, Sonia Donaldson, Martin Evans, Duncan Fraser, Aaron Goettel, Darren Haffner, Stephen Hair, Elizabeth Hanes, Al Holt, Lynn Ivall, Tim Koetting, David Lereaney, Patti LuPone, Christian Mena, Chris Nannarone, Erin O'Sullivan, Valerie Planche, Gordon Rix, Joyce Robbins, Jacqueline Robbins, Tamara Seeley, Joe Norman Shaw, Brenda Shuttleworth, Gillian Skupa, Lyle St. Goddard, Maureen Thomas
Filmed in: Calgary

Former ER *regular Gloria Reuben went on to star in the* TV *series* The Agency *and* 1-800-MISSING. *Brian Markinson later appeared in a number of* TV *series, including* Dark Angel, Angels in America, *and* Touching Evil.

CROSSFIRE TRAIL 92 min. (United States)
Turner Network Television
Producers: Tom Selleck, Michael Brandman, Steven J. Brandman, Thomas John Kane, Simon Wincer
Director: Simon Wincer
Cast: Tom Selleck, Virginia Madsen, Wilford Brimley, David O'Hara, Barry Corbin, Mark Harmon, Mark Acheson, Kyla Anderson, Brad Johnson, Christian Kane, Patrick Kilpatrick, Rex Linn, Joanna Miles, Carmen Moore, James Nicholas, Michael O'Shea, Ken Pogue, William Sanderson, Marshall R. Teague
Filmed in: Calgary

Based upon the Louis L'Amour novel, this film won the Bronze Wrangler Award for Best Feature Film at the 2002 Western Heritage Awards. Tom

Selleck became a TV *superstar with* Magnum PI *in the 1980s. Mark Harmon was starring in the medical drama* Chicago Hope *at the time and went on to play the lead in the mystery series* Navy NCIS *in 2003.*

WAYDOWNTOWN 87 min. (Alberta)
CTV, Telefilm Canada, Burns Film Ltd.
Producers: George Baptist, Brian Gliserman, Gary Burns, Sharon McGowan, Marguerite Pigott, Shirley Vercruysse
Director: Gary Burns
Cast: Fab Filippo, Don McKellar, Marya Delver, Gordon Currie, Michelle Beaudoin, Judith Buchan, Nick Cleary, Jennifer Clement, Mike Eberly, Derek Flores, Tobias Godson, Harris Hart, Tammy Isbell, James McBurney, Xantha Radley, Brian Stollery, Dan Willmott
Filmed in: Calgary

Nominated for a Genie award for Achievement in Direction, this film won three awards at the 2000 Vancouver International Film Festival. Fab Filippo went on to co-star in the popular cable TV *series* Queer as Folk.

1132 PLEASANT STREET (Alberta)
Director: Norm Fassbender
Cast: David McNally, Kate Ryan, Mark Gibbon, Christine MacInnis, Jean Pierre Fournier, Timothy Ryan, Christopher Lee Fassbinder, Cameron Forbes, Troy Anthony Young, Maralyn Ryan, Patricia Casey, James DeFelice, Jeff Haslam, Kathy Moran, Hal Cooke, Susan Neill
Filmed in: Edmonton

GRIZZLY FALLS 94 min. (United States/United Kingdom/Canada)
The Movie Network, Norstar Entertainment Inc., Grizzly Productions Ltd.
Producers: Georges Campana, Mark Damon, Jessica Daniel, Raylan D. Jensen, Allan Scott, Peter R. Simpson
Director: Stewart Raffill
Cast: Bryan Brown, Tom Jackson, Oliver Tobias, Richard Harris, Daniel Clark, Chantel Dick, Trevor Lowden, Marnie McPhail, Ken Kramer, Brock Simpson, Colin D. Simpson, James Bearden, John Tench, Hayden Simpson,

John Prentice, and Bart the Bear
Filmed in: Morley, Kananaskis Country, Toronto, and Vancouver

A few years later, Irish film legend Richard Harris would end his career playing Dumbledore in the popular Harry Potter *films.*

COIL 79 min. (Canada)
Quiet Us Films
Producers: J. J. Heffring, Jesse Heffring
Director: Jesse Heffring
Cast: Barbara Kozicki, Nathalie Matteau, Todd Hann, Alexis D. Smolensk, A. J. Demers, Tommy Campbell, Ursula Jordaan, Gregory D. Alvas, Scott Maxwell, J. J. Heffring, Karen Mueller Bryson
Filmed in: Calgary and Banff

2000

VIVA LAS NOWHERE 97 min.
(Alberta/United States)
Franchise Pictures
Producers: Josh Miller, Erik Anderson, Luis Colina, Kevin DeWalt, Tom Karnowski, Mark McGarry, Massimo Nouhra, Roma Roth, Demitri Samaha, Elie Samaha, Tracee Stanley, Andrew Stevens
Director: Jason Bloom
Cast: James Caan, Daniel Stern, Patricia Richardson, Sherry Stringfield, Daren Christofferson, Skerivet Daramola, Shaun Johnston, Lacey Kohl, Andy Maton, Larry Reese, Carrie Schiffler
Filmed in: Calgary

It won the New American Cinema Special Jury Prize at the 2001 Seattle International Film Festival. Movie tough guy James Caan's acting career dates back to the early 1960s with TV guest appearances and an uncredited part in Irma la Douce; *he became a superstar as Sonny Corleone in 1972's* The Godfather.

ANTHRAX 90 min. (Alberta)
Illusion Entertainment
Producers: Bruce Harvey, Giampaolo Sodano

Director: Rick Stevenson
Cast: Cameron Daddo, Ed Begley, Jr., Allison Hossack, Joanna Cassidy, David Keith, Brian Markinson, Kyla Anderson, Randy Birch, Lisa Christie, William B. Davis, Todd Hann, Ron Hartman, Kiel Harvey, Tara Howie, Jan Rubes
Filmed in: near Calgary

This film made newspaper headlines as a case of "life imitating art," following the anthrax scare that occurred after the September 2001 terrorist attacks on the United States.

SPEAKING OF SEX 96 min. (United States)
Le Studio Canal+, Omnibus
Producers: Steven A. Jones, Rob Scheidlinger
Director: John McNaughton
Cast: James Spader, Melora Walters, Jay Mohr, Nathaniel Arcand, Megan Mullally, Bill Murray, Lara Flynn Boyle, Kathryn Erbe, Mary Antonini, Hart Bochner, Robert Burton Hubele, Phil LaMarr, Terry Lawrence, Daniel Libman, Don MacKay, Bill Meilen, Anjul Nigam, Nick Offerman, Catherine O'Hara, Greg Pitts, Kathleen Robertson, Paul Schulze
Filmed in: Calgary

James Spader had previously appeared in films such as Stargate, Crash, *and* Sex, Lies, and Videotape. *Megan Mullally was starring in the sitcom* Will & Grace. *Bill Murray remains one of America's most popular comic actors, recently receiving an Oscar nomination for* Lost in Translation. *Catherine O'Hara is a veteran of the Alberta-filmed* SCTV *Network.*

HIGH NOON 88 min. (United States)
Rosemont Productions
Producers: Ted Bauman, David A. Rosemont, Karen Sharpe Kramer
Director: Rod Hardy
Cast: Tom Skerritt, Maria Conchita Alonso, Randy Birch, Susanna Thompson, Dennis Weaver, Michael Madsen, Judith Buchan, Colin A. Campbell, Bob Chomyn, Reed Diamond, Noel Fisher, Shaun Johnston, Terry King, Thomas F. Legg, Trevor Leigh, David Learaney, Jim Leyden, Andy Maton, Tom McBeath, Steven Eric McIntyre, Kate

Newby, Jim Rattai, Jacqueline Robbins, Joyce Robbins, August Schellenberg, Joe Norman Shaw, Jim Shield, Royal Sproule, Brian Stollery, Frank C. Turner, Matthew Walker, Brent Woolsey
Filmed in: Calgary

This remake of the classic 1952 Alan Ladd film was nominated for awards by both the American and the Canadian Society of Cinematographers. Tom Skerritt's long career includes many years starring in the TV series Picket Fences, *as well as roles in such films as* Alien, Top Gun, *and the original* M★A★S★H. *Michael Madsen's credits include* Reservoir Dogs, Die Another Day, *and* Kill Bill.

FOR ALL TIME 84 min. (United States)
Rosemont Productions International
Producers: Lynn Bespflug, David A. Rosemont, Richard Thomas, Susan Zachary
Director: Steven Schachter
Cast: Mark Harmon, David Lereaney, Mary McDonnell, Catherine Hicks, Larry Austin, Cody Brown, Philip Casnoff, Bob Chomyn, Paul Coeur, Bill Cobbs, Georgie Collins, Ed Evanko, Stevie M. Mitchell, Shaker Paleja, Romy Rosemont
Filmed in: Calgary

This film was nominated for two Golden Reel awards in sound editing categories at the 2001 Motion Picture Sound Editors Awards. Catherine Hicks was starring in the TV family drama 7th Heaven *at the time.*

DREAM STORM 97 min. (Alberta)
Alberta Filmworks
Producers: Tom Dent-Cox, Doug MacLeod, Jordy Randall
Director: Stacey Stewart Curtis
Cast: Tina Keeper, Tracey Cook, Peter Kelly Gaudreault, Graham Greene, Dakota House, Tom Jackson, Michael Horse, Jimmy Herman, Peter LaCroix, Kevin McNulty, Lubomir Mykytiuk, Michael Obey, Wilma Pelly, Yvan Ponton, Michelle Thrush, Timothy Webber
Filmed in: Bragg Creek

This was the third North of 60 *made-for-TV film.*

COME L'AMERICA 96 min.
(Alberta/Italy)

a.k.a. *Almost America*
Illusions Entertainment, Eagle Pictures SPA
Producers: Bruce Harvey, Anselmo Parrinello
Directors: Andrea Frazzi, Antonio Frazzi
Cast: Sabrina Ferilli, Cosimo Bani, Byron Chief-Moon, Frank Crudele, Henry Czerny, Massimo Ghini, Stefano Giulianetti, Guido Laurini, Tony Nardi, Veronica Niccolai, Joseph Scoren, Gioia Spaziani, Dominic Zamprogna
Filmed in: Calgary, Edmonton, and Italy

Nominated for two Genie Awards, it won for Best Achievement in Art Direction/Production Design. Sabrina Ferilli was once named the most-loved woman in Italy.

AFTER THE HARVEST 94 min.
(Alberta/Canada)
a.k.a. *Wild Geese*
Alberta Filmworks, Sarazin Couture Productions
Producers: Doug MacLeod, Pierre Sarrazin, Suzette Couture, Martha Fusca
Director: Jeremy Podeswa
Cast: Sam Shepard, Nadia Litz, Alberta Watson, Edanna Andrews, Liane Balaban, Patricia Benedict, Mairon Bennett, Jonathan Eliot, Lynn Ivall, Tim Koetting, George Leach, David Lereaney, Shawn Mathieson, Andy Maton, Doug McKeag, Evan Sabba, John White
Filmed in: Calgary

This film was nominated for four Gemini Awards, including acting nods for Nadia Litz and Alberta Watson. Sam Shepard received an Oscar nomination for his role in 1983's The Right Stuff. *Alberta Watson co-starred in the TV spy drama* Nikita.

RAT RACE 112 min. (United States)
Paramount Pictures, Zucker Productions
Producers: Sean Daniel, James Jacks, Richard Vane, Janet Zucker, Jerry Zucker
Director: Jerry Zucker
Cast: John Cleese, Rowan Atkinson, Lanei Chapman, Whoopi Goldberg, Cuba Gooding, Jr., Seth Green, Wayne Knight, Jon Lovitz, Amy Smart, Dean Cain, Gloria Allred, Marty Antonini, Jake Bendel, Jenica Bergere,

Exit Wounds: Starring Steven Seagal, this movies tells of an inner-city cop who discovers a web of dirty cops and corruption. Photo: Chris Large

Carrie Diamond, Andrew Kavovit, Jillian Marie, Breckin Meyer, Kathy Najimy, Paul Rodriguez, Kevin Rothery, Catherine Schreiber, Brody Smith, Dave Thomas, Vince Vieluf
Filmed in: Calgary, Drumheller, California, and Nevada

Rat Race was nominated for the Taurus Award for Best Aerial Work at the 2002 World Stunt Awards. One scene featuring Oscar-winner Cuba Gooding, Jr., was filmed during a Calgary Stampeders' football game. The character played by John Cleese, Donald Sinclair, is named after the man who inspired Basil Fawlty, the prissy hotel owner made famous by Cleese in Fawlty Towers.

ANATOMY OF A HATE CRIME
90 min. (United States)
Team Entertainment
Producers: Bill Bannerman, Lawrence Bender, Nicole Pennimgton
Director: Tim Hunter
Cast: Cy Carter, Ian Somerhalder, Chris Enright, Brendan Fletcher, Busy Philipps, Amanda Fuller, Aaron Goettel, David Hayson, Matthew Currie Holmes, John Innes, Rainer Kahl, Grant Linneberg, Douglas MacLeod, Kevin McNulty, Valerie Planche, Carrie Schiffler, Richard Stroh, Scott Urquhart
Filmed in: Calgary, Black Diamond, and Cochrane

It was nominated for the 2002 GLAAD *Media Award for Outstanding Television Movie. In 2004, Ian Somerhalder had a recurring role on the Warner Brothers series* Smallville. *Busy Philipps went on to co-star on* Dawson's Creek *for a few seasons.*

JET BOY 99 min. (Alberta)
Illusion Entertainment
Producers: Bruce Harvey, Nancy Laing
Director: Dave Schultz
Cast: Dylan Walsh, Kelly Rowan, Branden Nadon, Shawn Anderson, Randy Birch, Artur Ciastkowski, Matthew Currie Holmes, Tom Edwards, Chris Enright, Mark Gabruch, Lynn Ivall, David Lereaney, Nancy MacDonald, Bruce McDonald, Roy Neilson, Valerie Planche, Krista Rae, Tania Sablatash, Carrie Schiffler, Joe Norman Shaw, Stephen Strachan, Jordan Weller, Blair Wood
Filmed in: Calgary, Linden (Alberta), and Vancouver

Dylan Walsh went on to star on the cable-TV drama series Nip/Tuck; *Kelly Rowan had a co-starring role in the teen TV drama* The O.C.. *in 2003.*

EXIT WOUNDS 101 min. (United States)
NPV Entertainment, Silver Pictures
Producers: Bruce Berman, Joel Silver, Dan Cracchiolo, John M. Eckert, Ernest Johnson
Director: Andrzej Bartkowiak
Cast: Steven Seagal, DMX, Jill Hennessy, Isaiah Washington, Michael Jai White, Anthony Anderson, Tom Arnold, Eva Mendes, Jenny Celly, Shane Daly, Noah Danby, Rick Demas, Drag-On, Bill Duke, Naomi Gaskin, Rothaford Gray, Quancetia Hamilton, Jennifer Irwin, Daniel Kash, Christopher Lawford, Shawn Lawrence, Paolo Mastropietro, Bruce McGill, Dean McKenzie, Arnold Pinnock, Matthew G. Taylor, Mario Torres, David Vadim, Gregory Vitale
Filmed in: Calgary, Edmonton, and Ontario

It was nominated for a 2002 MTV Movie Award for Breakthrough Male Performance for singer DMX. A major gun battle involving cars, guns, and a helicopter with a smiley face painted on it was shot on Calgary's Centre Street Bridge, which was closed for restoration at the time. Months later, reshoots required the recently reopened bridge to be closed again, much to the chagrin of residents. If you watch carefully, you can see the seasons change between camera angles. Edmonton-born Jill Hennessy had co-starred on Law & Order for several years and soon after making this film got her own TV series, Crossing Jordan.

CHILDREN OF FORTUNE 96 min. (United States)
a.k.a. *Hard Rain*
CBS Productions
Producers: Andrew Baynes, Eda Lishman, Sheldon Larry
Director: Sheldon Larry
Cast: James Brolin, Virginia Madsen, Michael Moriarty, Amanda Fuller, Jack Ackroyd, Kyla Anderson, James Baker, Lorette Clow, Stephen Hair, Ron Hartmann, Vanessa Holmes, Eric Johnson, Barbara Kozicki, Kris Lemche, David Lereaney, Shaker Paleja, Lori Ravensborg, Joe Norman Shaw, Michael David Simms, Gemma Smith, Brian Stollery, Susan Van Boeyen, Denise Willis-Jones
Filmed in: Calgary and Drumheller

It was nominated for a 2001 Canadian Society of Cinematographers Award. James Brolin has a long career in TV and film, including Marcus Welby, MD, *and* Pensacola: Wings of Gold.

PAPA'S ANGELS 83 min. (United States)
CBS Television, Bakula Productions, Marian Rees Associates
Producers: Scott Bakula, Eda Lishman, Dyan Conway, Anne Hopkins, Marian Rees, Tom Spiroff
Director: Dwight H. Little
Cast: Scott Bakula, Eva Marie Saint, Lachlan Murdoch, Cynthia Nixon, Marty Antonini, Kirsten Bishop, Sean Easton, Tom Heaton, Jenny-Lynn Hutcheson, Pamela Johnson, Terry King, Tim Koetting, Shane Meier, Brandon James Olson, Valerie Ann Pearson, Kimberly Warnat

Filmed in: Calgary and Banff

It was nominated for an Emmy Award for its music. Best known for his long-running science fiction series Quantum Leap, *Scott Bakula took the helm in 2001 of TV's most famous starship in* Star Trek: Enterprise. *Cynthia Nixon was co-starring in the hit made-for-cable-TV series* Sex and the City, *when she made this film.*

THE INVESTIGATION 98 min. (Canada)
Muse Entertainment
Producers: Jamie Brown, Michael Prupas, Bernard Zukerman
Director: Anne Wheeler
Cast: Nicholas Lea, Reece Dinsdale, Lochlyn Munro, David Warner, Jack Ackroyd, Dax Belanger, Paul Coeur, Francis Damberger, Duncan Fraser, Michael Hogan, Shaun Johnston, Rainer Kahl, Hrothgar Mathews, Douglas MacLeod, Joe Norman Shaw, Michael St. John Smith
Filmed in: Calgary

David Warner is a noted British character actor who first gained notoriety in the 1966 film Morgan: A Suitable Case for Treatment. *His most-popular film was the billion-dollar-grossing* Titanic *in 1997.*

THE WAR BRIDE 103 min. (United Kingdom/Canada)
DB Entertainment, Random Harvest Pictures, Vanguard Entertainment
Producers: Douglas Berquist, Christopher Courtney, Alistair MacLean-Clark, Jordan Randell, Molly Orr Rosenberg, Melvyn Singer, William Talmadge
Director: Lyndon Chubbuck
Cast: Anna Friel, Brenda Fricker, Aden Young, Julie Cox, Loren Dean, Molly Parker, Schyler McLaren, Gabrielle McLaren, Caroline Cave, Keeley Gainey, Claudie Blakley, Benjamin Boyd, Dorothy A. Haug, Petina Hapgood, Lynda Boyd
Filmed in: Edmonton and London, England

Nominated for seven Genie Awards, including Best Picture, it won for Art Direction/Production Design and Costume Design. Anna Friel is a popular British actress, best known for her role on the TV soap opera Brookside.

DAYBREAK (Alberta)
Gullwing Entertainment Inc., Spineless
Entertainment, Stainless Steel Productions
Producers: Randal Atamaniuk, Ryan
Hanson, Allan Horyn
Director: Randal Atamaniuk
Cast: Collin Doyle, Aaron Talbot, Cameron
McLay, José DeSousa, Darcy Shaw, Elda
Pinckney, Ethan Reitz, Ernst Eder, Wayne
Pederson, Darrell Hough, Michael Pequin,
Ata Smailey, Rick Swan, Ron Roggé, Felix
Fibi, Drake Dyck, Jill Light, Chantal Eder,
Marcus Onischak, Ryan Hanson
Filmed in: Edmonton and Redwater

2001

COVER STORY 92 min. (United
States/Alberta)
Cover Story Films, Alladin Entertainment
Producers: Diane Daou, Chad Oakes,
Michael Frislev, Tony Vincent
Director: Eric Weston
Cast: Elizabeth Berkley, Jason Priestley,
Costas Mandylor, J. R. Bourne, Lorette Clow,
Diego Diablo Del Mar, Joey DePinto, Paul
Dunphy, Brian Gromoff, Douglas MacLeod,
Andy Maton, Chris Nannarone, Brian Stollery
Filmed in: Calgary

Elizabeth Berkley starred in the infamous film
Showgirls *in 1995. Canadian Jason Priestley is
best known for his role in the TV drama* Beverly
Hills 90210. *Paul Dunphy is a well-known
Calgary TV weatherman who has played bit roles
in a number of made-in-Alberta productions.*

WASTED 96 min. (United States)
MTV Network, New Line Television
Producers: Bill Bannerman, Maggie Malina,
Todd Wertman
Director: Stephen T. Kay
Cast: Nick Stahl, Summer Phoenix, Aaron
Paul, Brittney Irvin, Andrew Airlie, Frank
Cassini, Lorette Clow, Dana Crawford, Tanis
Downey, Paul Dunphy, Stephen T. Kay, Tony
Massil, Doug McKeag, Ty Olsson, Krista Rae,
Derek Richards, Katie Rowan, Jacqueline

Samuda, Joe Norman Shaw, Frank Takacs,
Ingrid Tesch, Barbara Gates
Filmed in: Calgary and Black Diamond

Wasted *won the 2003 Prism Award in the catego-
ry of Movie or Miniseries for Television. Nick
Stahl went on to co-star opposite Arnold
Schwarzenegger in* Terminator 3: Rise of the
Machines.

**THE HITCHER II: I'VE BEEN
WATCHING** 96 min. (United States)
Producers: David Bixler, Alfred Habler,
Charles R. Meeker
Director: Louis Morneau
Cast: C. Thomas Howell, Kari Wuhrer, Jake
Busey, Marty Antonini, Randy Birch, Tom
Carey, Darcy Dunlop, Duncan Fraser,
Mackenzie Gray, Stephen Hair, Shaun
Johnston, Terry King, Douglas MacLeod,
Brett Manyluk, Austen Meadows, Janne
Mortil, Valerie Planche, Jim Rattai, Stephen
Strachan
Filmed in: Calgary and Drumheller

*C. Thomas Howell reprised his earlier role in this
belated sequel to the 1986 horror hit. It was nominated for a 2004 Saturn Award for Best DVD
Release. Former MTV host Kari Wuhrer starred in
the popular late-1990s science fiction series* Sliders.

100 DAYS IN THE JUNGLE 120 min.
(Alberta)
ImagiNation Productions
Producers: Nicolette Saina, Matthew
O'Connor, Tom Rowe, Mary Anne
Waterhouse
Director: Sturla Gunnarsson
Cast: Michael Riley, Nicholas Campbell,
Aidan Devine, Jonathan Scarfe, Peter
Outerbridge, Brian Markinson, Brenda
Fletcher, Hugh Thompson, Adrien Dorval,
Nathaniel Arcand, William B. Davis, Patrick
Gilmore
Filmed in: Edmonton and Costa Rica

*This film won the 2003 Gemini Award for Best
TV Movie or Miniseries. Michael Riley has starred
in such series as* Power Play *and* This is
Wonderland. *Nicholas Campbell has won
acclaim for his mystery series* Da Vinci's Inquest.

ROUGHING IT 98 min. (United States)
Hallmark Entertainment
Producers: Robert Halmi, Jr., Tom Benz,
Larry Levinson, Stephen H. Berman, Stephen
Bridgwater, Brian Gordon
Director: Charles Martin Smith
Cast: James Garner, Robin Dunne, Adam
Arkin, Eric Roberts, Ned Beatty, Adam
Storke, Jill Eikenberry, Charles Martin Smith,
Kyla Anderson, Jim Baker, Kira Bradley,
George Buza, Paul Coeur, Graeme Davies,
Diego Diablo Del Mar, Tom Glass, Ron
Hartman, Gina Holden, Leslie Hopps, Kirk
Jarrett, Ranier Kahl, Hal Kerbes, Dave
Leader, David Lereaney, Ryan Luhning, Blu
Mankuma, Steven E. Miller, Billy Morton, J.
D. Nicholsen, Valerie Planche, Winston
Rekert, Wayne Robson, Peter Rumpel, Greg
Spottiswood, Jewel Staite, Brian Stollery,
David Ward
Filmed in: Calgary, at the CL Ranch, and
Drumheller

*This was nominated for a Golden Reel Award by
the Motion Picture Sound Editors and for a
Writers Guild of America Award. Based on the
writings of Mark Twain, it had veteran actor James
Garner in a leading role. Director Charles Martin
Smith also acted in such films as* The
Untouchables, Never Cry Wolf, *and* The
Buddy Holly Story.

AGENT OF INFLUENCE 98 min.
(Alberta)
Alberta Filmworks, Galafilm Productions
Producers: Randy Bradshaw, Francine
Allaire, Doug MacLeod, Arnie Gelbart
Director: Michel Poulette
Cast: Christopher Plummer, Marina Orsini,
Ted Whittall, Shaun Johnston, Cas Anvar,
France Arbour, Adrien Burhop, Noël Burton,
Mark Camacho, Paul Coeur, John Dunn-
Hill, Norman Edge, Alain Goulem, Gregory
Hlady, Al Holt, Yves Longlois, Terry
Lawrence, Douglas MacLeod, Bonfield
Marcoux, Lori Ravensborg, Pierre Rivard,
Kurtis Sanheim, Ari Snyder
Filmed in: Calgary

*Nominated for six Gemini Awards, it won for Ted
Whittall's performance. Christopher Plummer is
one of Canada's most accomplished actors, with a*

career ranging from Shakespeare *to* Star Trek. *He
made this film around the time he appeared in the
Oscar-winning film* A Beautiful Mind.

FUBAR 76 min. (Alberta)
Busted Tranny
Producers: Michael Dowse, David
Lawrence, Melanie Owen, Marguerite Pigott,
Mark Sloane, Paul Spence
Director: Michael Dowse
Cast: Paul Spence, David Lawrence, Gordon
Skilling, Tracey Lawrence, Sage Lawrence,
Eric Amber, Sr., Laurie D'Amour, Brian
Dowse, Jim Lawrence, Carmen Lewis, Dr. S.
C. Lim, Rose Martin, Roxanna Oltean,
Melanie Owen, Elizabeth Simon, Andrew
Sparacino, Margaret Spence, Anne Marie
Wheeler, Christopher Wright
Filmed in: Calgary

*This film was nominated for a 2003 Genie Award
for Best Achievement in Editing.*

WINTER KILL 91 min. (Canada)
Green Ice Productions
Producer: James Harvey
Director: Gilbert Allan
Cast: Camille Wainwright, Holly Backette,
Kelvin Beck, Chris Bolan, Roxanne Doctor,
Nicole Grainger, Shelley Harrison, Brent
Jans, Kris Loranger, Bronwyn Maria Martin,
Krista Nebloch, Bob Rasko, Barbara Schmid,
Dale Wilson
Filmed in: Edmonton

Camille Wainwright's credits include The Skull
of Pain, Catch Me If You Can, *and* Salem
Witch Trials.

STIFFED 83 min. (Alberta)
Number'd Films
Producers: Ziv Feldman, Cory Gelmon,
Michael Gelmon, Jasen Hamilton, Matt
Philipchuk, Lanny Williamson, Richard
Zywotkiewicz
Director: Richard Zywotkiewicz
Cast: Matthew Currie Holmes, Krista Rae,
Christy Greene, Tom Carey, Peter Strand
Rumpel, David Lawrence, Lori Ravensborg,
Terry King, Brian Martell, Lou Poulis, Sean
Bowie, Todd Hann, Marty Hanenberg, David
Trimble, Trevor Rueger, Tod J. Al, Nicole

Shawcross, Ziv Feldman
Filmed in: Calgary

SNOWBOUND 93 min. (United
States/Canada)
a.k.a. *White Lies*
Nomadic Pictures
Producers: Michael Frislev, Larry
Gershman, Alan Kaplan, Chad Oakes
Director: Ruben Preuss
Cast: Erika Eleniak, Monika Schnarre, Peter
Dobson, Jann Arden, Bill Mondy, Ken
Bolton, Mark Smith
Filmed in: Calgary and Whitehorse

One-time Playboy *Playmate Erika Eleniak is
best known for her series* Baywatch. *Jann Arden
is a popular singer-songwriter from Calgary, making her film-acting debut.*

SNOW DOGS 99 min. (United
States/Canada)
Walt Disney Pictures, Winterdance
Productions, Galapagos Productions
Producers: Casey Grant, Jordan Kerner,
Allison A. Millican, Christine Whitaker
Director: Brian Levant
Cast: Cuba Gooding, Jr., James Coburn,
Sisqó, Nichelle Nichols, M. Emmet Walsh,
Graham Greene, Brian Doyle-Murray, Joanna
Bacalso, Jean Michel Paré, Michael Bolton,
Jason Pouliotte, David Boyce, Alison
Matthews, Christopher Judge, Lisa Dahling,
Randy Birch, Donnelly Rhodes, Jim Belushi
Filmed in: Calgary, Canmore, Vancouver,
and Miami

*This was one of film-veteran James Coburn's final
films; he died in 2002. Nichelle Nichols is best
known as Lt. Uhura on* Star Trek.

ROLLERBALL 97 min. (United
States/Japan/Germany)
MGM, Atlas Entertainment, Yorktown
Productions, Toho-Towa
Producers: Vince McMahon, John
McTiernan, Charles Roven, Beau St. Clair,
Michael Tadross
Director: John McTiernan
Cast: Chris Klein, Jean Reno, LL Cool J,
Rebecaa Romijn-Stamos, Naveen Andrews,
Oleg Taktarov, David Hemblen, Janet Wright,

Pink
Filmed in: Lethbridge, Quebec, Wyoming,
San Francisco, Minnesota, and New York

*This is a remake of a cult 1970s science fiction
film. Executive producer Vince McMahon is the
owner of World Wrestling Entertainment.*

THE MATTHEW SHEPARD STORY
100 min. (United States/Canada)
Alliance Atlantis, NBC
Producers: Clara George, Ed Gernon,
Goldie Hawn, Peter Sussman
Director: Roger Spottiswoode
Cast: Stockard Channing, Shane Meier, Sam
Waterston, Kristen Thomson, Joseph Ziegler,
Yani Gellman, Makyla Smith, Jim Aldridge,
Wendy Crewson
Filmed in: Drumheller and Toronto

*Stockard Channing won an Emmy Award for her
performance. Executive producer Goldie Hawn
became a TV star in the 1960s on* Laugh-In *and
a movie superstar in the 1980s in* Private
Benjamin.

THE KNOCKAROUND GUYS 91 min.
(United States)
Lawrence Bender Productions
Producers: Lawrence Bender, Michael De
Luca, Julie Kirkham, Brian Koppelman,
David Levien, Brian Witten, Stan
Wlodkowski
Directors: Brian Koppelman, David Levien
Cast: Barry Pepper, Andrew Davoli, Seth
Green, Vin Diesel, John Malkovich, Arthur J.
Nascarella, Tom Noonan, Nicholas Pasco,
Shawn Doyle, Dennis Hopper, Andrew
Francis, Dov Tiefenbach, Catherine Fitch
Filmed in: Drumheller, Delia (Alberta),
Montana, New York, and Ontario

Vin Diesel became an action star with his films
The Fast and the Furious *and* XXX, *which
were made around the same time as this movie.
Seth Green starred in the TV series* Buffy the
Vampire Slayer *and the* Austin Powers *movies.*

JOHN Q 116 min. (United States)
Evolution Entertainment, Burg/Koules
Productions

Producers: Mark Burg, Howard Burkons, Dale De La Torre, Michael De Luca, Mathew Hart, Avram "Butch" Kaplan, James Kearns, Oren Koules, Richard Saperstein, Hillary Sherman
Director: Nick Cassavetes
Cast: Denzel Washington, Gabriela Oltean, Robert Duvall, James Woods, Ron Annabelle, Anne Heche, Eddie Griffin, Daniel E. Smith, Kimberly Elise, Laura Harring, Ray Liotta
Filmed in: Canmore, Ontario, Quebec, and Chicago

Oscar-winner Denzel Washington won the 2003 Image Award for his performance.

ARARAT 115 min. (Canada/France)
Alliance Atlantis Communications, Astral Films, The Movie Network, Telefilm Canada
Producers: Sandra Cunningham, Atom Egoyan, Robert Lantos, Julia Rosenberg, Simone Urdl
Director: Atom Egoyan
Cast: David Alpay, Arsinée Khanjian, Christopher Plummer, Charles Aznavour, Marie-Josée Croze, Eric Bogosian, Brent Carver, Bruce Greenwood, Elias Koteas, Simon Abkarian, Lousnak, Raoul Bhaneja, Arthur Hagopian
Filmed in: Calgary, Drumheller, and Toronto

Nominated for nine 2003 Genie Awards, this film won five, including Best Motion Picture and acting awards for Arsinée Khanjian (wife of director Atom Egoyan) and Elias Koteas.

2002

ANOTHER COUNTRY: A NORTH OF 60 MYSTERY 98 min. (Alberta)
CBC, Alberta Filmworks
Producers: Doug MacLeod, Tom Dent-Cox, Jordy Randall
Director: Gary Harvey
Cast: Tina Keeper, Dakota House, Timothy Webber, Marty Antonini, Simon Baker, Lawrence Payne, Jimmy Herman, Rainer Kahl, Greg Lawson, Brett Manyluk, David

McNally, Lubomir Mykytiuk, Lori Lea Okemaw, Wilma Pelly, John Ralston, Hugh Thompson, Ron White
Filmed in: Bragg Creek

This fourth made-for-TV movie continues the North of 60 saga.

BURN: THE ROBERT WRAIGHT STORY 98 min. (Alberta)
CTV, Monkeywrench Productions
Producers: Mary Young Leckie, Heather Goldin, Doug MacLeod, Randy Bradshaw
Director: Stefan Scaini
Cast: Jonathan Scarfe, Alan Scarfe, Kristin Booth, Sara Botsford, Karl Pruner, Mark Wilson, Paul Coeur, Lisa Christie, Greg Lawson, Jetro Spencer Barclay, Tom Carey, David Lereaney, Andy Maton, Brian Stollery
Filmed in: Calgary

MONTE WALSH 150 min. (United States)
Turner Network Television
Producers: John Albanis, Michael Brandman, Bobby Roberts, Stephen J. Brandman, Tom Selleck
Director: Simon Wincer
Cast: Tom Selleck, Isabella Rosselini, Keith Carradine, George Eads, Robert Carradine, Barry Corbin, William Devane, Wallace Shawn, Mary Antonini, Matt Cook, Tom Edwards, James Gammon, Tom Glass, Lori Hallier, Eric Keenleyside, Tim Koetting, John Michael Higgins, Joanna Miles, Rex Linn, Ken Pogue, Shane Pollitt, Rick Ravanello, William Sanderson, Peter Skagen, Marshall Teague, Zack Ward
Filmed in: Calgary, at the CL Ranch, Longview, and Redwater

This film was nominated for an Emmy for sound editing. Co-star Isabella Rossellini, the look-alike daughter of Ingrid Bergman, was one of the world's top fashion models before taking up acting in the 1980s. Keith Carradine continued his long association with westerns by playing Wild Bill Hickok in the 2004 made-for-cable-TV series Deadwood.

OPEN RANGE 145 min. (United States)
Touchstone Pictures, Cobalt Media Group, Beacon Pictures
Producers: Kevin Costner, David Valdes,

Jake Eberts, Armyan Bernstein, Craig Storper
Director: Kevin Costner
Cast: Kevin Costner, Robert Duvall, Annette Bening, Michael Gambon, Michael Jeter, Patricia Benedict, Abraham Benrubi, Guy Bews, Chad Camilleri, Tom Carey, Alexis Cerkiewicz, Lorette Clow, Kim Coates, Diego Del Mar, Diego Luna, Peter MacNeill, Dean McDermott, Billy Morton, Julian Richings, James Russo, Kurtis Sanheim, Cliff Saunders, Greg Schlosser, Patricia Stutz, Ian Tracy, Rod Wilson, Alex Zahara
Filmed in: Calgary, Morley, and Longview

Annette Bening received a Golden Satellite Awards nomination for her performance. Kevin Costner reportedly suffered a burst appendix while shooting the film. Michael Jeter, whose accomplished career included roles in The Green Mile, Patch Adams, The Fisher King, *and even* Sesame Street, *died not long after making the film.*

FUGITIVES RUN 96 min. (Alberta)
a.k.a. *Don't Call Me Tonto*
Producers: Lars Lehmann, Eda Lishman, Chad Oakes, Jack Clements, Michael Frislev
Director: "Alan Smithee"
Cast: David Hasselhoff, Steven Cree Molison, Michael Moriarty, Gordon Tootoosis
Filmed in: Calgary

David Hasselhoff is best known for his long-running TV series Baywatch. *"Alan Smithee" is a fictitious name applied when a director requests he not receive credit for the film.*

THE GREAT GOOSE CAPER 101 min. (United States/Alberta)
Studio 8 Productions, Voice Pictures Inc.
Producers: Angelo Bassi, Alex Brown, Jamie Brown, Pablo Dammicco, Bryan Gliserman, Wendy Hill-Tout, Jeff Lester, Terry Potter, Colin Neale, Jackie Quella, Patrice Theroux, Michelle Wong
Director: Nicholas Kendall
Cast: Chevy Chase, Kari Matchett, James Purefoy, Joan Plowright, Tom Arnold, Isabella Fink, Cheyenne Hill, Greg Lawson, Max Morrow, Hugh Portman, Lori Ravensborg
Filmed in: Calgary

Joan Plowright, who was married to Sir Laurence Olivier, received an Oscar nomination for her performance in Enchanted April. *American comic actor Tom Arnold provided the voice of the goose. Kari Matchett appeared several times on the critically acclaimed, but short-lived Fox series* Wonderfalls *in early 2004.*

THE INCREDIBLE MRS. RITCHIE 98 min. (United States/Alberta)
Normadic Pictures, Prophecy Entertainment
Producers: Phil Alberstat, Nick Cassavettes, Jim Reeve, Chad Oakes, Steve Robbins, Jana Edelbaum, Peter Foldy, Michael Frislev, Walter Josten
Director: Paul Johansson
Cast: Gena Rowlands, James Caan, Kevin Zegers, Justin Chatwin, Lorette Clow, Cameron Daddo, Darcy Dunlop, Leslie Hope, Brenda James, David Lereaney, Douglas MacLeod, Jeremy Raymond, David Schofield, Peter Skagen, Heather Wahlquist
Filmed in: Calgary

This film was nominated for a 2003 AMPIA award for Best Make-Up. Gena Rowlands, mother of executive producer Nick Cassavettes, received Oscar nominations for her performances in A Woman Under the Influence *and* Gloria.

A PROBLEM WITH FEAR 92 min. (Alberta)
Burns Film Ltd., Fear Alberta Ltd., Micro Scope Media
Producers: George Baptist, Luc Déry, Sharon McGowan, Shirley Vercruysse
Director: Gary Burns
Cast: Paulo Costanzo, Emily Hampshire, Willie Garson, Camille Sullivan, Benjamin Ratner, Keegan Connor Tracy, Marnie Alton, Donna Brunsdale, Lee Cameron, Jennifer Clement, Sarah Lind, James McBurney, Jeremy Raymond, Peter Strand Rumpel, Brian Stollery
Filmed in: Calgary and Montreal

This film was nominated for two Genie Awards, including one for Emily Hampshire's performance. Keegan Connor Tracy went on to co-star in the UPN series Jake 2.0.

12 MILE ROAD 120 min. (United States/Alberta)
Fox Television Network, CBS Inc.
Producers: Lisa Demberg, Wendy Hill-Tout, Avi Levy, Michelle Wong, Laurie Marie Parker
Director: Richard Friedenberg
Cast: Tom Selleck, Wendy Crewson, Maggie Grace, Beverley Breuer, Patrick Flueger, Anna Gunn, Tim Henry, Tegan Moss
Filmed in: Calgary

Patrick Flueger received a Best Young Artist Awards nomination for his performance. Hamilton-born Wendy Crewson had a recurring role on the Fox spy drama 24 during the 2003–04 TV season.

WORD OF HONOR 120 min. (United States/Alberta)
The Greif Company, Voice Productions Inc.
Producers: Howard Braunstein, Clara George, Leslie Greif, Michelle Wong, Wendy Hill-Tout, Don Johnson, Michael Jaffe, Tiffany McLinn, Lance H. Robbins, Troy Westergaard, John Matthew
Director: Robert Markowitz
Cast: Don Johnson, Jeanne Tripplehorn, Sharon Lawrence, John Heard, Arliss Howard, Peter McNeill, Michael Adamthwaite, Che Ayende, J. R. Bourne, J. Adam Brown, William B. Davis, Victor Ertmanis, Adam Frost, MacKenzie Gray, Zoe Heath, Barclay Hope, Christopher Jacot, Ron C. Jones, Reamonn Joshee, James Kirk, Greg Lawson, David Lereaney, Bill MacDonald, David Parker, Dan Petronijevic, Shawn Roberts, Robert N. Smith, Peter Stebbings, Stephen Warner, Jayson Williams
Filmed in: Calgary and Okotoks

It was nominated for a 2003 Golden Reel Award by the Motion Picture Sound Editors. Jeanne Tripplehorn's credits include Timecode, Mickey Blue Eyes, *and* Basic Instinct. *Sharon Lawrence spent much of the 1990s co-starring in* NYPD Blue.

JOHNSON COUNTY WAR 240 min.
Miniseries (United States)
Hallmark Entertainment, Larry Levinson Productions
Producers: Robert Halmi, Jr., Larry Levinson, Brian Gordon, Frank Q. Dobbs,
Stephen Bridgewater, Mary Church, Diana Ossana, Larry McMurtry
Director: David S. Cass, Sr.
Cast: Tom Berenger, Luke Perry, Adam Storke, Michelle Forbes, Burt Reynolds, Rachel Ward, Henry Beckman, Stephen Bridgewater, Christopher Cazenove, Paul Coeur, Jack Conley, Adrien Dorval, Bunk Duncan, Ron Hartman, Tom Heaton, Jimmy Herman, Chris Ippolito, Kirk Jarrett, Hal Kerbes, Tim Koetting, Doug Lennox, David Lereaney, Blu Mankuma, Fay Masterson, Silas Weir Mitchell, Stevie Mitchell, Billy Morton, John F. Parker, Ken Pogue, J. C. Roberts, Lyle St. Goddard, William Samples, Joe Norman Shaw, Stephen Warner
Filmed in: the Calgary area and at the CL Ranch

Luke Perry is a veteran of such TV series as Beverly Hills 90210 *and* Oz. *Michelle Forbes had supporting roles in TV's* Homicide: Life on the Street *and* Star Trek: The Next Generation. *Tom Berenger's film career dates back to the mid-1970s and includes films like* In Praise of Older Women, Platoon, The Big Chill, *and* Born on the Fourth of July.

PURPLE GAS 81 min. (Alberta)
Gullwing Entertainment Inc., Stainless Steel Productions, Cactus Earl Entertainment, Jex Orfax Productions.
Producers: Dana Andersen, Randal Atamaniuk, William Minsky
Director: William Minsky
Cast: Dana Andersen, Josh Dean, Belinda Cornish, Donovan Workun, Jacob Banigan, Ron Pederson, Jodie Lightfoot, Mark Meer, Jana O'Connor, Chester Andrich, Brad Bouchard, Kris Christianson, Ian Rowe.
Filmed in: Edmonton and Rochester (Alberta)

X2 133 min. (United States)
a.k.a. *X-Men 2*
Twentieth Century-Fox, Marvel Enterprises
Producers: Avi Arad, Tom DeSanto, Ross Fanger, Kevin Feige, David Gorder, Stan Lee, John H. Radulovic, Selwyn Roberts, Lauren Shuler Donner, Bryan Singer, Ralph Winter
Director: Bryan Singer

Cast: Patrick Stewart, Hugh Jackman, Ian McKellen, Halle Berry, Famke Janssen, James Marsden, Anna Paquin, Rebecca Romijn-Stamos, Brian Cox, Alan Cumming, Bruce Davison
Filmed in: Kananaskis Country, New York, British Columbia, Manitoba, and Ontario

This is the hugely successful sequel to the 2000 hit X-Men. *Patrick Stewart and Ian McKellen are both identified with two other popular entertainment "franchises"—*Star Trek *and* The Lord of the Rings, *respectively.*

SHANGHAI KNIGHTS 114 min. (United States/United Kingdom/Czech Republic) Touchstone Pictures, Jackie Chan Films Ltd., Roger Birnbaum Productions
Producers: Stephanie Austin, Gary Barber, Roger Birnbaum, Jackie Chan, Willie Chan, Jonathan Glickman, Edward McDonnell, David Minkowski, Solon So, Matthew Stillman, Scott Thaler
Director: David Dobkin
Cast: Jackie Chan, Owen Wilson, Donnie Yen, Aiden Gillen, Fann Wong, Tom Fisher, Gemma Jones
Filmed in: Calgary, the CL Ranch, the Czech Republic, London, and Los Angeles

Although most of the film was shot in Europe, some of the scenes in this sequel to Shanghai Noon *were filmed in Alberta.*

MIRROR 80 min. (Canada/Argentina)
Producer: Leyla Sahin
Director: Hakan Sahin
Cast: Ugur Polat, Travis Vanhill, Ljubo Bakic, Lambert Leoften, Ken Olson, Catherine Mazer, Cengiz Ternelli
Filmed in: Zama (Alberta)

AAPKO PEHLE BHI KAHIN DEKHA HAI (India)
Anubhav Sinha Productions, Super Cassettes Industries
Producers: Anubhav Sinha, Bhushan Kumar
Director: Anubhav Sinha
Cast: Priyanshu Chatterjee, Farida Jalal, Om Puri, Arundhati Roy, Saakshi
Filmed in: Calgary and Switzerland

2003

(Several of the films listed below have yet to be released as of May 2004; some information including final titles, running times, and credits may be subject to change.)

WHITECOATS 97 min. (Alberta)
Minds Eye Pictures
Producers: Josh Miller, Kevin DeWalt, Andrew Alexander
Director: Dave Thomas
Cast: Dan Ackroyd, Christine Chatelain, Maury Chakin, Dave Foley, Matt Frewer, Ingrid Kavelaars, Pat Kelly, Viv Leacock, Janet McLean, Peter Oldring, Scott Olynek, Carly Pope, Saul Rubinek, Dave Thomas
Filmed in: Edmonton

Canadian Dan Ackroyd rose to fame on Saturday Night Live *and became a film star with such hits as* The Blues Brothers. *Matt Frewer made his film debut in* Monty Python's The Meaning of Life *before achieving stardom as Max Headroom.*

THE LEGEND OF BUTCH AND SUNDANCE 120 min. (United States/Alberta)
Viacom Productions, Nomadic Pictures, Once Upon a Time Films, Toybox
Producers: Stanley M. Brooks, John Fasano, Michael Frislev, Greg Gugliotta, Chad Oakes
Director: Sergio Mimica-Gezzan
Cast: David Rogers, Ryan Browning, Rachelle Lefevre, Michael Biehn, Susan Ruttan, Mara Casey, Mark Consuelos, John Fasano, Blake Gibbons, Michelle Harrison, Greg Lawson
Filmed in: Calgary

THE LAZURUS CHILD 118 min. (Alberta/United Kingdom/Italy/United States)
Illusion Entertainment, Morgan Creek Productions, Eagle Pictures
Producers: Bruce Harvey, David Brown, Ciro Dammicco, Ronald Bass, Christopher Milburn
Director: Graham Theakston
Cast: Andy Garcia, Francis O'Connor, Angela Bassett, Harry Eden, Christopher

Shyer, Daniella Byrne, Jaimz Woolvett, Kyla Anderson, Mark Caven, Julian Christopher, Alexa Fox, Nicholas Gecks, Andrew Kushnir, Robert Joy, Greg Lawson, Justin Louis, Andy Maton, Stephen McHattie, Ciaran O'Driscoll, Shonah Mhene
Filmed in: Calgary and London, England

Cuban-born Andy Garcia has appeared in such films as The Untouchables *and* The Godfather, Part III, *and the 2001 remake of* Ocean's Eleven. *Angela Bassett was nominated for an Oscar for her portrayal of Tina Turner in* What's Love Got to Do with It.

HOLLYWOOD WIVES: THE NEW GENERATION 120 min. (United States/Alberta)
Patriarch Pictures, Voice Productions, Puma Productions
Producers: Jackie Collins, Wendy Hill-Tout, Tom Patricia, Randi Richmond, Renée Valenti, Michelle Wong, Michael Jaffe
Director: Joyce Chopra
Cast: Farrah Fawcett, Melissa Gilbert, Robin Givens, Dorian Harewood, Jeff Kaake, Stewart Bick, Peter Cockett, Pascale Hutton, Eric Johnson, David Joseph, Dallas La Porta, Greg Lawson, Kandyse McClure, Robert Moloney, Peter Oldring, Jack Scalia, James Thomas
Filmed in: Calgary

Calgary's luxurious homes doubled for Beverly Hills mansions in this production based on the Jackie Collins novel.

DISTANT DRUMMING: A NORTH OF 60 MYSTERY 98 min. (Alberta)
Alberta Filmworks
Producers: Doug MacLeod, Tom Dent-Cox, Jordy Randall
Director: Dean Bennett
Cast: Tina Keeper, Dakota House
Filmed in: Calgary and Bragg Creek

This is the fifth film based on the North of 60 *TV series.*

CHASING FREEDOM 98 min. (Alberta)
Alberta Filmworks, Court TV
Producers: Tom Dent-Cox, Judy Ranan,

Noreen Halpern, John Morayniss, Jordy Randall, Paul Ackerly
Director: Don McBrearty
Cast: Juliette Lewis, Layla Alizada, Brian Markinson, Philip Akin, Alison Sealy-Smith, Veena Sood
Filmed in: Calgary

Juliette Lewis's film credits include Natural Born Killers, Strange Days, Kalifornia, *and* Cold Creek Manor.

PICKING UP AND DROPPING OFF 120 min. (United States/Alberta)
Jaffe/Braunstein Productions, Is or Isn't Entertainment, Wildrice Productions
Producers: Michael Jaffe, Dan Bucatinsky, Lisa Kudrow
Director: Steven Robman
Cast: Scott Wolf, Amanda Detmer, Rachelle Lefevre, Kathy Baker, William Chaney, Greg Lawson, Eddie McClintock, Brian Stollery
Filmed in: Calgary

Executive producer Lisa Kudrow starred in Friends, *one of the most popular TV sitcoms of all time.*

CHICKS WITH STICKS 98 min. (Alberta)
Earth to Sky Pictures, Nightingale Productions
Producers: Nancy Laing, Debbie Nightingale, Christina Willings, Suresh Gupta, Kate Miller, Arrika Russell, Jessica Russell
Director: Kari Skogland
Cast: Margot Kidder, Jason Priestley, Tanya Allen, Jessalyn Gilsig, Vanessa Holmes, Pascale Hutton, Shaun Johnston, Kevin Kruchkywich, Juliette Marquis, Michie Mee, Marie-Chantal Perron, Andrew Chalmers
Filmed in: Calgary

GINGER SNAPS II: UNLEASHED 98 min. (Alberta)
49th Parallel Productions, Combustion Inc.
Producers: Peter Block, Paula Devonshire, John Fawcett, Grant Harvey, Steven Hoban, Jason Lee, Noah Segal
Director: Brett Sullivan
Cast: Emily Perkins, Katherine Isabelle, Tatiana Maslany, Janet Kidder, Susan Adam,

Brendan Fletcher, Pascale Hutton, Patricia
Idlette, Eric Johnson, Shaun Johnston, Lydia
Lau, Jake Makinnon, David McNally,
Michelle Beaudoin
Filmed in: Edmonton

*This is the first of two back-to-back sequels to the
popular 2000 horror film, which was shot in
Ontario.*

GINGER SNAPS BACK 98 min. (Alberta)
a.k.a. *Ginger Snaps III: The Beginning*
Combustion Inc.
Producers: Paula Devonshire, Grant Harvey,
Steven Hoban, Noah Segal
Director: Grant Harvey
Cast: Emily Perkins, Katherine Isabelle,
Nathaniel Arcand, J. R. Bourne, Hugh
Dillon, Adrain Dorval, Brendan Fletcher,
David La Haye, David MacInnis, Tom
McCamus, Matthew Walker, Kreg Mcminn
Filmed in: Edmonton and Fort Edmonton

FAMILY SINS 100 min. (United States)
a.k.a. *A Matter of Family*
Sony Pictures Entertainment
Producers: Ricka Kanter Fisher, Susan
Levitan, Peter Lhotka, Bettina Sofia Viviano
Director: Graeme Clifford
Cast: Kirstie Alley, Deanna Milligan, Will
Patton, Kathleen Wilhoite, Kevin McNulty,
David Richmond-Peck, Patrick Gilmore,
Kyla Anderson, Steve Braun, Darcy Dunlop,
Erin Karpluk, Greg Lawson, Viv Leacock
Filmed in: Calgary

Kirstie Alley began her film career in Star Trek II:
The Wrath of Khan *and is best known for her
work on the sitcom* Cheers *and the* Look Who's
Talking *film series.*

THE CLINIC 100 min. (United States)
Animal Planet
Producers: Wendy Hill-Tout, Irene Litinsky,
Michael Prupas, Rolf Scheider, Robert
Vaughn
Director: Neill Fearnley
Cast: Jonathan Scarfe, Mike Farrell, Ione
Skye, Bruce Davison, Reamonn Joshee,
Sebastian Spence
Filmed in: Calgary

*This film was written by actor/director Charles
Martin Smith.*

DREAMKEEPER Miniseries (United
States/Canada)
Hallmark Entertainment, Sextant
Entertainment Group
Producers: Georgina Lightning, Ron
McLeod, Matthew O'Connor
Director: Steve Barron
Cast: Nathaniel Arcand, Tantoo Cardinal,
Keith Chief Moon, William Daniels, Dakota
House, Jimmy Herman, Gordon Tootoosis
Filmed in: around Drumheller and in New
Mexico, Arizona, and South Dakota.

*This won Best Film at the 2003 American Indian
Film Festival.*

TV Series Made in Alberta

Numerous television series have also been based in Alberta over the years. These are just a few of them.

SECOND CITY TV (Canada) 1976–84
a.k.a. *SCTV, SCTV Network 90*
Old Firehall Productions, Allarcom Productions, CBC
Producer: Bernard Sahlins
Cast: John Candy, Joe Flaherty, Eugene Levy, Andrea Martin, Catherine O'Hara, Rick Moranis, Dave Thomas, Martin Short
Filmed in: Toronto and Edmonton

SCTV launched the careers of some of the most popular comic actors of the 1980s and 1990s. It was exported to the US, where it aired on late-night TV in the early 1980s.

THE LITTLE VAMPIRE (United Kingdom/Canada/West Germany) 1986
Allarcom Productions, TVS Television
Producers: Tony Allard, Richard Nielsen, Nic Wry
Cast: Joel Dacks, Gert Fröbe, Michael Gough, Susan Hogan, Jim Gray, Michael Hogan, Christopher Kent, Marsha Moreau, Lynn Seymour, Christopher Stanton
Filmed in: Edmonton

This was one of Gert Fröbe's final acting roles; the German actor was best known for playing James Bond villain Auric Goldfinger. Michael Gough was a veteran British actor who would soon gain fame as Alfred the butler in Tim Burton's 1989 version of Batman.

STINGRAY (United States) 1986–87
Stephen J. Cannell Productions
Producers: Stephen J. Cannell, Tom Blomquist, Lawrence Hertzog, Frank Lupo,

Jo Swerling, Jr., Herbert Wright
Cast: Nick Mancuso
Filmed in: Calgary and Vancouver

Stephen J. Cannell was a popular producer of TV action series in the 1970s and 1980s, including The Rockford Files, The A-Team, Riptide, *and* Hunter. Stingray *was one of his few flops at the time.*

THE RAY BRADBURY THEATRE (United States/Canada) 1989–92
Atlantis Films, Allarcom Productions, Alberta Motion Picture Development Corp., Western International Communications
Producers: Ray Bradbury, Peter Sussman, Larry Wilcox
Cast: Ray Bradbury
Filmed in: Edmonton and Calgary

The first few seasons of the series (1985–88) were filmed in the US Episodes in this Twilight Zone-*like series were based upon Bradbury's short stories.*

NORTH OF 60 (Alberta/Canada) 1992–99
Alliance Films, CBC Television
Producers: Wayne Grigsby, Tom Dent-Cox, Robert Lantos, Peter Lauterman, Doug MacLeod, Barbara Samuels
Cast: John Oliver, Tina Keeper, Tom Jackson, Tracey Cook, Gordon Tootoosis, Dakota House
Filmed in: Kananaskis Country, near Bragg Creek

This extremely successful series spawned a number of made-for-tv films after its conclusion. John Oliver left the series after the first season. The

Viper: Spectacular stunt scenes such as this one were a trademark of the series, which originally filmed in Calgary but relocated to Vancouver to avoid winter weather. Photo: Chris Large

series was nominated for Gemini Awards in 1994 and 1997. During the show's run, Tom Jackson guest starred on an episode of Star Trek: The Next Generation.

DESTINY RIDGE (Alberta/Canada)
1993–95

Alliance Films, CanWest Global
Producers: Anne Marie La Traverse, Peter Lhotka, Larry Raskin, Andy Thomson
Cast: Richard Comar, Raoul Trujillo, Nancy Sakovich, Elke Sommer, Rebecca Jenkins
Filmed in: Jasper

German actress Elke Sommer was a popular TV and movie personality in the 1960s and 1970s. Nancy Sakovich went on to co-star in Psi Factor: Chronicles of the Paranormal *and* Doc.

LONESOME DOVE: THE SERIES and LONESOME DOVE: THE OUTLAW YEARS (United States) 1994–96
Producers: John Ryan, Les Kimber, Suzanne De Passe, Rick Drew, Robert Halmi, Jr., Steven North
Cast: Scott Bairstow, Christianne Hirt, Eric McCormack, Paul Johansson, Bret Hart, Paul Le Mat, Diahann Carroll, Billy Dee Williams, Dennis Weaver, Graham Greene, Kelly Rowan, Tracy Scoggins, Guylaine St-Onge
Filmed in: Calgary and at the Copithorne Ranch

An entire fictional town was built northwest of

Calgary for these two TV series, which were produced back-to-back using mostly the same cast. Both series were based on the very popular 1989 miniseries Lonesome Dove, *and at the time were considered among the highest-profile TV series ever filmed in Alberta. The series won a 1997 Genie Award for Best Performance by an Actor in a Guest Role. Bret Hart is a well-known professional wrestler.*

JAKE AND THE KID (Alberta/Canada)
1995–97

CanWest Global
Producers: Arvi Liimatainen, Peter Lhotka
Cast: Benedict Campbell, Lorne Cardinal, Thomas Cavanagh, Robert Clothier, Stacy Grant, Patricia Harras, Shaun Johnston, Fred Keating, Julie Khaner, Greg Lawson, Jenny Levine, David McNally, Brian Stollery, Brian Taylor
Filmed in: Edmonton

This was the second TV series based on W. O. Mitchell's novel; the first was produced by the CBC in 1961. The late Robert Clothier is best remembered as Relic on the long-running TV series The Beachcombers. Jake and the Kid *was nominated for two 1998 Gemini Awards, winning for Patricia Harras's performance.*

VIPER (United States) 1996
Pet Fly Productions
Producers: Robert Benjamin, Danny Bilson, Howard Chaykin, Paul De Meo, Darrell Fetty, Barbara Kelly, Mark Lisson, Tommy Thompson
Cast: Jeff Kaake, Dawn Stern, Heather Medway, Joe Nipote, J. Downing
Filmed in: Calgary, Airdrie, Black Diamond, Vulcan, and British Columbia

A revival of a short-lived series that was cancelled in 1994, much of the 1996–97 season of Viper was shot in Calgary, and the production team became notorious for closing down the city's Deerfoot Trail for filming. According to the Calgary Sun, *the production team spent $20 million in Calgary before choosing to relocate to Vancouver for the remainder of the series.*

HONEY, I SHRUNK THE KIDS: THE TV SHOW (United States) 1997–2000

Walt Disney Television
Producers: Leslie Belzberg, Ed Ferrara,
Cathy M. Frank, Jonathan Hackett, John
Landis, Jim Lincoln, Kevin Murphy, Peter
Scolari, Dan Studney
Cast: Peter Scolari, Barbara Alyn Woods,
Hillary Tuck, Thomas Dekker, Bruce Jarchow
Filmed in: Calgary

*This series was one of the first major ongoing
Hollywood productions to be based out of former
military buildings vacated when the Canadian
Armed Forces pulled out of CFB Calgary. Based
on a pair of popular family movies, starring Rick
Moranis, the series was nominated for three
Daytime Emmys in technical categories, winning
the 2001 award for Outstanding Achievement in
Sound Mixing.*

MENTORS (Alberta) 1999–present
Mind's Eye Pictures, Anaid Film Productions
Producers: Kevin DeWalt, Will Dixon, Josh
Miller, Margaret Madirossian
Cast: Chad Krowchuk, Stevie M. Mitchell,
Sarah Lind, Belinda Metz
Filmed in: Edmonton

*It was nominated for the 2003 DGC Team Award
by the Directors Guild of Canada.*

MYTHQUEST (Canada) 2001
Minds Eye International, Myth Quest
Productions, David Braun Productions
Cast: Christopher Jacot, Joseph Kell, Wendy
Anderson, Meredith Henderson, Kevin Foley,
Shaun Johnston, Bill Switzer, Matthew
Walker, Leslie Malton

Index

Names of directors are in **bold,** for example, **Altman, Robert**.
Names of movies are in *italics*, for example, *Bye Bye Blues.*
Page numbers in ***bold italics*** indicate photos, for example, Ives, Burl, ***63***, ***64***, 64–68.